KT-423-415

Principles and Practice of Group Work in Addictions

Many professionals working across a variety of addictions settings find themselves working in groups and tackling complex issues; however, there is often very little initial training or on-the-job support to help them in this challenging task. *Principles and practice of group work in addictions* has been written with the aim of addressing the key areas in working with drug and alcohol misuse, while providing practical solutions to the more common problems that emerge in group work.

Drawing on the expertise of clinicians who work in the field of addictions, this book offers readers practical advice for everyday practice. Divided into three sections it covers:

- Core group work in addictions
- Practical issues and solutions to common problems
- Specific issues within the field of addictions.

Principles and practice of group work in addictions is illustrated throughout with practical case examples, providing the reader with an insight into group work in this area. The book will supply guidance for mental health professionals including clinicians, psychologists, nurses and medical staff who encounter group work in addictions for the first time, as well as provide further knowledge and support to those who already work in the field.

Robert Hill is a consultant clinical psychologist working at South London and Maudsley NHS Foundation Trust. He has worked in the mental health and academic sector for the last 20 years and published extensively in the field.

Jennifer Harris is a clinical psychologist working at South London and Maudsley NHS Foundation Trust. She has a particular interest in addictions and health psychology.

Principles and Practice of Group Work in Addictions

Edited by Robert Hill and
Jennifer Harris

Routledge
Taylor & Francis Group

LONDON AND NEW YORK

First published 2011
by Routledge
27 Church Road, Hove, East Sussex BN3 2FA

Simultaneously published in the USA and Canada
by Routledge
711 Third Avenue, New York NY 10017

Routledge is an imprint of the Taylor & Francis Group, an Informa business

© 2011 Selection and editorial matter, Robert Hill and Jennifer Harris;
individual chapters, the contributors.

All rights reserved. No part of this book may be reprinted or reproduced or
utilised in any form or by any electronic, mechanical, or other means, now
known or hereafter invented, including photocopying and recording, or in
any information storage or retrieval system, without permission in writing
from the publishers.

Trademark notice: Product or corporate names may be trademarks or
registered trademarks, and are used only for identification and explanation
without intent to infringe.

British Library Cataloguing in Publication Data
A catalogue record for this book is available from the British Library

Library of Congress Cataloging-in-Publication Data
Principles and practice of group work in addictions / edited by Robert Hill
and Jennifer Harris.
     p. cm.
   Includes bibliographical references and index.
   ISBN 978-0-415-48684-2 (hardback) – ISBN 978-0-415-48685-9 (pbk.)
   1. Substance abuse–Treatment. 2. Drug abuse–Treatment. 3. Alcoholism–
Treatment. 4. Group psychotherapy. 5. Social group work. I. Hill, Robert,
1962- II. Harris, Jennifer, 1972-
   RC564.P764 2011
   362.29–dc22

                                                                    2010048525

ISBN: 978-0-415-48684-2 (hbk)
ISBN: 978-0-415-48685-9 (pbk)
ISBN: 978-0-203-81481-9 (ebk)

Typeset in Times by Garfield Morgan, Swansea, West Glamorgan
Printed and bound in Great Britain by TJ International Ltd, Padstow,
Cornwall
Cover design by Lisa Dynan
Cover image by Lucjan Kowaleski

Contents

Contributors

Nancy Akrasi, Honorary Assistant Psychologist, Beresford Project, South London and Maudsley NHS Foundation Trust

Catherine Atnas, Clinical Psychologist in Training, Surrey Doctoral Training Programme in Clinical Psychology, University of Surrey

Tim Brown, Substance Misuse Worker, Acute Assessment Unit, Maudsley Hospital, South London and Maudsley NHS Foundation Trust

Monique Cloherty, Clinical Psychologist, Neurodisability Service, Great Ormond Street Hospital NHS Trust

Rachel Davies, Lead Occupational Therapist, Priory Secure Services, Farmfield Hospital, The Priory Group

Elly Farmer, Clinical Psychologist, Central and Northwest London NHS Trust

Brett Grellier, Counselling Psychologist, Lewisham Psychological Therapies Service, South London and Maudsley NHS Foundation Trust

Jennifer Harris, Clinical Psychologist, Lambeth Drug and Alcohol Service, South London and Maudsley NHS Foundation Trust

Robert Hill, Consultant Clinical Psychologist, Lead Psychologist for Inpatient Units, Acute Assessment Unit & Bethlem Addiction Service, South London and Maudsley NHS Foundation Trust

Jane Hutton, Consultant Clinical Psychologist, South London and Maudsley NHS Foundation Trust and Department of Psychological Medicine, King's College Hospital NHS Foundation Trust

Francis Keaney, Consultant Psychiatrist, Acute Assessment Unit & Beresford Project, South London and Maudsley NHS Foundation Trust

Marcus Koch, Deputy Clinical Team Leader, Inpatient Addictions Service, Bethlem Royal Hospital, South London and Maudsley NHS Foundation Trust

Ryan Little, Assistant Psychologist, Croydon Memory Service, South London and Maudsley NHS Foundation Trust

G. Alan Marlatt, Professor of Psychology at the University of Washington and Director of the Addictive Behaviors Research Center

Laura Marshall, Clinical Psychologist in Training, Surrey Doctoral Training Programme in Clinical Psychology, University of Surrey

Ann McDonnell, Solution Focused Brief Therapist, Rethink, Wimbledon, London

Tim Meynen, Consultant Clinical Psychologist, Lead Addictions Psychologist for Greenwich, South London and Maudsley NHS Foundation Trust

Luke Mitcheson, Consultant Clinical Psychologist, Lead Addictions Psychologist for Lambeth, Lambeth Community Drug & Alcohol Team, South London and Maudsley NHS Foundation Trust

Martin Naylor, RMN, Clinical Nurse Leader, Bethlem Addiction Service, Bethlem Royal Hospital, South London and Maudsley NHS Foundation Trust

Ernestine Nhapi, Charge Nurse, Bethlem Addiction Service, Bethlem Royal Hospital, South London and Maudsley NHS Foundation Trust

Andrew Parker, Consultant Addictions Psychiatrist, Independent Practice, Capio Nightingale Hospital, London

Claire Parry, Lead Occupational Therapist Addictions, Addictions Division, South London and Maudsley NHS Foundation Trust

Peter Ryan, Professor of Mental Health, School of Health and Social Sciences, Middlesex University

Deepti Shah-Armon, Consultant Clinical Psychologist, Central and Northwest London NHS Trust

Josephine Shaw, Charge Nurse, Formerly of Bethlem Addiction Service, Bethlem Royal Hospital, South London and Maudsley NHS Foundation Trust

Megan Underhill, Clinical Psychologist in Training, Salomons Doctoral Training Programme in Clinical Psychology, Canterbury Christ Church University

Shamil Wanigaratne, Consultant Clinical Psychologist, Head of Addictions Psychology, Addictions Resource Centre, South London and Maudsley NHS Foundation Trust

Martin Weegmann, Consultant Clinical Psychologist, Addiction Treatment Centre, Queen Mary's University Hospital, South West London & St George's Mental Health Trust

Siobhan Wilson, Senior Occupational Therapist, Bay of Plenty District Health Board, Whakatane, New Zealand

Acknowledgements

We are enormously appreciative of all the hard work and thought the contributors have put into their chapters. We would like to thank Ann for her work editing and commenting on the draft chapters, the anonymous reviewer from Routledge who provided many useful suggestions and Shamil for his continuing support and encouragement over the years. Finally, we are tremendously grateful to all the groups we have worked with and learned from over the years. Thank you to you all.

RGH – To my parents

&

JCH – For my beloved LaLaM

Foreword

Robert Hill and Jennifer Harris are to be congratulated for organizing and publishing this excellent resource for those who are engaged in group work in the treatment of addiction problems. The book is divided into three main sections: core considerations (describing different group treatment approaches), practical considerations (management of group activities), and specific considerations (such as cultural issues and co-morbidity). Readers are given access to a total of nineteen chapters, each of which makes a unique contribution to the depth of our knowledge and understanding of group process. I highly recommend this book to all readers who are involved in group work, including therapists, 12-step practitioners, and researchers who are involved in evaluating the effectiveness of various group approaches.

Many of the therapeutic values of group work are outlined in the Introduction section, 'Why Run Groups at All?' A list of eleven 'curative group processes' (originally developed by Yalom) are described, all of which are critical factors in helping us understand why group work can be an effective treatment approach for people with addiction problems. I would like to focus on a few of those points that I have found to be salient in my own work in developing and implementing group interventions for clients seeking help in changing their addictive behaviors.

One central question is understanding the advantages of group work as compared to individual treatment. Although it is certainly true that many individual approaches can be effective with many clients (especially people with co-morbidity problems and those seeking pharmacological treatment), there are a number of unique advantages of the group approach that may further enhance the process of recovery. In our own work with relapse prevention, we have found the group format to be more effective in various treatment outcome studies than one-on-one treatment. Why is that?

Perhaps the most effective ingredient in group work is the social support and facilitation of compassion for both oneself and others in the group. Given the stigma associated with having an addiction problem (shame, guilt, moral rejection), to participate in a group of others who are 'all in the same boat' can be a very powerful force. Social support and the enhance-ment of self-acceptance occurs in groups ranging from 12-step programs (no therapists) to other programs that are directed by therapists. In relapse prevention, therapists often tell me that the group format allows clients to give each other feedback and support as they are trained in learning new skills to cope with relapse triggers, urges, and craving. This group process provides many opportunities for vicarious learning, as various clients share their stories about past relapses and current plans for recovery. It's clear that the group cohesiveness and social bonding adds to the therapeutic alliance that clients and therapists often experience. Overall, a group approach that is designed to facilitate interpersonal compassion and personal acceptance is much more effective than group programs that are intended to confront and humiliate clients into changing their 'bad habits'.

In our relapse prevention programs, we offer clients an opportunity to participate in a group program that meets once per week to complete an eight-week course. The course is designed to provide clients with an overview of the relapse and recovery process, and to teach and share skills that can help clients 'stay on the wagon'. In our newly developed program (Mindfulness-Based Relapse Prevention), clients are taught meditation practices that can serve as a 'meta-cognitive' coping skill to cope effectively with urges/craving, as well as provide them with stress-management skills. Given that it takes time and practice to establish effective coping skills, a course format guides clients through the learning process, one class at a time.

Other group programs are available for clients to attend at any time (e.g., 12-step groups), rather than waiting for a new course to begin before they can start treatment. Some clients attend both a group course and an open self-help group to benefit from the combined advantages of both approaches. In our mindfulness course, therapists are asked to maintain their own meditation practice, so that they can share their personal experi-ences with their clients as they share theirs – this enhances a collaborative union between therapists and clients, as compared with a 'top-down' approach in which therapists tell their clients 'what to do'. Therapists are encouraged to meet clients 'where they are at' and to provide support for them, regardless of where they stand in the 'Stages of Change' motivational process.

Group work can be implemented with clients who have different goals, including abstinence and harm reduction. In relapse prevention, we encour-age clients in abstinence-based treatment programs to stay in the group, even if they experience setbacks. If someone experiences a lapse, therapists try to engage in a 'relapse management' process to get the client back on track, rather than giving in or dropping out.

In closing, I found reading this book to be a valuable and enlightening experience. So many good group work programs are included, along with relevant discussions of practical matters and implementation issues.

Many thanks to all the authors who contributed to this significant and clinically valuable overview of various group work approaches!

G. Alan Marlatt, Ph.D.
Professor and Director
Addictive Behaviors Research Center
University of Washington
Dept. of Psychology

Introduction

Why run groups at all?

Robert Hill and Jennifer Harris

This is a book about addiction and groups. When we talk about addiction we are referring to individuals who are using drugs and/or alcohol at either a harmful or dependent level. Often individuals who have made contact with a service will be offered treatment and support in some sort of group setting. This is a book for people working with such groups.

'The group' has long held a prominent place within the field of psychiatry, and even if its popularity has waxed and waned, it has never entirely departed from the radar. Groups have a particularly powerful pedigree within addictions, indeed both Alcoholics Anonymous (AA) and Narcotics Anonymous (NA) are primarily focused on like-minded individuals coming together to share their experiences in a group context. Accordingly, many professionals who choose a career in addictions find themselves called on to do group work. Others find themselves needing to design groups or offer some form of consultative expertise in group work. The setting for such work may be within inpatient wards, outpatient settings, day centres, rehabilitation centres, prisons or other forensic facilities. Groups can cater for alcohol-dependent clients, drug-dependent clients or a mix of the two; some groups will focus on abstinence, while others focus on harm mini-misation. Some will be skills-based, still others knowledge-based or insight-based. Group work may be short-term or long-term, time-limited, struc-tured or unstructured, and based around a number of psychotherapeutic approaches such as psychodynamic, cognitive behavioural, humanistic, or solution-focused approaches. Furthermore, groups may deal directly with the addiction, with the many mental health difficulties that individuals with substance dependence experience, or with some of the correlates of addic-tion, such as low self-esteem, anger, or impulsivity. If one adds to this the fact that groups can occur at different stages of treatment and can be either self-contained or modular based, then the issue of complexity in running groups becomes clear.

Despite there being a long and respected association between addiction treatment and group work, it is worth standing back and questioning the function of group work in addictions and asking the question 'Why run groups at all?' While many effective interventions, such as residential treatment, AA, and cognitive behavioural therapy (CBT), contain substantial amounts of group work, it is not clear whether the group merely acts as the delivery vehicle for these activities or whether the group is integral to them. The role of group work in addictions is therefore complex and while the evidence for effective group work is difficult to isolate from other components of a treatment package, the assumption held by many of those delivering groups is that they are a useful and effective means of doing 'something'. This 'something' can be multifaceted, from the delivery of information to the exploration of feelings, to the teaching of skills, and so forth. Thus, regardless of the specified objectives of the group, it is almost certain that hidden somewhere will be some assumptions about the beneficial value of groups. These may be related either to the therapeutic value of groups or to the economic/resource argument in favour of running groups. However, it is also important to be clear about the counter-arguments against running groups, most notably issues surrounding client acceptability, staff competency/confidence, and issues concerning client co-morbidity.

The therapeutic value of groups

The group work literature often speaks of 'therapeutic factors' or 'curative group processes', and broadly speaking these might be thought of as explaining how the group may be a medium for help. It is important to remember that any 'factor' or 'process' that arises in a group has the power to be positive (and therefore therapeutic or curative) or negative (and therefore 'counter-therapeutic'). There are two associated facets of group therapy that promote the operation of therapeutic factors. The first of these are the 'conditions for change', i.e., those 'aspects of the group structure and procedures without which the therapeutic factors could not operate' (Bloch & Crouch, 1985, p. 5). These include, for example, the need for an audience for self-disclosure, the act of verbal participation, and a shared sense of motivation. The second of these are 'techniques', often confused with therapeutic factors; these are 'devices available to the therapist to promote the operation of therapeutic factors' (Bloch & Crouch, 1985, p. 6).

   Providing a space to explore shared issues, the offering of mutual support, developing self-understanding and testing out new behaviours, reducing social isolation, and increasing self-acceptance through social comparison are all examples of ways in which groups can foster therapeutic value (Whitaker, 1985). Yalom (1995) provides a useful description of what he calls curative group processes, that is to say his understanding of what group members found helpful about group therapy. While these factors are not specific to addiction, we have briefly highlighted how these may be salient for clients undergoing group work for their addiction:

1   Instillation of hope. This might be hearing that treatment (e.g., detoxi-fication) can be helpful and that change is possible. Hope is an important factor in enhancing motivation by generating optimism and confidence that changes can be made. This can be particularly powerful when hope is demonstrated by other group members, i.e., the 'peer group'.

2   Universality. This typically relates to finding out that others are experiencing similar difficulties and that individuals are not alone in their struggles. This can be especially powerful in reducing feelings of isolation, shame, and guilt—particularly salient and handicapping emotions for substance misusers.

3   Imparting of information. This could be didactic information provided by the facilitators or group members; it could relate to any aspect of recovery such as health education, craving, coping with high-risk situations, mental health, managing difficult emotions, support, and so forth. This could also mean receiving and giving suggestions known to be effective strategies for handling problems. Imparting such infor-mation is particularly important for clients who are pre-contemplative of change in order to help increase the discrepancy between behaviours and goals (Prochaska & DiClemente, 1983).

4   Altruism. Many substance misusers feel worthless and inadequate. The group can present a valuable opportunity for clients to find that they can give something of value to others and feel useful. It is also a chance for clients to show unselfish concern for someone outside themselves.

5   The corrective recapitulation of the primary family group. Many of those with addiction difficulties have experienced neglectful, disrupted or abusive early relationships. The group can represent the original family with authority figures and sibling figures, and reactivate pre-viously suppressed emotions. Group work gives an opportunity to belong to a supportive 'family' and a chance to work through 'unfin-ished business' and re-orient behaviour patterns to an adult context.

6   Development of socializing techniques. Group work is an opportunity to be with others, listen, and talk. Many substance misusers have had their social development/learning interrupted or clouded by substance use, or have become socially isolated. Groups are a chance to test out and develop interpersonal skills such as conflict resolution, self-disclosure, and the offering of emotional support.

7   Imitative behaviour. Groups offer individuals a chance to observe helpful, successful or desirable behaviours by others (such as risks with self-disclosure or assertiveness), witness events unfold, and later feel safe to try new behaviours out for themselves.

8   Interpersonal learning. This can mean experimenting with new ways of relating to others and having the rare opportunity for direct or indirect feedback from others about how we come across. It can be a chance to

learn how to interact more honestly and deeply with others. It is believed that the group becomes a social microcosm that displays typical patterns of being with others.

9 Group cohesiveness. Regularly being part of a group may help those in recovery feel that what they say and do is important to others, similarly that what others say is important to them. Substance misusers typically show extremes in relation to their concern for others and this can express itself both in terms of under and over involvement.

10 Catharsis. Group work is useful as a space to vent and explore feelings and gain relief. This may be particularly important for a client group who are typically socially isolated, estranged from families/support, experience distressing/traumatic life events and who have shut off emotions through substance misuse. Although catharsis alone is not sufficient for symptom or behavioural change, it can be an important part of overall therapy.

11 Existential factors. Groups can be useful in helping members come to terms with basic features of their existence as human beings, for example the fact that we are all ultimately alone, that we cannot escape pain, that we all die, that we are responsible for our actions and yet we also may not have control over life. If substance misuse is a flight from reality, then a reorientation back towards reality in a supportive context is clearly essential.

While these potential benefits are directly aimed at clients, they do also help to legitimize the treatment process for staff as well. Understanding the potential value of groups can foster among staff an increased sense of personal accomplishment and sense of meaning in their work. Undertaking group work can also afford staff learning and development in the following three areas.

Firstly, staff running groups can benefit from working with other facilitators and observing different skills and approaches. This is particularly true where staff with different levels of experience work together or where the facilitators are from different disciplines. Working in a group allows skills to be honed and evaluated on an ongoing basis. Related to this is the fact that successful group work requires both continual skill development and up-to-date knowledge in order that it retain its relevance to clients. Groups thus keep staff engaged in their core work and require the ongoing development of professional competence.

Secondly, groups often induce anxiety in staff, and learning to understand and use such anxiety is another benefit of running groups. It appears clear that even the most experienced clinician has some degree of anxiety when undertaking group work. This relates not to the content, which the experienced facilitator is well used to, but to the process of running a group. Every group has within it the possibility of new encounters and new processes, something that the facilitator is expected to work with effectively. Normalizing these feelings and recognizing that 'process' as opposed to 'content' anxiety is normal can help to energize staff and help them understand more about their own vulnerabilities.

Thirdly, groups allow staff to understand rather more deeply the social difficulties that clients may have and thereby increase staff empathy or accurate understanding. Sometimes staff can gain a false impression of the client's capabilities and motivations when they meet in a one-to-one situation. After all, in a one-to-one session there is a primary focus on the client's needs, with no distractions and no competing, alternative or negative viewpoints being expressed. In the group context all of these are liable to happen and the group context is perhaps closer to the client's real-world experiences than individual therapy.

The economic argument for groups

The second major reason why group work continues to be promoted within the field of substance dependence is an economic one. It is recognized that it is not possible to provide individual therapy for every client seeking treatment and help. This is particularly important as the UK, along with the majority of both developed and developing countries, is witnessing a dramatic increase in the number of people who are either dependent or using alcohol or drugs at harmful levels. This increase, which shows no signs of abating, is going to continue to exert significant pressure on the NHS and as a result we need to be constantly on the look out for the best ways of working with clients to decrease the risks of relapse and enhance their skills and resources for recovery.

The ability to deal with large numbers of people with similar problems in a group setting with one or two therapists is simply far more cost-effective than trying to provide such therapy on a one-to-one basis. Moreover, even if there were sufficient funds available to undertake this task, it is by no means clear that there are sufficient therapists able to undertake one-to-one work at the level required with the numbers of people involved. The economic necessity of running groups should not however, detract from their additional value. The therapeutic factors already identified cannot always be replicated outside the group context. This is an important consideration for staff, as it can be particularly easy to reject group work on the basis that it is simply being used as a cost-saving exercise. Where it does save costs, this is not its primary function.

Arguments against group work

There are perhaps three clear arguments that can be put forward against the running of groups for clients with substance dependence or problematic use. These are the issues of client acceptability, staff competency or confidence, and client co-morbidity.

The first argument against running groups is one based on consumer satisfaction; some clients dislike groups irrespective of whether the group is reported to be helpful. It could be argued that a truly client-centred health service would be not only helpful and effective, but also liked. This is an ethical question in its own right and is at the centre of the dilemma of how to offer patient choice in a system that by its very nature must restrict choice. It is also a particularly salient question with regard to substance dependence, where there can be a general tendency to prioritize wants over needs (Ellis, McInerney, DiGiuseppe, & Yeager, 1989).

The second issue concerns the staff members who are required to facilitate groups with clients. While there are a number of staff members who are highly skilled in group work and actively seek this out as an area of work, there are many staff who find the thought of group work highly stressful and the actual experience even worse. While it is sometimes possible to avoid groups, in the current context of treatment provision this is quite difficult and staff are often asked to undertake groups without either the motivation or skill to do this job well. The result is that staff stress goes up and the functioning of the group can sometimes deteriorate, leading to an even more stressful experience. One of our reasons for writing this book is to make it easier for staff to approach and deal with all the issues that can confront them when running groups.

The third issue concerns the question of co-morbidity and the fact that the majority of clients attending substance misuse treatment centres have other psychological or psychiatric difficulties to contend with. The group as a vehicle for addressing substance misuse problems may be too simplistic in that it does not reflect the true interaction between addiction and psychological distress. For many clients one can see that the development of the substance dependence is secondary to other non-substance-related difficulties, difficulties that are often encountered in childhood and adolescence (Hill, Moran, Cooper, & Bearn, 2006). The group therefore has to be about more than just the addiction. However, we would argue that groups, when well run, incorporate most of those factors identified by Yalom (1983, 1995) and lie beyond the simple confines of substance dependence.

Why groups can be so powerful

Substance dependence is in many respects the greatest of levellers; it brings people to similar places whatever their background. Individuals seeking treatment often articulate shared beliefs or thoughts about their addiction. For instance, there is often a belief in the power of knowledge to change and transform. While we would not want to minimize the importance of such knowledge, it is rarely sufficient for change to occur, as many health education campaigns clearly show. The majority of clients know a long time before seeking treatment that they have a problem, yet often their ambivalence about doing anything about it is the main reason for the continuation of their behaviour. Clients can also become helpless in the face of their addiction, believing that there is nothing that they can do to change. This isn't always the result of ambivalence: sometimes clients are both willing and ready to change, but not able. Additionally some clients get stuck somewhere in the 'unfairness' of it all, seeing others who may use substances in a similar way, but who seemingly do not have the same problems. Such resentment, coupled with a long-held behavioural strategy of always seeking to fulfil 'desire', can decouple the individual from seeking change. Others still may hold onto the cherished belief that things can return to normal, either through controlled use or through occasional use. Others may take a step towards change by stopping use, but find that they have neglected to make other equally important changes to their life. Sometimes some of these beliefs remain fixed, but generally exposure to therapists and particularly other clients in treatment begins to undermine the strength and power of these beliefs. The group can exert an extremely powerful influence in this regard.

Why then is the group so powerful in changing embedded beliefs? Firstly, whatever form the group takes, it is based in a 'here and now' confrontation with reality. Norman Denzin (1987) has argued that one of the key features of addiction is the desire on the part of the individual to change their relationship with time, he particularly viewed alcoholism as a Dis-Ease of Time. Understood in this way, alcohol is used as a means of escaping either into the safety of the past or into a phantasy of the future. Both types of escape are viewed as inauthentic. Authentic time is lived in the present, and the group provides a powerful forum for just such authenticity.

Secondly, groups provide reality checks, either through the giving of factual information or through the sharing of personal experiences. Many members regard the AA or NA 'fellowship' as a powerful dynamic allowing for the safe and supportive expression of feelings in a group that is 'open' but comes together because of shared commitments. The group also exists as a learning environment for the pursuit of optimism. Indeed, the recounting of life histories in AA acts as a powerful reminder of what has been and of what could be. Glidden-Tracey (2005, p. 136) talks about 'learning from vicarious experience', by which she means the learning from others of both success and failure. This is the model that is employed by Twelve-Step groups and is at the heart of the telling of a person's 'life story'.

Thirdly, if the formation of groups often highlights individual vulnerabilities and strengths, it is through becoming part of a group that the individual can come to recognize the importance of social support. Such support can help to sustain and make change possible. Indeed, social support is well known to be an effective buffer against stress that undeniably rises when one seeks to change old patterns of behaviour (Ryan, Dawson, & Hill, 2008).

Fourthly, groups have the power to explore and assist both with attachment difficulties (Flores, 2004) and emotional regulation (Khantzian & Albanese, 2008). Attachment Theory (Bowlby, 1997) postulates that through our early care-giving experiences we develop internal working models about oneself, other people, and the world. Many substance misusers have experienced disrupted or abusive early relationships, thereby influencing the sorts of beliefs they are likely to have about, for example, their self-worth, getting their needs met, how to manage feelings, how trustworthy other people are, and so forth. Reading and Weegman (2004) describe how substance misusers have an unhealthy attachment to chemicals and that detachment from chemicals and attachment to treatment are necessary steps for recovery. Group participation may facilitate this attachment process and present an opportunity for group members to explore and develop self-insight into patterns of behaviour, coping, and emotional regulation.

Overriding all of these specific functions, group therapy recognizes that we are essentially social beings with a need to form healthy attachments with other people. Often the person with a drug or alcohol problem is the last to acknowledge that they have a problem and the impact of substance misuse touches many other people first, whether family, friends, work colleagues. Indeed, to view substance dependence solely as a problem of the individual is undoubtedly both restrictive and potentially harmful, for it is in the interactions of daily living that both substance use and sobriety take place. The therapeutic group can play a powerful role in helping individuals to move beyond intellectual acceptance of a problem to emotional recognition, understanding, and ultimately change. It is the power of the group experience in addiction that is often commented on by clients in treatment. While there is little doubt that such experiences can be painful for some, particularly those who have used alcohol or drugs to mask their social anxiety, it is also the case that the group provides a level of equality and shared experiences that is unusual in other areas of life.

Rationale for the book

Many professionals working across a variety of addictions settings find themselves working in groups and tackling complex issues. However, there is often very little initial training or on-the-job support to help staff with this challenging task. Psychologists, nursing and medical staff may receive some exposure to the principles of group work in their initial training and a few may have sought out further specialized professional training in group work. However, even these will receive very little training in the specifics of running groups with a substance dependent population. Furthermore, it is often the case that the more experienced the staff member, the less likely they are to run groups on a routine basis. Consultant psychiatrists and consultant psychologists are probably the least likely members of a staff team to work with groups. Paradoxically, the staff member who is most likely to run a group is often the one with the least amount of experience. Thus, newly qualified nurses are more likely to run groups than more senior staff. Additionally, staff members who have not undergone any initial professional training such as nursing assistants, drug and alcohol workers, and psychology assistants are often relied on to facilitate group work.

Those interested in developing their knowledge and skills in group work can gain a great deal from some extremely important and useful texts such as those written by Irving Yalom (1983, 1995) and Dorothy Stock Whittaker (1985). Other useful texts include those by Barnes, Ernst, and Hyde (2000), Bensen (2000), Brown (2004), Doel and Sawdon (1999), Rutan, Stone, and Shay (2007), and Tudor (1999). However, these general texts do not aim to cover salient issues within group work in addiction treatment and newer or less experienced clinicians may find it difficult to adapt these to the addictions field, particularly when offering more short-term group programmes.

There is a small body of literature specific to group work in addictions; however, this does tend to be for an American audience and is often substance-specific or focuses on one particular theoretical approach to group work. The two most well-known clinicians dealing with group work and addictions are Philip Flores of Atlanta, Georgia and Edward Khantzian of Harvard Medical School. Flores (1996) has written seminal works on how to combine the principles of AA with psychodynamic theory. Edward Khantzian and his colleagues (Khantzian, Halliday, & McAuliffe, 1990) provide an interesting and informative description of his team's adaptation of psychodynamic techniques to address the core difficulties of cocaine users over the course of a six-month group programme.

Velasquez, Maurer, Crouch, and DiClemente (2001) provide an excellent practical manual for anyone wishing to offer groups based on the trans-theoretical model of change and relapse prevention strategies. They help-fully offer structured handouts, although their remit does not cover a wider discussion of group issues and thus presupposes group competence regard-ing process issues. Baruch Levine and Virginia Gallogly (1985) have written a useful text about group work for alcoholics containing information both on the function and difficulties when running groups for clients with alcohol dependence. Ivan Elder (1990) has written a more general, albeit brief, book on how to conduct group therapy with addicts; there is much to recommend this book, however its main function does seem to be to introduce Elder's own model of long-term group work called the 'Force Friendly' model. David Brook and Henry Spitz's (2002) edited collection on group therapy for substance abuse is arguably the closest to an introductory book. This covers many interesting areas, including working with adolescents and older adults, but is rather medically oriented with an obvious focus on the structure of American healthcare treatment.

Books written by UK authors are few and far between; indeed, that by Reading and Weegman (2004) stands alone as a UK text. This edited book covers a range of interesting topics relating to group work that will stimulate more experienced clinicians or those with a particular knowledge of psychodynamic approaches.

Overview of the book

Principles and practice of group work in addiction has been written with the aim of addressing what we believe to be some of the key areas in addiction work while providing practical solutions to some of the more common problems that can emerge when doing group work.

We have divided the book into three main sections, which correspond in some ways to the tasks of the group. In Part I, we deal with core components of group work in addictions, in Part II, practical issues and solutions to common problems, while Part III focuses on special considerations. Each section contains a number of separate chapters written by practitioners working in the field.

Of course, in an ideal world anyone called on to do group work would receive extensive training and support prior to facilitating any group. However, we do not live in an ideal world and sometimes people are thrown in at the deep end. While we do not recommend this as a model, this book will hopefully act as a lifeline for those who find themselves in such a situation as well as a source of knowledge and support for those whose introduction has been rather more considered. We hope that this aim is successful and that the benefits of increased knowledge of and confidence in group work in addictions will have other benefits for both staff and clients dealing with this most human of conditions.

References

Barnes, W. R., Ernst, S., & Hyde, K. (2000). *An introduction to groupwork: A group-analytic perspective* (2nd ed.). Basic Texts in Counselling & Psychotherapy. London: Routledge.

Bensen, J. R. (2000). *Working more creatively with groups* (2nd ed.). London: Routledge.

Bloch, S., & Crouch, E. (1985). *Therapeutic factors in group psychotherapy*. Oxford: Oxford University Press.

Bowlby, J. (1997). *Attachment and loss*. London: Pimlico.

Brook, D. W., & Spitz, H. I. (2002). *The group therapy of substance abuse*. New York: Harworth Medical Press.

Brown, N. W. (2004). *Psychoeducational groups: Process and practice* (2nd ed.). London: Brunner-Routledge.

Denzin, N. K. (1987). *The alcoholic self.* New York: Sage.

Doel, M., & Sawdon, C. (1999). *The essential groupworker: Teaching and learning creative groupwork.* London: Jessica Kingsley Publishers.

Elder, I. R. (1990). *Conducting group therapy with addicts: A guidebook for professionals.* Blue Ridge Summit, PA: Tab Books.

Ellis, A., McInerney, J. F., DiGiuseppe, R., & Yeager, R. J. (1989). *Rational emotive therapy with alcoholics and substance abusers.* New York: Pergamon Press.

Flores, P. J. (1996). *Group psychotherapy with addicted populations: An integration of twelve-step and psychodynamic theory.* New York. Haworth Medical Press.

Flores, P. J. (2004). *Addiction as an attachment disorder.* New York: Rowman & Littlefield.

Glidden-Tracey, C. E. (2005). *Counseling and therapy with clients who abuse alcohol or other drugs.* London: Sage.

Hill, R. G., Moran, P., Cooper, W., & Bearn, J. (2006). Early childhood maladjustment and adherence with inpatient drug detoxification treatment. *Journal of Substance Use, 10,* 1–7.

Levine, B., & Gallogly, V. (1985). *Group therapy with alcoholics.* London: Sage.

Khantzian, E. J., & Albanese, M. J. (2008). *Understanding addiction as self medication: Finding hope behind the pain.* New York: Rowman & Littlefield.

Khantzian, E. J., Halliday, K. S., & McAuliffe, W. E. (1990). *Addiction and the vulnerable: Modified dynamic group therapy for substance abusers.* London: The Guilford Press.

Prochaska, J. O., & DiClemente, C. C. (1983). Stages and processes of self-change of smoking: Toward an integrative model of change. *Journal of Consulting and Clinical Psychology, 51,* 390–395.

Reading, B., & Weegman, M. (2004). *Group psychotherapy & addiction.* London: Whurr.

Rutan, J. S., Stone, W. N., & Shay, J. J. (2007). *Psychodynamic group psychotherapy.*: The Guilford Press.

Ryan, P., Dawson, I. & Hill, R. G. (2008). *Managing stress and violence at work.* Brighton: Pavilion Publishing.

Tudor, K. (1999). *Group counselling.* Professional Skills for Counsellors series. London: Sage.

Velasquez, M., Maurer, G. G., Crouch, C., & DiClemente, C. C. (2001). *Group treatment for substance abuse: A stages-of-change therapy manual.* London: Guildford.

Whitaker, D. S. (1985). *Using groups to help people.* London: Routledge.

Yalom, I. D. (1983). *Inpatient group psychotherapy.* New York: Basic Books.

Yalom, I. D. (1995). *The theory and practice of group psychotherapy* (4th ed.). New York: Basic Books.

Part I

Core considerations in addictions group work

Introduction to core considerations

This first part of the book, 'Core considerations in addictions group work', explores what may be considered the core components of group work when working with individuals with drug and alcohol problems. The first chapter helps to set the scene for the book as a whole by offering readers a first-hand account of the role of groups in recovery. Tim Brown gives a fascinating account of his thinking about group work from multiple perspectives: as a client, as someone undertaking training in drug and alcohol work and currently as a staff member facilitating groups. We hope this 'insider' perspective offers some inspiration to those involved in or thinking about group work.

'Motivation' might be considered pivotal to our work within addictions, and indeed motivation is a theme that runs throughout the book. Without proper consideration of motivation, all other efforts can fail. Luke Mitcheson and Brett Grellier draw on their extensive experiences to offer a refreshing commentary on motivation, with practical ideas on how to apply motivational interviewing principles to the group setting.

One of the most commonly used approaches to group work is the relapse prevention model developed by Alan Marlatt in 1978, and this has been one of the mainstays of addictions treatments ever since. In Chapter 3, Shamil Wanigaratne and Francis Keaney, both NHS consultants, discuss how our understanding of addiction and relapse prevention has moved forward in the twenty years since the publication of *Relapse Prevention for Addictive Behaviours* (Wanigaratne, Wallace, Pullin, Keaney, & Farmer, 1990). Reflecting both on their own experience of running groups and on the most up-to-date theory and research, they provide a succinct overview of the field as well as some practical suggestions for those undertaking group work.

In Chapter 4, Martin Naylor and Ryan Little discuss their experiences of promoting physical health within an addictions context. They usefully summarize the policy context of health initiatives before discussing a number of core health-promotion groups for substance misusers. While more emphasis has been placed on health promotion for problematic drug use, the ideas incorporated in this chapter can lend themselves to clients with alcohol problems.

Often individuals in treatment are faced not only with changing their drug and alcohol use but also with the additional task of changing their lifestyle, support network, and self-identity. In Chapter 5, Siobhan Wilson and Claire Parry, both experienced occupational therapists, discuss ways in which groups can help clients to focus on these important questions of life meaning and self-identity in a way that promotes self-understanding, optimism, and the development of positive social networks.

Chapter 6 gives some background to the approach of mindfulness, along with some practical information about how to run mindfulness groups within an addiction service. Robert Hill, Jane Hutton, Marcus Koch, and Ann McDonnell discuss some of the issues that have arisen when introducing mindfulness to clients in an addiction centre, before concluding with suggestions as to how to explore the practice of mindfulness further. All of the authors practise mindfulness themselves and Jane Hutton is an active trainer of both clients and staff in the practice of mindfulness.

Chapter 7 considers how professionals working in addictions services can introduce clients to Twelve-Step approaches. A case example from an inpatient detoxification ward is provided. Andrew Parker, a consultant psychiatrist, provides a very clear overview of Twelve-Step groups and how we as professionals might correct myths about these mutual help groups and support clients to take the best from this valuable resource. A case study from a group he established entitled 'Mind the Gap' will, we are sure, provide an excellent template for staff who wish to introduce clients to Twelve-Step groups as well as correcting a number of myths about Alcoholics and Narcotics Anonymous.

Clearly there are a number of other areas that we could have included in a section entitled 'Core considerations in addictions group work'. Thus, space allowing, we would have included a separate chapter on managing emotions. However, we hope that Chapter 6 on mindfulness and Chapter 17 dealing with acceptance and change provide some insight and techniques for managing one's emotions.

Reference

Wanigaratne, S., Wallace, W., Pullin, J., Keaney, F., & Farmer, R. (1990). *Relapse prevention for addictive behaviours*. Oxford: Blackwell.

Chapter 1

From patient to practitioner

A personal journey

Tim Brown

Editors' note

When debating and reflecting on what might be included in this book, we were very keen for readers to have a personal account of what groups can offer clients during their recovery. We are therefore very grateful to our colleague, Tim Brown, who currently works as a substance misuse worker on an inpatient detoxification unit. He generously gave his time to be interviewed so that we might hear about the role that groups played in his journey from service-user to co-facilitator of groups on an Acute Assessment Unit.

* * *

Disposing of the empty bottles became a bit of a problem. I'd go out at night dropping them off into various wheelie bins. I found myself thinking 'I can't put too many in Mrs So-and-So's this week, otherwise the bin men might start thinking she's got an alcohol problem. How many did I drop in 29's last week? I don't think I've done 33's for a while. . .'

These were the words spoken by a client in a support group on the ward I am currently working on. Clients were reminiscing about their day-to-day lifestyles prior to admission.

Ring any bells?

Just a bit. They rang cathedral-sized bells in my head as I was facilitating that particular group. For until about four and a half years earlier it could have been me speaking. Same street numbers, same thoughts, same feelings of furtiveness and guilt. It was the first time since I had completed my training as a substance misuse worker that a client had articulated a situation that I myself had previously been in.

In fact four and a half years ago, I did say those words. In a group. In treatment. And I expected people to laugh, or scoff, but they didn't. They listened and nodded and smiled and I had their support. Just as now, our client had her peers' support. And mine.

Tim, looking back to when you were in recovery, what sort of groups did you attend then?

Before I started the day programme, I attended three groups a week for six weeks. I did six weeks' worth of Harm Reduction (that was just for alcohol), a Men's Group and another group, I forget what it was called but we played this board game, and if you landed on a certain square then you had to say something, I suppose as a way of sharing experiences or whatever. My biggest memory of that group was that one week, when it was sunny weather, I'd got there early, and so I went over to the pub and had a lime-and-lemonade. And then in the group talked about that and got the first sort of 'You mustn't do that!' and all that sort of stuff.

What was that like for you, hearing that from the group?

Horrible, very horrible. At the time I didn't realize it was very Twelve-Step based. The group wasn't, but the flak I was getting was very Twelve-Step based and it was a pretty uncomfortable group. I remember going home and feeling very 'Grrrr' and all that sort of stuff.

What do you think of that now?

I suppose now I'd know a bit more about where their reaction was coming from and I've also learned so much more about myself since then that I couldn't have articulated then, because at the time I thought 'What's all this all about?'

When you heard you were going to be attending groups, what did you think, feel about that? Were you apprehensive, excited?

I suppose, yes, I was, it was all new stuff, I hadn't been to any groups before. Those initial groups weren't particularly large. Certainly there were two or three people in the Harm Reduction Group and they weren't always the same people. I don't think I had much fear about 'What am I going to say?' or anything like that. That was very much a learning group for me; I came across people who seemed to have different problems, which again with hindsight, I realized were sort of mental health problems that I knew nothing about at the time. And, people in that group would come and go, they wouldn't be there the next week and I would think 'Well, what's happened to them then?' and I didn't really understand that. The Men's Group was quite interesting. Again, I didn't really understand why they had the Men's Group, but they also had a Women's Group going on at exactly the same time in another room. I guess that was about covering areas that men didn't want women in, or women didn't want men in, or whatever. There were always fewer in the Men's Group than the Women's Group, which was interesting.

Do you think it was useful having a Men's Group?
Yes, yes, I think it was. Again it would vary so much, you know, because it was people who weren't on the day programme, so you had people who were still drinking, others who were trying to control their drinking, and others who were trying to give up. So it was a mish-mash of different people, and who were all there for different reasons. But again, with all these groups, even the one that was horrible, I sort of had the feeling of 'Well this is what I've got to do'. No one said that, but I felt it and I suspect it was them seeing how motivated I was.

What did you find helpful about those first groups you went to?
Well, I think, the fact that I wasn't alone, that whole thing about it not just being you and the mixture of different stories and different backgrounds, and hearing the different ways that people will try and handle it.

What was helpful about that?
Well . . . that no one's the same, well, I mean apart from the fact that we all have probably the same sort of problem, everyone's different, everyone has their own way of doing it. It was useful learning, watching how some people seemed to cope, and others didn't. But then again that feeds into now, you know. Every day I come into work and I never know who's still going to be here, who's suddenly decided they've had enough, whatever, so that sort of, again ties in.

It sounds like those first experiences prepared you for the changing nature of the groups here at work?
Yes, yes, absolutely. Another thing that was helpful about those groups was the joy of actually driving again as I needed to get behind a wheel to get there, being out and about, it was all sort of new, it was all about redis-covering things. So they were very much positive feelings. I was still having individual counselling once a week, so that was useful and it was good to talk things through. I only had four or five sessions, but I think that was probably all I needed. After about 6 weeks, I started the day programme proper, when things became much more structured. It was 4 days a week and there were the same people in each group and by then I was feeling much more confident.

From those groups, what would you say was useful for day-to-day living without alcohol?
From the day programme? Most of it, really. Again we went back through all the Harm Reduction stuff, which was no bad thing. We covered lots of facts and figures, the costs involved in alcohol, which I knew nothing about and found fascinating. We also covered the psychological and physical aspects of alcohol. We looked at anger stuff, I loved all that, it was all new

to me. Before these groups I thought that something happened and I got an emotion, I didn't realize that I thought about it and made sense of it, interpreted it. We also did assertiveness, covered all the background stuff like rights. What else did we do? Oh yes, problem-solving . . . things like don't bite it all off in one chunk, and all that. I really enjoyed the 6 weeks and it was then on a Monday morning that one of our number came in and he had lapsed over the weekend and I watched how the facilitator handled it. And as a result of that, we then did lapse versus relapse and all that sort of stuff. But, it was watching him, that was the first little sort of thing that went in there about (points to head) 'Ah, I think I fancy doing that.' So that's where I got the idea of 'Okay, I think I might have a go at this' came from. It was certainly only a very fleeting thought, and I didn't have a clue of how to do it or how to go about doing it, but that's where the idea came from.

The planting of the seed?
Yes, that was the planting of the seed. And then again, one of the practical things they did at the end of the course, we had a little a quiz, which was interesting, to see how much we had taken in. But it was all very gentle. And we made quite a good sort of group, the seven of us, we all got on pretty well. I mean they didn't all last, two dropped out before the end of the six weeks.

You said that you got on well. How did you develop that bond?
It just sort of grew really, I think, as people opened up and shared stuff with each other . . . One I still keep in touch with, admittedly only Christmas cards, but we're still in touch.

So you had individual counselling and attended groups. What do you think groups added to your recovery?
For me, it was three things really. It was the fact that I wasn't alone and therefore sharing experiences, even if they weren't similar, that was a big thing, for me. And through sharing those experiences, people saying 'Well I managed this once before, I stayed dry and this is how I did it'. Then there was learning stuff from other people. I realized that actually you learn almost as much from your peers as you do from the facilitator. Well you learn from both. So for me the groups were about learning from others, it was the not being alone, and also learning to articulate my own stuff that I suspect I'd kept locked inside. So they were the key elements really. Quite early on, I had this sort of vision, of me going back and grabbing the younger me and pulling him back through the thickets and brambles . . . and saying 'It's alright, it is alright on the other side but I've got to get you through here.' I don't know where that came from, but it was a very strong visual image. But I was very optimistic, both at the time and now looking

back on it. I had very few negative days there; in fact, it was one of the most positive times I think I've had in my life, really. And other things seemed to drop into place then. I was very lucky I had lots of support at home. I was sort of like a blotting paper really; I just soaked it all up, all this new stuff and being with other people who had the same problem.

That was a lovely description of what you found from the group, thank you. How did you then look into training?
That didn't happen quite then, it was a bit later on. I'd been semi-retired but then started thinking about going back to work. At the end of the group, they gave us details about an organisation called the Shaw Trust that helps people to get back into work. The first thing I started there was IT stuff; of course, my IT skills then were pretty much zilch.

Was the IT training run as a group?
Yes, well, sort of. It was sitting there in front of one of those things (points to PC), looking at it and swearing and thinking 'I don't understand this' while helpful people come round and showed me how to do it. I did that a couple of times a week. Again, it was also something to do; it was keeping me busy, which is part of what we do in the groups here, looking at how to keep busy. That was the autumn, then I went away and then at the end of that year I thought 'Right, if I am going to do anything about this, how do I go about this?' So I started looking into a counselling course and did a basic, one-term foundation course at Greenwich Community College. And that introduced me to basic counselling stuff; it introduced me to the whole idea of listening, confidentiality and being non-judgemental.

Did it make sense of things for you, what happened in groups and what facilitators did?
I don't know really. I don't think so. It was basics but new basics. After a few weeks we did 'triads', which I found terrifying, trying to 'listen' while a third person observed. But again, at that point I still didn't know how I was going to go about doing anything about becoming a drug worker. And then I'd gone into the Shaw Trust one day to do some IT work and my key worker said 'You're interested in becoming a drug/alcohol worker, aren't you?' and I said 'Well, yes, it's a theory'. He said 'Ring this number!' And that was Addaction's number and that was the next big step, which was becoming a trainee.

What sort of groups did you attend as part of your training?
My training was in two parts; there were two projects, the NEXT PROJECT and SMART SCHEME. The first project was over 12 weeks and was purely for ex-users who might or might not then go on and become workers. That was 2 days a week in groups and once a fortnight in a one-

to-one tutorial. The subjects we covered in the groups were 'Awareness of substance misuse', 'Theories of addiction', 'Boundaries', 'Assertiveness', 'Drugs and the law', 'Relapse prevention', and 'Giving and receiving feedback'. And then we did five subjects in the tutorials, which were the written stuff for the National Open College Network. The main subject was personal development. Actually personal development and reflection were the biggest parts of both courses. I guess really that was the whole ethos of both courses. We also covered 'Models of addiction', 'Basic awareness of different substances and alcohol', 'Harm reduction' and 'Interventions' which were motivational interviewing and CBT. We did a little bit of solution-focused therapy but not properly, which is a shame because that's something I'd like to have done more of.

The second project was very similar in set-up to the first, the only difference was that it was open to anyone, not just ex-users. It was specifically for people who wanted to go on and become drug workers. Also, the written part went towards the NVQ qualification and the course involved a placement here on the ward. It was spread over nine months and so it was in much more detail. At this time it also started coming together in terms of the practical aspects on placement and the theory back at the course base. Both courses were based on experiential learning, a 'learning by doing' approach. Although there was quite a lot of written stuff, that wasn't really what this particular group of trainers really concentrated on. It was very much reflection, self-awareness and developing through the group, throughout all the training to become a worker. Does that make sense? I think, out of the two courses only maybe three days at most in any way resembled a teacher giving facts. Whatever subject we did, we were nearly always broken up into groups or doing exercises, doing role-plays, learning that way. We got quite a lot of handouts too. But probably 95% of both courses were very much by 'doing it' rather than 'we're now going to sit here and learn that'.

That was a lovely description. I was thinking about that idea of 'learning by doing', and I wondered how safe you felt starting out by learning in a group? Pretty unsafe, well no, that's not the right word, I did feel safe but what I did feel, which I suspect a lot of other people also felt, was 'Everyone else is more interesting, brighter, have more interesting backgrounds, are braver in getting up and doing stuff' and all that. Funnily enough, before I came in today, I was thinking of an example. We would often break up in to mini-groups within the group, depending on what we were studying that day, and we nearly always were in different groups, which was good because that was how you got to know everyone. It would nearly always involve a case study or something like that, where someone would take on the facilitator role within the mini-group, someone would be writing something down on the sheet, and then we would present our thoughts to the large group. I was always the writer. Until they realized 'Hold on, why is he always doing that?' It was because I felt comfortable with that. So relatively quickly I realized, or I think it was made obvious, we would have to take a turn at doing everything, which of course gave me the beginnings of the idea of group dynamics. Because the ones who happily sit there and write away, like me, it's about comfort zones and we started thinking about comfort zones, which I'd never thought about before. So I notice it here, I pick up on the aspects that people in groups are happy to do and not do.

I was interested in hearing more about the personal development aspect of the course, and wondered how it prepared you for challenges that come up in your work?
I don't think it did consciously, because at that point I wasn't still 100% sure that's what I'd end up doing. I suppose, I became aware for example, particularly during the first course, I was the only alcohol user as opposed to drug user or both, and my own background felt very different to nearly everyone else in terms of age, in terms of life experiences, so in that way I think I was quite an odd man out, I think. So now I suppose if I see people here who for whatever reason stick out, I do sort of empathize with them. But I don't think I was aware of it as it happened; all I was aware of was that I felt that I stuck out a bit, that I was a bit too 'normal' (that horrible word, whatever it means), and therefore not interesting and didn't have much to offer and all that stuff. And so the stories that came out, the life styles were totally beyond me, they weren't anything that I knew anything about. Again as it happened it was wonderful training really, as it wasn't a great big shock to me when I came to work here.

It makes me think about how people can be 'put into' roles within a group.
Yes, at the time I didn't realize that, I guess. There was always the one who wanted to lead the mini-groups and always the one who had more to say than the others, the ones who were always bored, the ones who held back, of which I was one, but the facilitators knew that and actively worked with that. Which was one of the reasons they always broke us up into different groups.

It sounds like you picked up some useful facilitation skills?
Well, I think so, I was very aware when I did the group interviews for the second course that I used my own group experiences and I think that's what got me onto the course. I found myself in a mini-group with just two others, one of whom was trying to dominate the other and I don't know where it came from, but I just thought 'Oh no, no, no!' and I wrested the group away from him. It wasn't like me. Going back to the training, we did lose people from the course, people who decided they didn't want to become drug-workers, or couldn't manage the NVQ part, or some people

relapsed. The first course was a rolling course, after the four weeks, one or two people left and the following week, another two or three people arrived, which in itself was interesting because this reflects very much what happens here. We have a group that is very settled and then two or three of the clients leave and we get another two who, well, immediately disrupt the group that is left. On both courses we did a day on 'endings', which was very much about how you cope with endings because all of the 'I'll keep your number' and then don't and all that.

Although the trainers made sure the group was safe and focused, they were very much our groups. The focus was very much on we decide how the group goes. On the first course, there was a 'check in' to start with and a 'check out' at the end of each day. On the second course, we spent much more time and detail processing at the end of the day. That was something I never learned to do properly.

What makes you say that?
Well, either I'd be waiting to say something then someone else would say it before me and I'd have to think of something else today, or I'd think of what I really wanted to say when I walked through the door at home!

A matter of timing?
Yes, my timing is not very good. Even now I still can't do it. But you know, that was very much the ethos of the course; you're not allowed to go into your comfort zone. I remember them saying at the start of the course, you should feel raw, rung out by the end of every day and I did. Looking back on it, it was wonderful training for here and, in fact, for any place.

Could you summarize the benefits of having groups as part of your training?
Well, looking back now, I can't imagine it being done in any other way. The realization that everyone is different was so useful and that a group will have its own dynamics, something will happen in the group regardless, you could just sit there and something will happen, was also very good learning. We had one day just like that, it was very, very uncomfortable; for about half an hour no one knew what we were supposed to be doing and that was very deliberate! It was facilitated by one of the senior trainers; she was brilliant! So I realized that you just can sit there in the group and something will happen. I learned that it doesn't matter what the subject matter is, or what you're supposed to be talking about, because there will be dynamics around it.

Do you think only those people with experience of addiction can run groups for people with addiction?
No, I don't. But I do think probably the groups are slightly different.

In what way?

Well, soon after I started here on the ward, there was a member of staff who was an ex-user, although I didn't know this to start with. When I did groups with him he had an immediate rapport with the group that I couldn't quite put my finger on, which I then realized afterwards was because he was an ex-user. And so, the group had a different feel to it, in a way it was less sort of 'school like', less 'this is what we're going to teach you'. I probably couldn't have put that into words then, that's in hindsight.

How was that different compared with facilitating groups with people who aren't ex-users?

He was quite open, he self-disclosed. Which is another subject in itself. So I suppose in a way the argument for that, there is no pretence, so the group know and therefore, they think, 'Right, he's one of us'. So one difference with ex-users, at least you can get rid of that 'them and us' feeling, they feel you are on their wavelength. The group can have less of a classroom feel to it, in my view. But then the other side of it is perhaps people who haven't used can be more objective about issues that come up in the group and they can actually say 'Well, okay, I don't have that experience but. . . .' And it starts an interesting discussion. It works both ways.

Thinking more about self-disclosure, that of course has its pros and cons. I started off self-disclosing as I was encouraged to by the team here. So at first I thought 'This is great!' as it cut away all the 'them and us' stuff. But of course what it did lead to was 'How did you do it?' and questions like that. I quickly discovered that didn't really help the group as it was about me and it shouldn't be, it should be about them. And so I began to think it was less useful to self-disclose. Sometimes I long to, but I really think carefully 'Is that for me, Tim, or is that for them?' If it's for me then I forget it. But if it's for them, and it can help, then maybe I will, but I tend not to now. Now I think it can get a bit muddy, 'un-boundaried' when I self-disclose, so I don't tend to.

What do you enjoy about facilitating groups?

Watching the light bulbs come on, that gives me a real buzz. When they go 'Oh right, I hadn't thought about that!' I suspect it reminds me of when I felt light bulbs come on in my head! I like seeing the support they give each other. And sometimes, the group can be very inspiring, on both those levels when you watch them supporting one another and watch someone picking something up and saying 'Hold on . . . Oh right!' and then running with that and us saying 'Okay then, what do you think that means then? How are you going to develop that?' If they take it along a tangent, then I run with that, though sometimes I need to pull it back if it goes too far.

So that 'light bulb' moment could be one of the ways you know a group has been useful?
Yes, also sometimes they say, 'It's been a good group, thank you for that!' But then of course, sometimes, half of them sleep through it!

What's that like for you as a facilitator?
It's very difficult, but then of course you can understand why, particularly if they're in their first few days of treatment and the medication is building up. But that of course can agitate the others who are further down the line and they see someone nodding off all the time, and quite like the idea of dozing themselves but can't. I sometimes forget, but have to try to remember; the group are not all at the same stage of their treatment. Someone who's been here for two weeks is feeling very different to someone who's been in for two days, purely because of what's inside of them.

I remember you saying about your first course being a rolling programme: it sounds a bit like that.
Yes, the group dynamics change, as people leave and people come in. The group is never the same; you never quite know what the group will be like, as you've not necessarily had exactly that same group before. Just one new person may have gone and another has joined but it all feels different. And, so again it's watching, asking 'Who's the noisy one this time, who's the one who wants to take control? Oh, it isn't him this time, he's been usurped, it's this one instead. How's he going to deal with it?' I find it quite interesting. So then you split the group up and then he can go back to being the dominant one again.

It reminds me of your training with the mini-groups which always changed.
Yes, all the time.

So there are lots of things going on in the group: how do you make sense of it?
I'm not sure really. I go with it. I've been quite lucky I've been able to work with people from different backgrounds and learn from that. I've also been able to facilitate with the same person for particular groups and have been able to build up a relationship. That's helped me a lot, especially in the early days, as sometimes there's not much chance to observe here before facilitating. We don't always take the same role in the group and we agree to swap sections of the group. That comes from working together regularly. But it can feel harder or less comfortable when I facilitate with someone new or someone who hasn't facilitated this group for ages or even any group for years and of course then their fear builds up.

What would you recommend to them?

It's very difficult, because if they genuinely haven't done that particular group, then I might suggest that I take the lead in running it; it's not ideal, of course. If I haven't done a group for a while, then I make sure I have a read through the manual and brush up on what the group is about. Of course, there are some groups that I prefer doing over others, but then I think that's the same for most people. I get a real buzz out of doing the CBT 'Thinking Choices' group and most people are terrified of it, but then again, in my case I suspect that's because I found CBT so useful when I was in treatment. CBT made such a big difference to me and I think that's why I enjoy doing that group now. I like the inner bully group, I call that the 'Who says?' group! I still get anxious before groups. Before I go in I tend to do the 'Well, what's the worst that could happen. . .?' And that sort of settles me down a bit. I wouldn't say groups are scary, but I do feel a certain edge beforehand. But for me, I think that's a helpful feeling. This probably links back to my theatre background; if there isn't an edge, it wouldn't be a good performance. But that's just me.

What would you recommend to people who are new to groups?

I would say take time to prepare it; of course, that can be hard to do. It also helps to have trust in the other person who's doing the group.

What makes for a good facilitator?

Trying to be aware of the quiet ones, trying to include everyone, trying to make the group as much for them and not trying to pretend we know more than they do, because of course we don't. I think a good facilitator tries to share their experiences and their knowledge. I try to share my experiences without sort of saying 'I've been in that same boat.' Giving the group something to think about or to investigate. Of course, it doesn't always work; sometimes they might not want to do a group, and you might not get through to them. Although sometimes having said that, something changes for them in the group, where the group was the space where someone floated an idea around that someone else picked up on. As a facilitator you can encourage someone to come up with an idea that someone else picks up on. I don't think you can predict how a group will go. You can go into a particular group thinking 'This will be all right', but then it goes as flat as a pancake and you come away wondering 'What happened there?' But I link that back to when I was performing, when one performance might go as flat as a pancake and I could spend hours analysing it, but then realize that it was a different audience and the spark just wasn't there, or perhaps in some cases I was trying too hard. Sometimes I bring those thoughts back to here, and think perhaps I was trying too hard, or they were, instead of just letting it happen, which in some cases it will, or in others it just won't happen at that time. You just have to accept 'Okay, perhaps it will be better this afternoon, or tomorrow.' There's no guarantee that a group will always work; that's something I learned from performing, that sometimes it just doesn't. It would be easy to beat yourself up, to think 'What did I do wrong?' It can help to have time afterwards to think about it. Another thing that is helpful for the group is to go at their speed so they can get the most out of the group. So you have to be aware of your speed and timings, you need to judge when that particular group needs more time on a section or has finished, and it might be different for each group. You learn by doing it really.

What else can help to support you and help you learn and develop?
Every now and again, I go through the group manual to remind myself of the group. Through doing the groups, I think about the bits that don't work and cut these out after discussing this with the rest of the team.

Thank you Tim, is there anything else you'd like to add?
I've found that the more you tell the group and involve them, right from the start, in why we're doing the group, the more likely you are to get their participation. When you say something like 'This is what we're doing', they end up asking 'Well, what's this all about then?' Also, I think it's useful to explain the links between the different groups here so the clients don't think each group is in isolation. I remember that in my course or training, either you pick it up yourself or someone else points it out. I remember joining up the dots and thinking, 'Oh, I see, that links in with that!'

The other major thing is that the group is the clients' chance for realizing they're not alone. I know that clients understand that when they're out on the patio having a smoke, but in the group it's in a slightly more formal setting. So they realize they're not alone and when they hear people speaking and they go 'Oh blimey, that's my problem', it's that first point of contact. And then, if we can float ideas around, or get them to float the ideas around, they can learn something from it and they can pick things up from others in the group. If you have someone here at the end of their stay and they help others who have just walked through the door, that's the beginnings of group support.

Tim, thank you very much.

Chapter 2

Motivation and change

The role of motivational interviewing in substance use groups

Luke Mitcheson and Brett Grellier

Introduction

Understanding what motivates our clients to take drugs and alcohol, and what motivates them to change these behaviours once they become problematic is, and will remain, a central preoccupation of anyone working in the field of addictions. Intuitive clinicians will know how therapeutic interventions must be able to respond to the subtle shifts in clients' struggles to control their behaviour, but they may have found it difficult to synthesize academic and theoretical perspectives on motivation into useful practical knowledge. Considering how motivation may be influenced, for better or worse, in the context of group work adds another level of complexity to what is already a complex issue. Heather (1992) has described addiction as a motivational problem, and we start by defining motivation before considering why motivation should be of interest in clinical work and specifically in group work. Through the prism of knowledge about how to enhance individual motivation to change, we consider what could be usefully applied in groups.

What is motivation?

Motivation is a concept that is commonly invoked as key in all that we do. We infer that it is 'motives' that steer us in certain directions over others. Motives are understood to be largely instinctual and are shared with the animal kingdom, e.g., the need/drive for shelter, food, and water. Along with these basic motives are social needs and curiosity motives. Social needs pertain to our motivation to feel part of a group or to form romantic relationships. Curiosity motives relate to the seemingly innate need for sensory stimulation. Scientists have discovered that our motivation to fulfil our basic needs is regulated by homeostatic systems in our body in much the same way that a thermostat maintains a consistent temperature in our homes. For example, our bodies send messages to the brain that say that we require glucose for our system to run optimally, and this activates particular areas of the brain that then motivate us to search for food.

How does this relate to addiction? The reasons why some individuals use and then become addicted to drugs are complex and relate to the inter-relationships of individual differences in terms of biological make-up, personality traits as well as social context (Mitcheson, Maslin, Meynen, Morrison, Hill, & Wanigaratne, 2010). This has led to integrative theories that incorporate physiological, psychological, and social perspectives, so-called bio-psycho-social theories (Orford, 2001; Wanigarante, 2006).

We can theorize how motivation can initiate initial experimentation with substances and subsequent addiction problems. Both social needs and curiosity motives can be understood as motivating initial experimentation with drugs and alcohol. The consumption of alcohol in many western societies is a common social practice and the motivation to be part of a social group will motivate the desire to drink alcohol. Similarly, in certain social groups the consumption of illegal drugs can also be viewed as a social norm or a way of gaining special status within a particular subculture. The curiosity motive needs little explanation: the desire to seek out novel experiences is understood to be innate in higher-order species.

The consumption of drugs and alcohol can also be understood in the context of the homeostatic system. If normal coping methods for excessively high or low levels of arousal are absent or perceived to be ineffective, then drugs might be used to counteract this. As the body becomes accustomed to external stimulation then homeostatic systems develop around the ingestion of drugs in order to maintain the equilibrium. The messages sent to the brain therefore motivate actions to obtain more drugs.

An important aspect of these ideas is the extent to which motivation is a trait or whether it is better understood as a mediating variable in the change process. Miller (1985) concluded there was limited evidence for viewing motivation as a trait, thereby undermining the idea that clients with substance use problems have a particular 'addictive' personality. It is now recognized that motivation is better understood as a more dynamic and fluctuating construct.

Most practitioners with even a passing interest in addictions are likely to have heard of Prochaska and DiClemente's (1983) transtheoretical model of change. This model proposed that individuals pass through a number of stages: pre-contemplation, contemplation, decision (preparation), action, and maintenance. Individuals were proposed to either remain at the maintenance stage or to relapse, which would then send them back to the pre-contemplation stage. In later work Prochaska and DiClemente (1996) suggested a spiral model in which individuals could move back and forth across all stages. This model has been extremely influential in the addictions field and an assessment of an individual's stage of change has been used to inform the type of intervention applied. While these assessments might not reveal anything more startling than whether the individuals are more or less ready to change their behaviour. This fact alone requires us to challenge the 'one size fits all' approach. This is worth keeping in mind when thinking about running groups and is discussed later. It follows that certain interventions may be better suited to clients at different times. For example, contingency management approaches that attend to extrinsic rather than intrinsic motivation would be appropriate at the pre-contemplation stage, whereas in the maintenance phase, where motivation is optimal, mindfulness-based approaches could be indicated. Despite the ubiquity of this model, there has been little empirical evidence to support the distinct stages. However, in practice, this model does provide a framework for a dialogue with individuals that helps them to conceptualize their own experience of change and can help services develop a more nuanced approach to service design.

Partly in response to some of the deficiencies of the stage model of change, West (2006) has developed the PRIME theory. This is a dynamic model that attempts to provide a conceptualization of the motivational factors for change across five interacting levels. PRIME is an acronym for 'Plans', 'Responses', 'Impulses/inhibitory forces', 'Motives', and 'Evaluations'. This theory has integrated aspects of previous theories of addiction and may provide researchers with the opportunity to empirically test its principles, with the hope that it could influence future clinical interventions.

At this stage, given the theoretical ambiguities and lack of research to support a consensus about the role of motivation in the change process, practitioners might well ask whether the construct of motivation is a help or a hindrance to planning and running groups. Perhaps it is then useful to take a step into practice-based evidence to what experienced practitioners would consider to be self-evident. This would include the notion that some clients seem to be more motivated to change than others, but also that within individuals the desire for change also fluctuates over time. Motivation to change can also be imposed. Extrinsic motivation, such as ultimatums from courts or concerned family members, will not be universally effective for all people and this indicates that internal or intrinsic motivation will also need to be attended to. As a consequence of these subtle changes and shifting motivations, it is a reasonable conclusion that certain interventions are likely to be more helpful than others at particular times with particular individuals. This presents a fundamental conundrum to thinking about motivation in the context of group work: if motivation is so individually specific, how can it be directly worked with in groups?

In order to answer this question we focus on the theory and application of an individual counselling method known as Motivational Interviewing (MI) (Miller & Rollnick, 2002). We are not advocating a simple translation of these ideas to groups but believe there is a wealth of experience behind these ideas that can point us in the right direction when thinking about enhancing motivation through group work.

Motivational interviewing: core philosophy and principles

Motivational interviewing (MI) is a particular form of skilled communication designed to enhance intrinsic motivation to change and is closely associated with the work of Miller and Rollnick (1986). The core philosophy of MI is most closely aligned with Carl Roger's humanistic theory of motivation (Rogers, 1957). The humanistic theory of change rests heavily on the assumption that humans are intrinsically motivated to move towards what is good and fulfilling for them. This assumption has yet to receive any compelling supporting evidence and social constructionist writers have argued strongly against this supposed innate drive (e.g., Gergen, 1999). However, we are interested here with how MI works in practice.

The initial description of MI was not derived from a philosophical or theoretical base, but rather from retrospective analysis of some common principles that Miller had been using in his clinical practice that did not seem to fit with the cognitive behavioural model he was working with at the time (Miller & Rollnick, 2009). Later on, Miller and Rollnick (2002) paid more attention to the philosophical principles, in particular humanistic philosophy, while recognizing differences between MI and Roger's (1961) person-centred counselling. The most striking difference is MI's role of directing conversation towards a motivational discourse, or 'change talk', that is in opposition to Rogers' approach that values non-directiveness. Similarly, theoretical explanations of the process of change have come as a result of empirical findings and links have been made to the social psychological theories of cognitive dissonance (Festinger, 1957), reactance (Silvia, 2005), and self-perception theory (Bem, 1967; Laird, 2007). We also find a social constructionist perspective useful, in which the principles that direct communication create a novel discourse that opens up the possibility of change.

The core principles of MI are the expression of empathy, developing discrepancy, rolling with resistance, and supporting self-efficacy. Based on the principles of Rogerian person-centred counselling, it is believed that the communication of a non-judgemental empathic understanding of the client and their difficulties facilitates change. Key to this principle is the acceptance that ambivalence about change is a normal part of human experience. The developing of discrepancy, relating to the theories of cognitive dissonance, is guided by the belief that change is motivated by a perceived discrepancy between present behaviour and important personal goals or values. For example, a client for whom retaining custody of their child depends on quitting drug use will find their current behaviour is in direct opposition to their goal of preventing their child being taken into care. Returning to the first principle, it is important that the arguments for change come from the client rather than the counsellor. It is the counsellor's role to open up possibilities in dialogue for the client to discover why it is important for them to change in order to achieve their personal goals. The third principle, rolling with resistance, guides the counsellor away from arguing for change, but instead acknowledging the client as the primary resource for finding answers and solutions. For example, if the client expresses that he is never going to be able to change, then the counsellor would empathically reflect this back rather than being caught in the 'why don't you'/'yes . . . but' trap. Finding yourself in this trap is a sign that you need to respond differently and get out of this communication dead end.

The final guiding principle of supporting self-efficacy relates to the client's own belief in their ability to make changes. The emphasis here is on the client's responsibility for choosing and carrying out change, with the counsellor skilfully communicating their belief in the client's ability to change. This can be achieved in a number of ways, e.g., reflecting back to the client areas in their life where they have been able to make positive changes and then asking open-ended questions that help the client to discover transferable skills that they can apply to their current situation. In summary, MI can be understood as optimizing conditions for clients to become ready, willing, and able to make change (Rollnick, Miller, & Butler, 2008). The willingness for change is attended to through the creation of cognitive dissonance in which, through the empathic understanding and developing of discrepancy, the 'why' of change is created. The ability to make changes is attended to through the development of self-efficacy through which the client becomes confident that they know 'how' to change. The readiness to change is created when the 'why' and 'how' reach an optimum point: the reasons for change are clear and compelling and the client's confidence in their ability to make the changes is assimilated.

Motivational interviewing with groups

There is sufficient evidence for MI-based approaches to be recommended by the NICE psychosocial guidelines for drug misuse (National Institute for Health and Clinical Excellence, 2007) and the core ideas are well known across the addictions field. Why not then directly apply MI to working in groups? Indeed, this very question was posed by Walters, Ogle, and Martin (2002) in their chapter entitled 'Perils and possibilities of group-based motivational interviewing', where they clearly inject a cautionary note into a simple application of MI to working with groups. In contrast to individual applications of MI, the evidence base for group-based MI is thin and one study reported worse results compared with simply giving feedback to people on their alcohol consumption (Walters et al., 2002).

Why might this be? Essentially, and despite appearances, MI is a complex and subtle counselling approach requiring the therapist to be sensitive to an individual's ambivalence and therefore to adapt style and intervention accordingly. Even in sessions with individuals, research has shown that therapists following a MI protocol can, when the protocol is discordant with the client's ambivalence, lead those clients to become more resistant to change (Amrhein, Miller, Yahne, Palmer, & Fulcher, 2003). While it may be theoretically possible to do MI in groups, in reality the sheer complexity of this would suggest otherwise. Walters and colleagues (2002) highlight a number of the processes occurring within a group, some of which we have represented diagrammatically in Figure 2.1 with a 'group' of two clients.

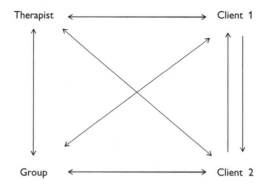

Figure 2.1 Processes for a therapist to consider in group work.

Attending to these processes in a more typical group of eight or more people adds to the complexity. If we accept that doing MI for individuals in groups as devised may be beyond the capability of most practitioners, is there still a way to make use of some of the wisdom inherent in the interventions associated with this approach? We believe there is, and would refer back to the introductory chapter of this book and Yalom's (1975) curative group processes. To varying degrees, these curative processes are relevant to all of the core dimensions of motivation; importance, confidence, and readiness to change. The group can take less motivated individuals with them on the change process, provide arguments for change and undermine reasons for no change. But equally, when things do not go so well, these processes highlight how groups might undermine advances on these dimensions.

In the language of MI, resistance from some powerful group participants can have a demoralizing effect on others and the desire for cohesiveness may lead participants to undermine the therapist's attempts to roll with this resistance. Participants may seek to avoid dissonance both internally and within the group too, leading to an entrenchment of no-change or at least the status quo. An example from our experience of this process occurring is clients glorifying drug taking in groups with a selective focus on the positive aspects of using, even when undergoing a voluntary drug detoxification.

Despite these risks we know that interpersonal pressure can work the other way too: the majority could shift the individual less ready for change towards change and reinforce this with the public commitment to change that a group facilitates. Recognizing the power of the group to enhance and create motivation, but also understanding that the group can do exactly the opposite, is essential. This is relevant where enhancing motivation is either an explicit focus of the group or an implicit aim within the wider context of a group. We consider these issues further with reference to the four principles of MI.

Express empathy

The challenge in a group context is maintaining equity of empathy to participants presenting diverse and conflicting views and ideas. This can in part be addressed explicitly in the setting of ground rules at the start of the group. Ideally, this would be done by asking participants which ground rules they would like to see in operation and agreeing the role of the facilitator and participants in monitoring and enforcing such rules. It is our experience that the essence of ground rules can be distilled down to a basic respect for each other, such that each person's right to express an idea or opinion does not demean or belittle another participant. The more the group owns the ground rules, the more the participants are likely to adhere to them, thus giving some space for the facilitator to attend to more subtle differences within the group. Walters et al. (2002) suggest that strategies used to work with resistance, such as giving attention to the views that you want to amplify, using reflective listening, and acknowledging the difference of opinion in summary statements, can be useful. Like a conductor of an orchestra, the facilitator is highly active in monitoring the group process and directing the group to 'perform', i.e., fully participate. Rollnick et al. suggest that it can be helpful to 'encourage the quiet, soften the loud' (2008, p. 171). This can be done by drawing less vocal participants into the discussion with direct questions and by asking more assertive participants to summarize their key points for the group to consider.

Key to expressing empathy is recognizing the strengths and limitations of each participant and using these strategically in facilitating the group process. Despite the intention to create a supportive group that is tolerant of divergent opinion, there will inevitably be moments when you as the facilitator will have to take control of the group to keep it safe and move in a positive direction. Although this will lead to some participants expressing a loss of empathy, reminding the group of the core purpose of the group or the programme the group is part of (i.e., the meta-meaning of why people are in the group) may be required.

Develop discrepancy

Confrontation is the implicit goal of MI, but confrontation is not direct because this increases resistance to change. Instead, MI attempts to elicit the reasons for change from the client rather than attempting to persuade him or her that change is necessary (Miller & Rollnick, 2002; Tober & Raistrick, 2007). Theoretically, peers in a group have experiences to draw on that may enable them to challenge each other in a more direct and legitimate way than a professional would be able to do. When this works, it can be a short-cut to resolving ambivalence, the group norm providing a powerful motivator to consider different ways of thinking and being. We say theoretically because, unless skilfully managed, this can also be experienced as punishing and alienating and lead to participants withdrawing from the group and entrenching a position of no-change with the added burden of loss of self-esteem. Participants may also seek to maintain equilibrium in the group, to avoid conflict, and re-norm in a way that minimizes the extent and nature of difficulties participants may be presenting. Such behaviour can entrench a negative group position of no-change. Using the group to enhance discrepancy can be akin to handling a volatile explosive like nitro-glycerine—highly effective in the right circumstances but not without danger!

To avoid mishaps, we suggest some thought is given in the preparatory phase of the group to who is going to be in the group and what you as facilitators are hoping to achieve. In a cohesive, well-motivated group the ability to enhance discrepancy within the group will be better tolerated than in a group in which participants have more mixed levels of motivations. Rollnick et al. (2008) note that one of the traps to guiding in groups is conducting multiple individual consultations. In the right circumstances, inviting comment from other participants on another's ambivalence, in such a way that allows an expression of empathy, may be useful, for example asking 'Who else has felt stuck like this?' or 'How did things shift?' Walters et al. (2002) suggest that breaking a group up into smaller working units with strategic placing of more motivated participants with others who may be less motivated can be useful too.

Roll with resistance

It is inevitable that resistance will be experienced in the group and that facilitators will be indirectly and directly challenged as obvious figures of authority and advocates of change. Of all the principles of individual MI, it is our experience that this is the most difficult to translate to a group setting. As Walters et al. (2002) highlight, the risk is that the group may re-norm around the more powerful and resistant participants. The facilitator is then set up to respond to bring the group back round to a more positive atmosphere. The battle-lines are thus drawn. There is no easy solution to avoid this. At times the facilitator will need to be highly active and intervene. In extreme circumstances this may even require the facilitator to ask people to leave the group. The ground rules highlighted above may reduce the risk of a negative re-norming of the group occurring, as will the individual MI techniques for managing resistance. If it is one or two individuals being particularly resistant, then simply ignoring them and attending to the other participants may be effective. More direct interventions might include inviting alternative views with the aim of using the group norm to shift the resistant participants from their entrenched views. Rolling with resistance may be easier with two facilitators, so that there is support to step in and steer the group in another direction.

Inevitably there will be times when group facilitators will leave the group feeling that things have not gone well. This is when post-group reflection becomes crucial. In this space it may be helpful to reflect on what happened and what the resistance experienced was all about. To usefully understand it in motivational terms, rather than thinking a client or group is 'unmotivated', instead consider whether the behaviours exhibited were due to a lack of awareness of a problem or of a perceived need for change. Maybe there was simply a lack of interest in what you were offering as available treatment? The development of the MI approach challenges us to think about clients not as intrinsically unmotivated, but motivated for different things; the challenge to us as practitioners is to make what we offer relevant (Donovan & Rosengren, 1999).

Support self-efficacy

As with expressing empathy and developing discrepancy, groups also have the potential to help individuals develop self-efficacy, the 'how' of change. The facilitator's role is to harness the knowledge and experience in the room to support explicit conversations about change. Equally, the facilitator needs to be mindful of the group getting mired in conversations about failure and no-change. We find solution-focused thinking useful here. As a facilitator your task is to be very interested in the resources that people use and the knowledge they have gained from their struggles in overcoming addictive behaviour. Facilitators can invite group members to comment on each other's resources ('How do you think X did that?') as well as suggest things that have worked for themselves. Drawing on past successes and change experiences unrelated to substance use can be rich sources of ideas. Groups can be set up with these goals in mind. It is also useful to use the group to solidify commitment by encouraging public statements of commitment to actual change and explicit action.

Keeping in mind the four principles of MI can be a useful reference point during group work, even if the logistics and evidence base for doing pure MI remains to be established. More recent developments of MI have shifted to thinking about broader styles of communication. Rollnick et al. (2008) describe three of these: guiding, following, and directing. Each of these ways of communicating has a place within group work. A following ('going along with') style would best be suited to an exploratory open-ended group, and a directing ('taking charge') style to an educative group, for example one set up to deliver overdose training. Yet in both these groups, at times there will also be a place for the guiding style and indeed the guiding style should predominate in groups seeking to make participants fully active in the process. When talking to clients about the why, how, what, and when of behaviour change, the skill lies in structuring the conversation in a useful way that encourages the clients to take as much of the lead as possible.

As with MI, guiding with individuals utilizes four core counselling skills:

1   asking open questions
2   affirming your client's position
3   listening reflectively and
4   summarizing.

They facilitate the principles of MI and are a useful set of skills to use when running groups. Using these skills as a guiding style in your interactions can help to facilitate motivation to change and foster a therapeutic environment that maximizes the success of the treatment intervention.

Asking open questions

Using open questions as opposed to closed questions will encourage your clients to talk and think aloud in the groups. In doing this you are more likely to facilitate conversations in the group and get people active in the process. A couple of well-chosen, open questions can be sufficient to direct the group to the core purpose and get people active and contributing. Asking open questions emphasizes collaboration and active participation.

Affirming your client's position

This is one way of fulfilling the 'express empathy' principle of MI and the same provisos apply here too. Few clients start treatment completely ready, willing, and able to begin the difficult process of addressing their substance use. In spite of the problems that substance use may be causing in their lives, there will simultaneously be aspects of using that are valued and have positive or negative reinforcing qualities and that are therefore difficult to give up. It is important not to label or judge clients. Instead, empathizing with the dilemmas and difficulties your clients tell you about (their ambivalence) with responses such as 'That feels like quite a struggle' will help develop an atmosphere of trust and understanding. As a facilitator the challenge remains as to how far you can maintain this position with particular individuals in a group when this seems to be against the general therapeutic atmosphere.

Listening carefully and reflectively

A clear understanding of your clients' experiences will only happen through careful listening. Listening is an active process that communicates that you are interested in what your clients are saying and want to work with them to achieve change. Not listening carefully can result in your clients feeling misunderstood, rejected, and sceptical about treatment, reluctant to talk about what is going on, and perhaps disengaging. Reflecting back what your client has said, in a short summary, is a way of demonstrating that you have been listening. While it may not be possible to ensure that participants will listen to each other, a facilitator can still model how it can be done and set the tone of the group process.

Summarizing

Summarizing is a key part of MI and a key part of a facilitator's role in groups. It shows that you have been listening, provides an opportunity to check that nothing has been missed, allows you to emphasize key points from the discussion and enables you to move the group on in a different direction.

In many respects the difficulties of adopting MI in groups reflects the difficulties of running groups generally. We believe the rich source of ideas and therapeutic tools from the MI literature offers the potential to help better facilitate groups as well as keep in mind the shifting interpersonal dynamics that can impact on participants' motivations. The principles of MI, distilled down into a guiding counselling style and the basic communication skills outlined above, should be a cornerstone of any group facilitator's competencies. Excellent resources for both experienced and budding practitioners of MI can be found at www.motivationalinterview.org.

Conclusion

Motivation is not a fixed concept and it increases or decreases as a function of shifting personal, cognitive, behavioural, and environmental determinants. Thus, it is possible that a client's motivation may fluctuate throughout the course of a group or from one group to the next, or even during a single meeting. If this occurs, remember that motivation is not static, consciously owned, and controlled by the client, but an evolving interaction between therapist, client, the outside world, and the group.

The three key concepts in MI are that:

1 client motivation is critical for change
2 motivation is a dynamic rather than a static trait and
3 motivation is influenced by external factors, including the therapist's and the group's behaviour.

These three factors need to be attended to at all times, not only because of their importance in controlling behaviour change, but because we as therapists and group workers affect them just as much, if not more than the clients themselves.

References

Amrhein, P. C., Miller, W. R., Yahne, C. E., Palmer, M., & Fulcher, L. (2003). Client commitment language during motivational interviewing predicts drug use outcomes. *Journal of Consulting and Clinical Psychology, 71*, 862–878.

Bem, D. J. (1967). Self-perception: An alternative interpretation of cognitive dissonance phenomena. *Psychological Review, 74*, 183–200.

Donovan, D. M., & Rosengren, D. B. (1999). Motivation for behavior change and treatment among substance abusers. In J. A. Tucker, D. M. Donovan, & F. G. Marlatt (Eds.), *Changing addictive behavior: Bridging clinical and public health strategies* (pp. 127–160). New York: Guilford Press.

Festinger, L. (1957). *A theory of cognitive dissonance*. Evanston, IL: Row, Peterson.

Gergen, K. J. (1999). *An invitation to social constructionism*. London: Sage.

Heather, N. (1992). Addictive disorders are essentially motivational problems. *British Journal of Addiction, 87*, 828–830.

Laird, J. D. (2007). *Feelings: The perceptions of self*. New York: Oxford University Press.

Miller, W. R. (1985). Motivation for treatment: A review with special emphasis on alcoholism. *Psychological Bulletin, 98*, 84–107.

Miller, W. R., & Rollnick, S. (1986). *Motivational interviewing: Preparing people for change*. New York: Guilford Press.

Miller, W. R., & Rollnick, S. (2002). *Motivational interviewing: Preparing people to change addictive behaviour* (2nd ed.). New York: Guilford Press.

Miller, W. R., & Rollnick, S. (2009). Ten things that motivational interviewing is not. *Behavioural and Cognitive Psychotherapy, 37*, 129–140.

Mitcheson, L., Maslin, J., Meynen, T., Morrison, T., Hill, R., & Wanigaratne, S. (2010). *Applied cognitive and behavioural approaches to the treatment of addiction: A practical treatment guide*. Oxford: Wiley-Blackwell.

National Institute for Health and Clinical Excellence (2007). *Drug misuse: Psychosocial interventions*. NICE clinical guideline 51. London: NICE.

Orford, J. (2001). *Excessive appetites: A psychological review of addictions*. Chichester: Wiley.

Prochaska, J. O., & DiClemente, C. C. (1983). Process and stages of self-change of smoking: Towards an integrative model of change. *Journal of Consulting and Clinical Psychology*, *51*, 390–395.

Prochaska, J. O., & DiClemente, C. C. (1996). Towards a comprehensive model of change. In W. R. Miller & N. Heather (Eds.), *Treating addictive behaviours* (2nd ed., pp. 3–27). New York: Plenum.

Rogers, C. R. (1957). The necessary and sufficient conditions of therapeutic personality change. *Journal of Consulting Psychology*, *21*, 95–103.

Rogers, C. R. (1961). *On becoming a person*. Boston: Houghton Mifflin.

Rollnick, S., Miller, W. R., & Butler, C. C. (2008). *Motivational interviewing in health care: Helping patients change behavior*. New York: Guilford Press.

Silvia, P. J. (2005). Deflecting reactance: The role of similarity in increasing compliance and reducing resistance. *Basic and Applied Social Psychology*, *27*, 277–284.

Tober, G., & Raistrick, D. (2007). *Motivational dialogue: Preparing addiction professionals for motivational interviewing practice*. London: Routledge.

Walters, S. T., Ogle, R. & Martin, J. E. (2002). Perils and possibilities of group-based motivational interviewing. In W. R. Miller, & S. Rollnick (Eds.), *Motivational interviewing: Preparing people to change addictive behaviour* (2nd ed., pp. 377–390). New York: Guilford Press.

Wanigaratne, S. (2006). Psychology of addiction. *Psychiatry*, *5*, 455–460.

West, R. (2006). *Theory of addiction*. Oxford: Blackwell.

Yalom, I. D. (1975). *The theory and practice of group psychotherapy*. New York: Basic Books.

Chapter 3

Relapse prevention for the 21st century

Shamil Wanigarante and Francis Keaney

Editors' note

In 1990 Dr Shamil Wanigarante and Dr Francis Keaney co-authored a book called *Relapse prevention for addictive behaviours: A manual for therapists* with Jane Pullin, Wendy Wallace and Richard Farmer. Here the Editors ask Shamil and Francis to give us an update on the changing nature of relapse prevention work in addictions

* * *

Interview with Dr Shamil Wanigaratne

In 1990 you co-authored a book called Relapse prevention for addictive behaviours: A manual for therapists. *What made you write that book at that particular time?*
Dr Shamil Wanigaratne: That's quite easy because five years before we published our book, Alan Marlatt and Judith Gordon had published their book on relapse prevention. Although this was largely a theoretical book, it did have some chapters describing practice and we felt that here was a very clear model that had a lot of scope for clinical application. We developed a group programme based on the model, which was well received by the clients. Having run the group programme for a couple of years, we felt that our therapist manual was worth publishing. We felt that the Marlatt and Gordon model could be used both individually and in groups and also that we could contribute by applying and translating their model into routine clinical practice.

What was 'state of the art'/'cutting edge' relapse prevention in 1990?
Well, apart from Marlatt and Gordon's model, there were two other approaches around; one was Dennis Daley's and the other Terence Gorski's, and they were both based around Twelve-Step relapse prevention approaches, which had some similarities with the Marlatt and Gordon

model. There was also the Helen Annis relapse prevention model, which was in a way an elaboration of part of the Marlatt and Gordon model. If you take all three models that were around then, the Marlatt model was the Rolls Royce and was essentially pulling together a lot of the previous research and putting it together in a coherent way.

Would you say that our understanding of the psychology of addiction has changed much in the last 20 years?
I think it has, and it has changed quite a lot, in a number of areas. The most recent and probably the most important changes are the developments in our understanding of the biology of addiction, such that we now understand a lot more about the biological infrastructure of addictive behaviour. In terms of the psychology of addiction we would probably say that we are now more aware of what sits above the biological stratum, namely the neuropsychological basis and the way that executive functioning in particular impacts on addictive behaviour. Apart from these biological or neuropsychological aspects, a lot has changed with regard to theory and here I am thinking about Robert West's PRIME Theory, which sets out to explain motivation. Previous models have been based on linear modelling, but Robert West's is a more complex mathematical model built on chaos theory. Interestingly, at the same time, in Seattle Alan Marlatt and his associates, particularly Kate Witkiewitz, were revising his model and employing similar non-linear thinking. So there's a kind of quantum leap in psychological thinking about addictions. And once you've made that leap, it's not that difficult to accept that individual human beings don't function in a linear way and that the previous models were quite limiting. Also the new modelling can account for the complexity of individual cases of addiction, although ironically, because they are so broad and all encompassing, you have a problem of whether and how to use them effectively in clinical work. So this is how I would sum up in a nutshell the current state of the psychology of addictions, recognizing also that you shouldn't leave out the psychodynamic world and the proposition of the self-medication hypothesis. Linking addiction with trauma or post-traumatic models has also been an important development in the last 20 years and this would sit very comfortably with the new relapse model in terms of people's backgrounds, strengths and weaknesses. Another important approach to add in terms of clinical applications is Marsha Linehan's Dialectical Behaviour Therapy (DBT) work, particularly the focus on individual skill development and the management of emotions.

That leads on nicely to my next question, which is how has relapse prevention changed in the last 20 years?
Relapse prevention from its inception never excluded skills development, but if you look at what has changed since then, I think there has been a

shift from 'why'-type questions to 'how'-type questions. In other words, instead of focusing on explanatory models we are now focusing on how to help clients avoid slipping back. If we think of what was originally set out by Marlatt and Gordon, the essence of the model was about the maintenance of change and applying psychological knowledge to aid maintenance, then I think that the language of relapse prevention took over in a very medical way. We need to revisit this, so that relapse prevention today should be much more about the practical skills associated with change and how maintenance of change requires the strengthening of an individual's capacity to tolerate discomfort. Our knowledge of the biological world can help here with pharmaceutical interventions, but primarily we are concerned with the psychology of change, the importance of self-efficacy and of brief motivational-type interventions.

Your book continues to be widely read. However, despite repeated requests, you've never published a second edition. Why is that?
There is a reason for this. One is the criticism of the old model and whether life is all about high-risk situations, or whether there is more to life, as the current literature would suggest. Our knowledge of relapse prevention currently means that any new book needs to be a far more complex text and one with a huge emphasis on assessment and incorporating all the new discoveries—any such book would be out of date the moment you write it. Secondly, I think the changing field we have already talked about means that, if we were to write a new manual, it would have to incorporate all these developments and then it goes beyond the original cook-book type approach. So I certainly couldn't produce another book along the same lines. A new edition would have to be far more comprehensive and far more diverse, with the result that it probably wouldn't hang together nor be a simple text that clinicians could work with. One of my colleagues, Luke Mitcheson, has written a book that I have contributed to which addresses the skills aspect of relapse prevention, while also dealing with how to help clients change their cognitions. This book in a way fulfils the demand from some quarters for a revision.

The titles of your chapters in 1990 included anxiety, high-risk situations, thinking errors, psychological traps, assertion, decision making and problem solving, lifestyle balance and depression. If you were writing this book now, what would stay and what would go, and why?
First of all, I think all of these areas, even with the new model, are still valid, although many would need to be updated. For example, there have been enormous developments in cognitive therapy for both anxiety and depression in the last 20 years. The concept of high-risk situations has been subject to a lot of debate and I think it still has clinical utility. Lifestyle balance is of course one of the fundamental cornerstones of the Marlatt

model, but that too has changed. If my original book distilled the key elements of the Marlatt and Gordon model into applied clinical work, then I would say that a current book would incorporate more skills-based approaches and contributions from DBT, which as I have already said focuses much more on developing coping skills and strengthening one's repertoire of skills to deal with phenomena such as urges and cravings. In answer to your question, I would include a lot more skills stuff, I wouldn't drop any of the other chapters, but obviously the job would be to revise upwards in terms of what is currently known in terms of our evidence base.

What do you think current relapse prevention models do not account for in recovery from addiction?
That's a good question. If recovery is about empowerment and playing to one's strengths, then I think the new Marlatt model is rather more recovery-based than the old model that could be said to be more pathological/medical. To accommodate recovery, we need to give a lot more power back both to the individual and to society and systems. The attitudes of service providers have to change as well if we are to capture the essential philosophy of recovery. While the new model looks at the individual's abilities and skills and how to strengthen these, it also focuses on how to plug the gaps in areas where there are deficits. With empowerment and giving the individual back control, we are playing with metaphors and the term relapse prevention itself suggests a certain passivity in the individual. Interestingly this is not what was meant, as the original Marlatt model was very much about empowerment. However, I think in transposing it to a medical context it lost some of its meaning and got corrupted.

In 1990 you applied a metaphor of a 'fire drill'. What metaphor would you use now?
That's a difficult one. Fire drill is something you do once a year or a couple of times a year, which gives you a template or a blue print on how to act in case there is a fire. This is very important and has saved lives in real fires. With what we know now, relapse prevention needs a plan of action and something more ongoing. Daily exercise or meditation practice should be very much part of relapse prevention. While this was encapsulated in the lifestyle balance aspect of relapse prevention, the emphasis was on doing a course of relapse prevention or getting the drill right. In some ways metaphors are dangerous because they take on a life of their own and are often taken literally. It's a difficult one and I may want to come back to that. It's very difficult to think of a simple metaphor.

Obviously this is a book focusing on group work in addictions, so I'd like to ask you what are the important factors to consider when translating the relapse-prevention model into a group setting?

Our original book, while relevant to both individuals and groups, arose out of our experience of running groups and was geared more towards group work. As I said before, we developed our application in a group setting because we felt that groups were a very powerful way of delivering relapse prevention. They were a powerful way of delivering increased awareness, of developing support and empathy and of getting people to share ideas. Although I hate to use medical metaphors, if you want to get drugs quickly into someone's system it is better to give them an injection rather than oral medication. Groups are a bit like that, they are simply more powerful. That said, I wouldn't rule out individual work; in fact you might argue that the newer model of relapse prevention is more suitable for the individual because it focuses on an individual's strengths and weaknesses. However, the group element can substantially add to this through the impact of group dynamics.

Are there any specific factors that you need to take account of when using relapse prevention in groups?
The biggest factor you have to take account of in groups is the fact that not everybody is in the same place. There is a kind of homogeneity of assumption in relapse prevention work, whereby you assume a certain level of motivation or understanding and pitch the group there. In reality there will be some people who are in tune with what's going on and some who are struggling, and that's a problem for clinicians and group facilitators. The other issue along with different levels of motivation is heterogeneity in terms of co-morbidity and different psycho-pathologies. So the assumption of homogeneity is always going to be a problem and of course in clinical practice if we pitch a group too high or too low we lose people. Some people may also have neuro-cognitive deficits and the old relapse prevention model assumes a lot of capability in terms of executive functioning. This is a problem particularly among dependent drinkers, where there is often a lot of damage in the pre-frontal area. Executive functioning doesn't recover particularly easily and therefore the question of whether we are doing something that is way above an individual's capabilities or abilities becomes particularly salient. Knowing this, it may be better to focus on a more physical/biological level rehabilitation or remediation before we incorporate complex thinking or planning into our group programmes.

In your experience, what are the benefits of offering relapse prevention within a group context rather than on an individual basis?
The plusses of a group are empathy, support, strength in numbers and clients feeling that they are with people who are going through the same thing as them. All of these factors make groups particularly powerful. Of course, we need to be clear about whether we are talking about the new or the old model. As we speak, there is very little application of the new model

into any clinical work and I think it is a challenge to see which aspects can be incorporated into groups and evaluate this, and that in some ways is quite exciting. But what is certain is that there is a body of evidence and knowledge that supports group work based on linear models or more high-risk situations, and I think to strengthen this approach with skills and competencies, while at the same time addressing the deficit issue and bringing in more lifestyle and mindfulness aspects, are exciting possibilities.

What makes for a 'good enough' group facilitator? And, can you give any tips both to those starting out in their career and those who are more experienced but wish to develop their skills?
The simple answer is confidence, but of course how does one get confidence? Confidence either comes from knowledge or experience, often both. Knowledge we can train, which means that someone who is going to do relapse prevention work needs to understand what it's all about, so a good theoretical knowledge of the principles is essential. You can train people on that, you can teach them. Experience one only gets by driving it and riding it, and there is absolutely no short-cut to experience. However, if one is forearmed with knowledge and theory, then this undoubtedly helps to facilitate and process experience in a more structured way, which should lead to greater confidence.

How do you know when a relapse prevention group has been effective?
Well, from a group perspective, if there is energy, interaction, questioning and you can see that people are participating, then you think that is effective. That might be wrong, people might just be responding without making any sort of intellectual or emotional connection to the material. The flip side of this is that people who are silent may be listening quite carefully and you should not assume that because people are not interacting that they are not benefiting, but generally you feel it to be effective where people are interacting and do respond. Again there are no short cuts for longitudinal outcome measurement and looking at process issues in terms of outcome. Again it's a two-way process as well, because it's important what the therapist thinks about the session, but we also know in the literature that if we get clients and therapists to rate sessions then they don't often match. What therapists think was a good session, clients may rate as not, so there are no simple answers to these questions.

In what ways have the needs of people with problematic substance use changed over the last 20 years, and how do you think this impacts on group work?
Most models are based on a single addiction or single substance use assumption. Now we find that most substance users are poly substance users and it is unclear whether our thinking and assumptions apply to them all. If you look at it another way, the evidence base for effectiveness for

interventions seems to follow on a sort of purist substance line, probably because it is easier to research single groups. In reality those groups don't often exist. So I think what we are mainly talking about is the poly substance use phenomenon and I don't know how you address that in relapse prevention work, whether you focus on one substance or whether you focus on giving up substance use completely or switching entirely to the question of recovery.

While there is a high level of co-morbidity in both psychiatric and substance-using populations, addressing substance use may not be a priority within psychiatric settings. In such services, how would groups play a role? Which key concepts would best be included in such groups?
We know that certain substances actually exacerbate and precipitate relapse in, say, psychotic conditions and that there may be a causal link as well in, for example, cannabis use and dosage of cannabis use. What we find in our colleagues in the mental health side is a reluctance or lack of confidence in their own ability to bring up the issue of substance use or to address it, and that requires skills and confidence. I think groups should be much broader and instead of calling them relapse prevention we should aim to get clients discussing ideas; these may take the form of focus groups. We should then deliver motivational and relapse prevention interventions that don't go under the relapse-prevention banner. I think we should encourage clients to have open and honest discussion about their substance use and then you can apply some of the theoretical models to that process, the most obvious one would be motivational interviewing. What I have found with a dual diagnosis population is a kind of paradox in that substance misuse treatment settings seem to have a whole narrative around 'do not use drugs' or 'stop using drugs', whereas mental health settings seem to have a narrative around 'use the drug we give you and don't use other drugs'. Clients with mental health problems often believe that the drugs that they choose to use themselves are beneficial, while the drugs that are medically prescribed make them ill with side-effects, so those two narratives have never been fully explored and addressed.

As a clinical psychologist, what do you feel clinical psychology has to offer group work in addictions?
Well, clinical psychology at the end of the day is the application of scientific psychology into clinical practice. If you work from a scientist–practitioner model, you collect practice-based evidence, drawn from our experiences of how we apply certain techniques and learn from them. I think this approach has absolutely everything to offer to the clinical field. In terms of group work, I think that clinical psychology training itself doesn't have a huge group component, but perhaps that is something that clinical psychology training itself should address.

As a practising psychologist, in what way would you highlight the particular benefits of adopting a psychological perspective to treating addictions?
You have got to continue to think in biopsychosocial terms. We have addressed the biological dimension, but we haven't talked much about the social element, although group work does, I think, have a huge social dimension. The psychological dimension focuses on the individual, whether this be personality risk factors, cognitive style, cognitive deficits or mood issues. Psychologists still need to function at all three levels and be aware of and work with other colleagues. That's why we shouldn't be separatists and a way of approaching this is to train colleagues on the psychological dimensions of substance misuse so that everyone, regardless of discipline, delivers good effective care.

Finally how would you sum up relapse prevention for the 21st century?
Relapse prevention in the 21st century is based on acknowledgement of the addictions phenomenon and awareness that relapse prevention is a lot more complex than anticipated. It has to acknowledge the quite significant roles played by biology; it has to incorporate social factors, individual strengths and find a place for motivation. So relapse prevention in the 21st century is, I think, a much more complex intervention that takes into consideration individual assessments, but also incorporates things like mindfulness, pharmacological treatments and group approaches. Like any century however, you have to live in the zeitgeist with the knowledge base that we have, but certainly I would like to think that we have moved on and are working on a multi-dimensional level. So the simple answer to what is relapse prevention in the 21st century is that we have moved from two-dimensional to three-dimensional relapse prevention.

Dr Wanigaratne, thank you very much indeed.

Interview with Dr Francis Keaney

In 1990 you co-authored a book called Relapse prevention for addictive behaviours: A manual for therapists. *What made you write that book at that particular time?*
Dr Francis Keaney: We were working in an NHS treatment unit and found that there weren't that many kinds of psychosocial interventions we could offer people and the choices were mainly abstinence-based or Twelve-Step-based. When I think back, one of the key aspects that occurred to me was that there was an educational process in terms of understanding alcohol careers. In many of the people we saw, it was a bit like Cinderella or Sleeping Beauty, in a sense that all of a sudden after 20 or 30 years of heavy drinking, that our clients 'woke up' to the fact of their drinking and couldn't understand how they had got to this point. So, we were looking for

what was in the literature that might be useful from an educational point of view to explain some of the behaviours we saw in our clients, and what kind of practical strategies we could advise or offer people that could help them on their recovery journey. I think it helped that Shamil and I were coming from very different perspectives: I was coming from quite a medical background and he was very interested in psychosocial interventions.

What was 'state of the art'/'cutting edge' relapse prevention in 1990?
I'm not sure. There were certainly some group ideas out there based around AA and NA approaches, but as far as I was aware there were no general relapse-prevention ideas being adopted within the NHS at that time.

Would you say that our understanding of the psychology of addiction has changed much in the last 20 years?
Yes I would say that it has, but I would say this has been less in conventional psychiatry or psychology and more in our understanding of what's called the process of addiction, as opposed to simple chemical dependence. In this case it's the rehabs in the USA that are leading the way, like Betty Ford or the Meadows, and I can recommend looking at their websites to understand this approach more.

How would you say that relapse prevention has changed in the last 20 years?
That's a good question. I don't know if it really has or not; I'm not too familiar with the current literature. If I understand correctly, Marlatt has written a new edition of his book, where he focuses on being present, on being more mindful. But I don't think there is a great deal of evidence out there to support the efficacy of relapse prevention. It seems to me and what I find disappointing is that people talk a lot about delivering relapse prevention, but I'm not always convinced that these skills are really being put into action. And I think until we move into a situation where we are required to evidence base what we do in therapeutic terms, which could be taping, video-taping, letting other people watch how you work, we are stuck. If you were thinking about it from another way, what would be the evidence base for relapse prevention, in a very operational way? I think you might look to see what kind of aftercare services are offered and whether any of these include relapse prevention groups.

Your book continues to be widely read. However, despite repeated requests, you've never published a second edition. Why is that?
For me, I haven't got the time, but if I did have time then I would write a very different edition that incorporated ideas about helping people to think differently about change.

The titles of your chapters in 1990 included anxiety, high-risk situations, thinking errors, psychological traps, assertion, decision making and problem solving, lifestyle balance and depression. If you were writing this book now, what would stay and what would go, and why?

I think that these areas are still key: High-risk situations, thinking errors, psychological traps and lifestyle balance. The one that jumps out at me more than anything else is around making good decisions and having strategies for understanding how people make decisions. I think this is very much related to the current ideas going around about DBT, mindfulness and mentalization that I think could do with coming into the addiction's field more. The other area I would focus on is drinking careers, although some of our clients might not view it as such. This might mean using some type of timeline to work with clients so that they could reflect on various aspects of their lives in terms of their drinking careers. This might help to redress some of the distortion and deletion in our clients' thinking, and help them understand the impact of alcohol on their lives and physical and psychological health. This seems to me to be similar to when you are asked to write a life story in rehab, so, somehow that seems to help on reflection. I think that we bring clients into treatment and suddenly ask them to talk about psychological ideas when not all of them may be able to or used to doing this. So this is where, in our book, I don't think we stepped into other people's shoes and into their thinking sufficiently. I would want to add in something more about seeing recovery from the client's perspective; that's what I meant by mentalization. We didn't wish to come from a point of blame and guilt, but often a lot of these things can be pointing out at what's not good about you and what you have done badly and people stop, they switch off. So it's coming from a very different place. And I think we can learn a lot from these newer ways of thinking. That's all.

What do you think current relapse prevention models do not account for in recovery from addiction?

Well, perhaps there is a danger that people will see CBT work as the answer to everything, but it may not suit everyone. It can form part of your skills base, but it is only one way of seeing things. I also worry that many CBT programmes on offer are too structured, too manualized and not fluid enough. I would like to see a lighter approach to models, where people can take the parts that suit them.

In 1990 you applied a metaphor of a 'fire drill'. What metaphor would you use now?

I think a metaphor would have to be something to do with, something like a 'BlackBerry®', current technology that wasn't there 20 years ago. The world of communications has changed dramatically since 1990 and I wonder how can we use these? I think it might be a communication metaphor. That's as far as I can take it right now.

Obviously this is a book focusing on group work in addictions, so I'd like to ask you what are the important factors to consider when translating the relapse prevention model into a group setting?
I think there are a number of factors. One of the things is that, as you are probably aware, people will bring to the group all kinds of issues, or sides to themselves that they may or may not reveal on a one-to-one basis. And so, an important factor is to have some awareness of group dynamics. As a facilitator one needs to have the skills and confidence to facilitate the group in a way that is useful for all the members there and crucially help people to feel safe. I think one must be able to assess how much an individual can use the group, pay attention to others and reflect on information. This might also be to do with understanding people's learning styles. I think that if you don't know anything about teaching and learning styles, you're in trouble. People have various learning styles and so you need to consider, are you using the right language? Are you explaining it well? Are you engaging people? Are they being engaged? Are they interested? That type of thing.

In your experience, what are the benefits of offering relapse prevention within a group context rather than on an individual basis?
Since so many of our services are being cut, groups like AA/NA, rehab groups, day programme groups and so on are a way to get greatest volume through for least cost. So bearing that in mind, maybe some of the benefits of NHS services offering groups is at a very simple level to facilitate socialization, and to facilitate somebody being comfortable, because many of them say 'I've never been to a group like this before' and it's just to help people to get over some of their phobias and shyness around groups. I also think that some of the benefits relate to peer influence and modelling. So you know, people may listen to you as a professional, but maybe it reaches them more when one of their own peers asks them questions or describes certain situations. I think that the process of giving and receiving feedback is very interesting. Also I mention benefits about socializing and being part of something; I think belonging seems to be very important for people, particularly as our client group often feel stigmatized and outside of things. Certainly, if you run groups that involve carers of users, it's an eye-opener for family members who come along as they haven't realized the extent of the issue and problem.

What makes for a 'good enough' group facilitator? And, can you give any tips both to those starting out in their career and those who are more experienced but wish to develop their skills?

I think one of the key things is good communication skills. A facilitator needs to be able to communicate with clarity and notice or judge whether people have been able to really listen to what you're saying and then to be able to change your communication accordingly to suit the group. This means being really observant to all the kinds of subtle messages that people give out and that's not easy in a group when there are several other people you need to pay attention to as well. And also people come with different states of mind, angry, upset, self-pity, so you need to know how to manage a whole range of emotional states. I think a good facilitator is task-focused and explains 'This is what we're here for, this is what we're going to focus on and so on'. Not everyone would like that, because they want to chat and joke and all that. I think you also need to know about defence mechanisms; it's helpful to know how humans use the groups and things like that. I think it's useful to know how to convey different messages; you know' from how to be approachable to knowing how to appear credible.

For those starting out, I would say have a think about the groups you belong to, at home or socializing or whatever; this often involves being part of a group. If you can, think of how you are in those situations, because you may be very good in those situations. It's all to do with context. I think one of the things that I've been interested in from the group point of view is that you may have a timetable, an agenda coming into the group, some-thing that you are task-focused on, but there is something very important about being slowed down, and about being very present in the group. This means that you are very congruent and very present in the group and can pick up on and respond to other people's states of mind. Sometimes, you may just have to respond to something very important going on in the group. Sometimes you may need to jettison your whole timetable and your agenda. So although earlier I mentioned being very task-focused, being present might be the task. It's also helpful to have a good co-facilitator who will notice things that you won't and who will also be able to comment on you if you are good at giving and receiving feedback. That also helps enormously I think, because you may not be right in what you say. Sometimes we have videotaped the groups and looked at them afterwards.

For those who want to develop their skills, I think it might be useful to go on training where you are part of a group yourself, so that you can see it from the customer's point of view and where you have to talk about yourself in some way in public.

How do you know when a relapse prevention group has been effective?
One of the things that you might notice is that people adopt the language, they use certain words. So if they understand a concept such as a high-risk situation, they might say 'I went to a funeral' or 'I went into a pub yesterday' and use the term 'high-risk situation', so this shows they have some understanding of the actual language. I think the second thing is that

when they kind of reflect on what's happened to them over the last week, besides using the language they'll be able to explain some of the concepts, for example, like backing yourself into a corner and you have no choice but to drink (i.e., seemingly irrelevant decisions), and they say something like 'When I think about that, I now understand the risk'. They may start to describe situations where they have lapsed or relapsed, but it hasn't gone on for very long. So they might say something like 'Before this group I'd start drinking and six or nine months later I'd seek help and now its three days or three weeks later'. Something's changed for them. It's also about curiosity. You might start to notice an increasing curiosity about process, people might ask questions in a different way; that tells you that something is going for them. This might be what I call questions of clarification like 'Can you explain. . .?' or 'Do you mean this or that?'

In what ways have the needs of the substance misuse population changed over the last 20 years, and how do you think this impacts on group work?
It seems to me we are getting people who cannot be managed in primary care, so that rather than criteria relating simply to severity and complexity, it's more about who can manage them. If you think about needs being distributed across the normal distribution, we are seeing the right-hand tail end of the curve, the more severe end, and more and more of them. Twenty years ago we would see a combination, a mixture of people. This means we have people who are psychologically and physically more unwell involved in the group process. We have to simplify or adapt groups for people with cognitive impairment, for example. Secondly, there's something about funding issues; services have a lot less time to work with people.

While there is a high level of co-morbidity in both psychiatric and substance misuse populations, addressing substance misuse may not be a priority within psychiatric settings. In such services, how would groups play a role? Which key concepts would best be included in such groups?
Groups would raise awareness and could be used to discuss how people self-medicate to alleviate symptoms and the effect of such strategies.

As a psychiatrist, what do you feel psychiatry has to offer group work in addictions?
One idea I have, perhaps this would be an unusual view, is we could combine group work with pharmacological interventions. So you could have people on antabuse, nalteroxone, this is for alcohol, but you could have them on nalteroxone for drug use as well. I think psychiatrists can offer an awareness of borderline behaviour, awareness of personality disorders, awareness of how mental health states affect one's ability to feel reasonably well, anxiety and depression, those types of practical issues. They could also offer physiological explanations about areas such as 'Why aren't I sleeping for the

first year after I detox? 'What's this business of liver disease and Hepatitis C; how does it affect me?' Another area they can contribute, although this might apply to any of the professions, is they can offer continuity of care if they stay in one place. I think this is really important for general recovery of adults in mental health, where psychiatrists actually know the clients. But in our current system of funding where we have to move people on so quickly, those type of relationships are no longer available, the chronic year after year reviews and that type of thing.

As a practising psychiatrist, in what way would you highlight the particular benefits of adopting a psychiatric perspective to treating addictions?
Well I think the thing about it is, if you look at any part of the care pathways, psychiatrists can identify psychotherapeutic interventions that will be helpful.

Finally how would you sum up relapse prevention for the 21st century?
You might wish to put it this way, that you learn more from failing than from succeeding or as Samuel Beckett put it 'Try again. Fail again. Fail better.'

Dr Keaney, thank you.

Recommended reading

Annis, H. M. (1990). Relapse to substance abuse: Empirical findings within a cognitive-social learning approach. *Journal of Psychoactive Drugs, 22*, 117–124.

Bliss, P., Murphy, K., & Ricketts, T. (2002). Relapse prevention group work: A clinical evaluation. *Journal of Substance Use, 7*, 78–84.

Carroll, K. M. (1996). Relapse prevention as a psychosocial treatment: A review of controlled clinical trials. *Experimental & Clinical Psychopharmacology, 4*, 45–54.

Daley, D. C., Marlatt, G. A., & Spotts, C. E. (2003). Relapse prevention: Clinical models and specific intervention strategies. In A. W. Graham, T. K. Schultz, & B. B. Wilford (Eds.), *Principles of addiction medicine* (3rd ed., pp. 467–486). Chevy Chase, MD: American Society of Addiction Medicine.

De Jong, W. (1994). Relapse prevention: An emerging technology for promoting long-term drug abstinence. *The International Journal of the Addictions, 29*, 681–705.

Gorski, T. T. (1990). The Cenaps model of relapse prevention: Basic principles and procedures. *Journal of Psychoactive Drugs, 22*, 125–133.

Irvin, J. E., Bowers, C. A., Dunn, M. E., & Wang, M. C. (1999). Efficacy of relapse prevention: A meta-analytic review. *Journal of Consulting and Clinical Psychology, 67*, 563–570.

Keller, D. S. (1996). Exploration in the service of relapse prevention: A psycho-analytic contribution to substance abuse treatment. In F. Rotgers, D. S. Keller, &

J. Morgenstern (Eds.), *Treating substance abuse: Theory and technique* (pp. 84–116). New York: Guilford Press.

Marlatt, G. A., & Donovan, D. M. (2005). *Relapse prevention: Maintenance strategies in the treatment of addictive behaviors*. New York: Guilford Press.

Marlatt, G. A., & Gordon, J. R. (Eds.) (1985). *Relapse prevention: Maintenance strategies in the treatment of addictive behaviors*. New York: Guilford Press.

Marlatt, G. A., & Witkiewitz (2005). Relapse prevention for alcohol and drug problems. In D. M. Donovan & G. A. Marlatt (Eds), *Relapse prevention: Maintenance strategies in the treatment of addictive behaviours* (2nd ed., pp. 1–44). New York: Guilford Press.

Mitcheson, L., Maslin, J., Meynen, T., Morrison, T., Hill, R., & Wanigaratne, S. (2010). *Applied cognitive and behavioural approaches to the treatment of addiction: A practical treatment guide*. Oxford: Wiley-Blackwell.

Morgenstern, J., & Longabaugh, R. (2000). Cognitive-behavioral treatment for alcohol dependence: A review of evidence for its hypothesized mechanisms of action. *Addiction, 95,* 1475–1490.

Wanigaratne, S. (2003). Relapse prevention in practice. *The Drug and Alcohol Professional, 3,* 11–18.

Wanigaratne, S., & Keaney, F. (2002). Psychodynamic aspects of relapse prevention in the treatment of addictive behaviours. In M. Weegman & R. Cohen (Eds.), *The psychodynamics of addiction* (pp. 117–132). London: Whurr.

Wanigaratne, S., Wallace, W., Pullin, J., Keaney, F., & Farmer, R. (1990). *Relapse prevention for addictive behaviours*. Oxford: Blackwell.

Witkiewitz, K., & Marlatt, G. A. (2004). Relapse prevention for alcohol and drug problems: That was Zen, this is Tao. *American Psychologist, 59,* 224–235.

Chapter 4

Promoting physical health through group work

Martin Naylor and Ryan Little

Introduction

Health promotion is increasingly important in the NHS and aims to support individuals in taking better control over factors that influence their health. The *NHS 2010–2015: From good to great* (Department of Health, 2009a) speaks of reducing avoidable ill-health through addressing the 'big four' lifestyle factors of smoking, alcohol, diet, and physical activity. It is recognized that these behaviours are important contributory factors in the development of chronic diseases and over 140,000 preventable deaths each year. The Department of Health has attempted to tackle these health behaviours through high-profile campaigns, such as the recent 'Change 4 Life' programme that encouraged healthy eating and the 2006 'Let's Get Moving' campaign that targeted physical activity. Such campaigns emphasize the individual's responsibility for maintaining their own health and that of their family. However, the *NHS operating framework for England (2010–2011)* also highlights the role of PCTs and local authorities in supporting individuals to make these lifestyle changes through 'schemes to promote physical activity, building on and complementing 5-A-Day activity and interventions such as the school fruit and vegetable programme' (Department of Health, 2009b, p. 21).

Alcohol and drug users will also benefit from such general programmes. However, it is important to recognize that there are additional demands for health promotion and disease prevention that are specific to this group. In this chapter we discuss three areas that we think are particularly relevant to those with drug and alcohol problems:

1   government health promotion initiatives
2   health promotion in a group setting and
3   core health promotion groups for substance misusers.

Government health-promotion initiatives

The government has a long involvement with campaigns that target alcohol and drug use and its associated harm. Some recent campaigns include: (1) the 2008 'Know Your Limits' campaign that aimed to raise young people's awareness of the risks of binge drinking; (2) the 2009 'Think' campaign that addressed the perils of drink driving; and (3) the 2001 'Know the Score' Scottish campaign that highlighted the dangers of cocaine use. One might also include campaigns targeting smoking, heart disease, and stroke within this category, such as 'Safe, Sensible, Sociable' (Department of Health, 2007). These campaigns aim to increase the general public's awareness of the risks of drug and alcohol use. They are also based on the premise that excessive use of alcohol or drugs will have a negative health impact and that any change in use will bring positive health benefits.

Models of care for alcohol misusers (Department of Health, 2006a) states that treatments targeting alcohol misuse should not only seek to achieve a reduction in alcohol-related harm, but also an improvement in health and social functioning. These strategies assume that any treatment addressing excessive alcohol consumption will in itself bring sufficient health benefits for the individual, negating the need for any further specific health promotion interventions. Hence, it is difficult to find any government targets or strategies that specifically focus on improving the physical health of those who misuse alcohol, although these might conceivably target neurological complications and liver disease.

In contrast, the government is far more specific in its targets to address physical health among drug misusers. *Models of care* 'advocates a far greater emphasis on the need to reduce drug related harm including risks of blood borne virus (BBV) infection, overdose and other infections . . . Harm reduction interventions are required for drug users before, during and after all structured drug treatment' (Department of Health, 2006b, p. 12). However, it should be remembered that these sessions often serve only as an introduction to the issues and are aimed at increasing participants' motivation and engagement into treatment as well as giving out essential harm-reduction advice.

The government places an important focus on brief interventions, since these can be cost effective, offered within existing treatment facilities, and have the potential to reach the greatest number of people, particularly those who may be at risk of developing moderate to severe problems later on. Brief interventions tend to be offered as part of a stepped care approach to those people who are at the start of their drinking or drug-use careers or who have not yet developed the complex physical and psychological problems associated with long-term heavy drinking or drug use. Brief interventions also tend to be directed at individuals on an opportunistic and, for the most part, individual basis, often directed at those who are beginning to think about, or are in the early stages of change.

Health promotion within a group setting

Traditionally, the most widely available source of therapeutic support for people with drug and alcohol misuse issues is offered within a group format, namely Alcoholics Anonymous (AA) and Narcotics Anonymous (NA). Davison, Pennebaker, and Dickerson suggest that the success of AA is 'testament to the potential strength and efficacy of mutual support' (2000, p. 209). Furthermore, such groups can be powerful in addressing associated difficulties such as shame, social isolation, and depression (Leshner, 1997).

It is also our experience that groups can be a time- and cost-effective format by which to offer health information. Group members value the group discussions that arise, since these allow participants to share their own experiences and knowledge, and learn from each other. In our experience, group members seem to value the opportunity to express their concerns to their peers in a supportive and stable forum, even at times discussing a topic that could potentially save their lives. We find that clients are more likely to recognize and accept behaviours as being unhelpful when they are challenged by their peers. Many clients are likely to have had negative experiences of authority figures, hence the group is useful for clients to elicit positive health ideals for themselves rather than simply accept/challenge those offered by staff members. Such peer group reinforcement seems to work positively for topics such as safer sexual practice, increased awareness and knowledge of exercise ideas/routines, improved sleep hygiene, overdose management, and harm reduction (safer injecting or drinking behaviours). A group format also allows clients an opportunity to solve problems together so that any solutions reached may be considered more salient, manageable, and meaningful.

Another benefit of offering health promotion within a group is that many perceived barriers to action (physical, social, economic, psychological) are normalized. Negative expectations can be minimized if the group members come to realize that although they may share the same barriers, they may still make gains in health behaviour. Being with others who are addressing similar problems can be a powerful motivating factor to engage with the group subject that might be otherwise too easily avoided or minimized in day-to-day life. Groups can be an efficient way to engage clients who might usually show resistance to approach a topic or consider behaviour change. Offering information in a group can defuse a sense of threat or accusation that clients might feel when talking about risky health behaviours in an individual session. In our experience, clients who mastered more tangible topics related to health promotion then seemed to be more willing and confident to engage with more intangible topics, such as challenging negative thinking, emotion regulation, and craving skills.

Health promotions groups

Throughout the course of their substance misuse, drug and alcohol users typically come into contact with a variety of agencies, such as accident and emergency departments, general practitioners, inpatient detoxification units, residential rehabs, day programmes, community drug and alcohol teams and prisons. It is likely that each agency will promote healthy living differently, according to their service philosophy, relevance to the agency, level of engagement with the client group, the team's degree of specialization (and how many other areas they are responsible for covering), and the length of time they have to offer treatment. While a busy accident and emergency department may only be able to help someone to move from a 'pre-contemplative' to a 'contemplative' state when they see someone following an alcohol-related injury, a residential rehab with a 3–6-month specialist addictions programme would be able to include regular health promotion groups covering a full range of subjects. In the following section we look at a number of health promotion groups and offer some suggestions of core topics within each and highlight pitfalls or useful formats. Interested readers might like to refer to Saloo and Styles' (2006) National Offender Management Service's interventions resource pack for useful group outlines.

We find that clients are generally more likely to remain interested and engaged in groups when they can actively participate within the group rather than be presented with information. Interactive techniques such as discussion, role-plays, games, quizzes, brainstorming, well-presented overheads and visual aids, handouts and work sheets, and practical participation are particularly important. It is recommended that any games or quizzes are based around the principle of errorless learning so that they do not reinforce myths or wrong information.

Overdose management

Overdose management groups should be on the programme of any organization offering addiction advice. When working with a client group with a high likelihood of relapse or, indeed, who are still using, it makes sense to give as much information as will best improve the chances of survival from overdose. However, how much you cover in these groups depends on how much time you have and the overall aims of the organization. When possible, it should include advice about recognizing the signs of overdose, how to manage the situation, including calling the emergency services, and training in the use of naloxone. It is also helpful to teach clients how to put someone in the recovery position or how to administer cardiac pulmonary resuscitation (CPR).

We have found overdose management to be a very powerful group for clients. It works well and gets much of its power as a subject from being delivered in a group format. A substantial number of clients will describe a time when they believe they have had an overdose and most will describe having witnessed an overdose, many of which resulted in death. Using statistics helps to back up clients' experiences, and increases the salience of the group training. The group provides a forum for clients to share what they understand about overdose and an opportunity to explore myths around overdose that have become received truth on the street. Group discussion and the sharing of experiences is a powerful part of this group.

Blood-borne viruses

A group on blood-borne viruses (BBV) is an essential part of any residential programme, such as inpatient detoxification units and prisons, or structured day programmes. High relapse rates on discharge from these agencies make it important that clients have a good grasp of the risks presented by hepatitis B, hepatitis C and HIV. Such services can take advantage of their insisting on compulsory attendance at BBV groups; the group format itself also maximizes the number of clients accessed, particularly when time may be restricted. While clients seem to have become more open about discussing hepatitis C within a group context over the last 10 years, there continues to be stigma associated with HIV. If clients do not wish to discuss issues within the group, we would offer an individual session and, where helpful, make a referral to a specialist service. A quiz might be an effective way to engage the group in the subject of BBV while also a way to correct unhelpful or risky myths.

Safer injecting

This is an essential topic of any agency working with people who are continuing to use drugs or who are in danger of relapsing. Where practical, this group can be helpfully linked with a group on BBV. Handouts and information displayed in treatment areas should be readily available to supplement groups and to inform those clients who are not engaging in the agency's group programme. It should also be noted that giving information on safer injecting can sometimes confuse or anger clients who feel that they are no longer going to use drugs. Safer injecting encompasses more than the practical issue of accessing clean needles, as many group members raise concerns about how to refuse sharing needles without causing offence. Such barriers may be overcome by encouraging the group to share their experiences of what has worked well.

Sexual health

Group work in sexual health can be used in all agencies offering specialist addictions advice. This is an area fraught with sensitivities that make it important to take time thinking about the information discussed. For the most part it is better to deliver the groups on a gender-specific basis and to cover broad topics with plenty of information on how and where to seek further advice. For female clients the areas for discussion would include information on safe sex, sexually transmitted diseases and contraception. Clients can be very judgemental of each other and will at times be critical of women who are pregnant or have children who have been taken into care; negative views around those who are sex working may also be expressed. For men the same areas should be covered as well as issues around impulsivity and equal responsibility for contraception. Both genders may express feelings of anger, guilt, and shame. Intended sexual behaviour (as measured by social-cognition models) appears to be an unreliable predictor of actual behaviour, probably due to its neglect of factors such as interpersonal interaction, high emotion, arousal, and of course substance use itself. Groups will therefore benefit from also focusing on interpersonal skills, assertiveness, and negotiation skills.

Balance sheet

While this is not immediately obvious as a health promotion group, we believe this can be very effective in a number of areas. The advantage of conducting this group is that it is a real client-participation event. In considering the following: (1) positives of using; (2) negatives of using; (3) positives of not using; and (4) negatives of not using, the facilitator will end up with a board or flipchart that contains the clients' own work. This can often give a very powerful message to clients, especially as there is usually a great imbalance between the responses for the positives and negatives of using. Physical health issues loom large in the responses and so can be used to support the need to focus on these in more detail.

Sleep hygiene

Running a group on sleep hygiene is helpful for a number of reasons. Problems with sleep are a major reason that clients find withdrawal from alcohol and drugs difficult, distressing, and often unbearable. Clients frequently cite their need for sleep as a powerful relapse trigger, hence understanding how human sleep patterns work and how drugs and alcohol disrupt sleep can help encourage some clients to persist with the progress they have made in detoxification rather than re-establishing old patterns. Many clients share their first-hand experience of relapsing as a consequence of seeking 'just one decent nights sleep', and this can benefit others who may be seeking to gain relief in a similar fashion. The group can also help to highlight the problem that hypnotic medications reinforce patterns of sleeplessness and dependence. Alternative strategies can be suggested and positive coping strategies can be elicited from all members of the group.

Healthy eating

Clients have a wide range of opinions and understanding about healthy eating. Some clients who have a reckless approach towards safer injecting and sex will be fastidious about what they eat. Others will have paid no attention to their dietary intake and lived on junk food and fast fixes of crisps and chocolate (if they have eaten at all). All treatment agencies that come into contact with addicted clients should be giving advice on healthy eating, whether through making leaflets and posters available, offering brief opportunistic interventions, or facilitating group work. It can be useful to back up messages about healthy eating in the treatment environment. This might range from offering cookery groups, balanced meals, having healthy snacks and beverages available, through to including gardening and food preparation groups as part of leisure or recovery activities. Again, if a lifestyle balance group is part of the programme, the importance of having regular times during the day to eat meals will already have been discussed.

Physical exercise

Factors such as medical conditions (e.g., ulcers, osteoporosis, amputation, hepatitis C, liver damage, HIV) and dietary reasons (e.g., reduced muscle mass, low energy reserves) impact on an individual's confidence and ability to take part in physical exercise, even everyday activities such as walking to the shops, climbing stairs, or playing with their children. Moreover, some clients may simply lack experience in exercise activities.

Since most introductory levels of exercise outside of addictions treatment take place in a group format, e.g., fitness classes, sports lessons, and fun-runs, it makes sense that services also offer exercise instruction in a group format. This not only offers continuity between treatment experiences and 'outside' life, it also lowers the cost per exerciser. Low-impact cardio-vascular fitness groups are a gentle way to re-build the body's tolerance for exercise by increasing the lactic acid threshold and encouraging a more efficient provision of energy to the muscles. Music can help motivate participation. Sports-based groups that are graded and adapted to meet any mobility limitations are also popular. Boxing can be an effective way to increase a sense of personal safety and add an element of attention/ concentration to an exercise routine. It can be useful to substitute heavy boxing bags with pads, so that clients can build technique and speed without risking impact injuries. Where pad work (or indeed any other technique) is performed on a individual basis, engaging a group to observe and talk about the boxing techniques seems to work well and also allows observers to absorb techniques prior to their 'turn'. Boxing pad work seems to offer a relaxing and calming effect for clients, rather than increase focus on aggressive or violent thoughts or behaviour. The calming effect seems especially noticeable for people with a history of physical abuse or assault. From a psychosocial perspective, many clients report not having tried this kind of activity since they were at school and this can add to the idea of 'starting afresh'.

On a cautionary note, it is inadvisable to conduct a fitness/sport session without prior accredited training. Even gentle exercise can induce increased blood pressure and hence it is recommended that a registered mental health nurse monitors (and records in the notes) blood pressure and beats per minute before and after an exercise session and that clients report their perceived exertions levels at regular intervals during exercise as well as note pain in their muscles, joints, or chest. As well as offering sessions for physical exercise, the treatment environment can support group messages about the importance of exercise through access or referral schemes to leisure facilities.

Smoking cessation

Clients may enter addictions services with the intention of changing their life completely and this can include quitting other risky behaviours, particularly cigarette smoking. Others may believe that smoking is a solace and that quitting tobacco will jeopardize their primary treatment (Hill, Cooper, Harris, Keaney, Fredericks, & Gossop, 2007). Nevertheless, all NHS premises have become smoke-free, with some temporary exceptions in addictions inpatients for restricted smoking. There is strong evidence that group therapy is more effective than self-help materials or no treatment in supporting smoking cessation, however it is unclear whether group therapy is more effective than individual counselling (Stead & Lancaster, 2005). A group might explore perceptions of smoking cessation in the context of substance treatment, offer information about effects of smoking, decision balance to enhance readiness, tasks to promote self-confidence and specific coping strategies for craving, lapses, and lifestyle changes. At a minimum, services can provide anti-smoking advice and nicotine replacement therapy as part of the individual's treatment.

Conclusions

The promotion of improved physical health through group work in addiction services should be considered a valuable addition to any detoxification or rehabilitation programme. Groups can maximize clients' own wisdom, although we need to ensure that myths are not perpetuated. Irrespective of an individual's long-term success with abstinence, health promotion during rehabilitation/detoxification offers an opportunity for individuals to learn and improve skills that lead to a healthier life and to reduce the harm and risks associated with continued substance misuse. Our view is that group work provides a way to get information across efficiently and effectively, and exploring the different dimensions and considerations around a drug/alcohol-free lifestyle enhances clients' motivation to remain abstinent and strive towards a more productive and fulfilling life.

References

Davison, K. P., Pennebaker, J. W., & Dickerson, S. S. (2000). Who talks? The social psychology of illness support groups. *American Psychologist*, *55*, 205–217.

Department of Health (2006a). *Models of care for alcohol misusers (MoCAM)*. London: The Stationery Office Limited.

Department of Health (2006b). *Models of care for treatment of adult drug misusers: Update 2006*. London: The Stationery Office Limited.

Department of Health (2007). *Safe. Sensible. Social. The next steps in the National Alcohol Strategy*. London: The Stationery Office Limited.

Department of Health (2009a). *NHS 2010–2015: From good to great. Preventative, people-centred, productive*. London: The Stationery Office Limited.

Department of Health (2009b). *The NHS operating framework for England 2010/11*. London: The Stationery Office Limited.

Hill, R. G., Cooper, W., Harris, J., Keaney, F., Fredericks, F., & Gossop, M. (2007). Don't you think we're giving up enough already: Attitudes of patients and staff in an inpatient addiction treatment service towards a proposed 'no smoking policy'. *Journal of Substance Use*, *12*, 225–231.

Leshner, A. I. (1997). Introduction to the special issue: The National Institute on Drug Abuse's (NIDA's) Drug Abuse Treatment Outcome Study (DATOS). *Psychology of Addictive Behaviors*, *11*, 211–215.

Saloo, F., & Styles, G. (2006). *National offender management service, integrated drug treatment system, the first 28 days: psychosocial support, interventions resource pack*. London: National Treatment Agency for Substance Misuse.

Stead, L. F., & Lancaster, T. (2005). Interventions for preventing tobacco sales to minors. *Cochrane Database of Systematic Reviews* Issue 1, Art. No. CD001497. DOI: 10.1002/14651858.CD001497.pub2

Chapter 5

Developing resources for recovery

Siobhan Wilson and Claire Parry

Introduction

This chapter explores the use of recovery-orientated groups on an inpatient detoxification unit for clients with drug and alcohol dependence. The chapter introduces key components of the recovery model and then outlines three groups that were developed to help clients explore their life roles, daily structure, and social networks. Throughout this chapter we use quotes from service users collected as part of a focus group on the inpatient addiction ward. We gratefully acknowledge their contribution and permission to use this material.

The recovery model

The concept of recovery is not new. In psychiatry and medicine, recovery has historically been referred to as the end of, or cure from, an episode of illness. Also, recovery has long been a central component of Alcoholics Anonymous (AA) and other Twelve-Step groups within the substance misuse field. In recent times, mental health and substance misuse services have adopted a broader concept of recovery, moving away from pathology towards sustained, solution-focused recovery.

The recovery philosophy originated in the United States and had two major influences: the Twelve-Step Alcoholics Anonymous and the independent living/survivor movements. Within the Twelve-Step model, individuals consider themselves to be 'in recovery' when they have abstained from drug and alcohol use. The underlying assumption is that addiction is a life-long disease and that people will have to work to maintain their sobriety.

The second influence came from the civil rights movement and independent mental health living movements in the USA. Being 'in recovery' in relation to serious mental illness was seen as a process that involved minimizing the illness and its effects on a person's life as the person tried to understand how to live with and manage an illness over time. Many of the barriers to recovery identified by mental health advocates have been social and political, for example exclusion and stigma. In the 1990s countries such as Australia and New Zealand adopted the recovery principle into the delivery of mental health services. More recently in the UK, the Department of Health has published policies endorsing the patient as the expert in their own care and encouraging more choice in relation to the care they receive (Department of Health, 2001, 2006).

A widely used definition of recovery comes from Anthony, who describes it as 'a deeply personal, unique process of changing one's attitudes, values, feelings, goals, skills, and/or roles. It is a way of living a satisfying, hopeful, and contributing life even within the limitations caused by illness. Recovery involves the development of new meaning and purpose in one's life as one grows beyond the catastrophic effects of mental illness' (1993, p. 14).

After studying personal accounts of recovery, Andresen, Oades, and Caputi (2003) suggested four key components in the process of recovery:

1   Finding and maintaining hope: believing in oneself; having a sense of personal agency; optimistic about the future.
2   Re-establishment of a positive identity: finding a new identity that incorporates illness, but retains a core, positive sense of self.
3   Building a meaningful life: making sense of illness; finding a meaning in life, despite illness; engaged in life.
4   Taking responsibility and control: feeling in control of illness and in control of life.

Substance misuse and recovery: where are we now?

Recovery from addiction is complicated, multi-faceted, and individually determined. Different clinical models have been used to conceptualize the route to recovery from substance misuse. Thus psychological, social, cultural, and individual factors have all been identified, but there is still uncertainty as to the actual processes involved. Some argue that addiction is irreversible and therefore a chronic relapsing condition like diabetes and asthma, and clients need to be abstinent to be in recovery (O'Brien & McLellan, 1996). Others have challenged the life-long, disease view of addiction, and suggest that addiction may be a 'temporary phase in the life course', with some clients being able to develop out of drug or alcohol use, with or without any medical or other interventions (Stall & Biernacki, 1986; McIntosh & McKeganey, 2001). Recently in the UK, there has been debate between those who believe that abstinence is essential to recovery and those who believe that recovery can be thought of as a broader concept that can include pharmacologically-assisted recovery (e.g., methadone maintenance).

For the purpose of this chapter, we are defining recovery in substance misuse from a 'both–and' perspective; that is to say, recovery encompasses building an individually fulfilled life regardless of whether someone is abstinent or in pharmacologically-assisted recovery.

In 2008, the UK Drug Policy Commission Recovery Consensus Group published a document entitled *A vision of recovery*. This document aimed to clarify what is meant by 'recovery' in the substance misuse field and to promote some forward momentum. While this does not solve the issue of how to commission and provide recovery-based services, it does offer a description of some key features of recovery:

- Recovery is a process.
- It is about accrual of positive benefits, not simply reducing harm.
- Recovery requires the building of aspirations and hope from the drug user, their families, and those providing support.
- It may be associated with a number of different types of support.
- Recovery must be voluntarily sustained in order to be lasting.
- Recovery requires control over substance use, i.e., a comfortable and sustained freedom from compulsion to use.
- Recovery maximizes physical, mental, and social health and well being.
- It is about building a satisfying and meaningful life.

The concept of recovery is still an evolving one, but it is being encouraged by government initiatives, such as the 2008 *Drug strategy 'Drugs: protecting families and communities'* (Department of Health, 2008). There is growing support for the idea that recovery is not just about removing substances from an otherwise unchanged life (Hill, 2010). Different people need different services at different points in their lives, and a variety of outcomes including improved health, stable accommodation, and involvement in work and leisure activities should be indicators of recovery, rather than solely abstinence.

One recent development has been the use of the International Treatment Effectiveness Project (ITEP) developed in the United States and brought to the UK by the National Treatment Agency. The project offers an evidence-based set of resources for use in key worker sessions that has demonstrated improvements in engagement and treatment outcomes. Clients and workers discuss and visualize the recovery process in a series of personalized maps that clients can use to identify their own personal resources as well as professional support available (Campbell, Finch, Brotchie, & Davis, 2007).

The role of groups in recovery

There is an underlying principle in recovery-orientated practice that peer support is of prime importance. Group work provides the opportunity for clients at different stages of recovery to share past experiences, strengths, and resources and to learn from one another. Clients report that the groups provide a sense of shared identity and understanding of the daily challenges faced in recovery. We therefore decided to include three recovery-focused areas into our inpatient group programme: (1) 'roles and identities'; (2) 'leisure'; and (3) 'building life enjoyment'.

The philosophy of recovery was built into the aims, objectives and outcomes of these three groups. All three groups were structured so that clients worked on their own recovery plans in order to instil hope and optimism for the future.

Within this context the groups were run as part of a compulsory group programme. Compulsory, staff-run groups are not ideal and do not fully embrace the recovery philosophy; however, they were written and facilitated with the guiding principle that the helping relationship between clinician and clients moves away from that of 'expert/patient' to one of 'coaches/partners in a journey'. In our experience, groups have worked more successfully when the facilitators have been able to move out of the 'expert' role to work in collaboration with the client. We also recommend that facilitators think about their own recovery values, experiences of recovery (e.g. from advers life events) and what helped or hindered them.

Roles and identities group

'Whereas before I was part of the drug culture, and my roles didn't mean much, all I was doing was scoring, getting money to score, and spending time around other users . . . but roles change and I am an uncle, a son, and I want to make some changes and focus on these.'

(Roy)

'I found the group helpful because it's important to think about what roles that you have got in life when you are off drugs . . . my roles have taken a back seat and you forget how important those roles are . . . it helps you to look forward.'

(Emma)

As the 'career' of a substance-misusing client progresses, their roles and identities may diminish; for example, roles such as worker, partner, and parent may become less of a priority or they become a barrier to substance misuse and are lost. For some users, addiction can become their major life role, providing the user with a sense of identity and meaning in their day as their occupational choices are reduced to the maintenance of their substance misuse (Chacksfield & Lancaster, 2008).

Biernacki (1986) suggests that in order for clients to move out of a drug-using identity, they have to realize their 'spoiled identity'. Central to recovery is the desire to rebuild a sense of self, and to do this change is required. Thus as McIntosh and McKeganey (2001) have noted, not only does the future need to look different and offer positive opportunities, it also needs to be achievable.

The roles and identities group aims to promote:

- Discovery of a positive identity.
- Future roles to add meaning to abstinence/maintenance.
- Contact with a wider support circle.
- Individual decision-making.
- Role participation (in a group or society), because this is linked with long-term psychosocial wellbeing.

Pitfalls and hints

As the group progresses, we often find that people will reflect on major roles such as parent or employee, where their responsibilities have diminished or sometimes disappeared altogether. We find that clients are often presented with the reality of all that they have lost through their addictive behaviours, and this can sometimes present a challenge in terms of instilling hope. As a result, some of our group discussions can become quite emotional. The role of the facilitator is to manage any emotions that arise, such as feelings of loss and sadness, while also instilling hope and optimism for the future. In our experience, there may be several ways of addressing this in the group, for example discussing the importance and value of roles in people's life experiences. A solution-focused approach helps move groups away from a focus on problems to one that more actively embraces solutions (Miller & Berg, 1995).

Since some clients can find it difficult to identify roles, there is some value to having a pre-prepared list of roles, as long as this is used as a prompt and not as a prescriptive list. Where possible, it is much more meaningful to elicit ideas from group members' own lived experiences and facilitate peer support when clients feel stuck or have difficulties identifying any current or future roles. In our experience, these groups have worked more successfully when the facilitator allows the group to make suggestions and give feedback to each other. If clients feel really stuck in identifying a role, it can be useful to suggest discussing the role of service-user.

We have found it helpful to acknowledge that roles and identities change, and similarly that the value attached to these will change over time (e.g., the roles of care-giver, parent, and sibling may have different significance at different life stages). We encourage clients to focus on what is important to them during the current life stage.

As with many aspects of change, attention to detail is essential. The more specific goals are, the easier they are to act on and re-evaluate. We have learned that clients are more likely to incorporate goals into their recovery when they have focused on a couple of roles, understand why these are important in their recovery and have specified how they see these roles as developing. The use of SMART goals (specific, measurable, achievable, realistic, and time-specific) can be adopted into this group to ensure clients feel that their goals are achievable (Drucker, 1954).

Leisure group

> 'I genuinely think it's finding something else that you enjoy that stimulates your mind, that you get a natural high off and you get a buzz from rather than taking drugs . . . it's all about finding that something.'
> (Ross)

> Picking up an interest or hobby again . . . can be every bit as important to recovery as clinical or therapeutic interventions.
> (Drug Scope and Adfam, 2009, p. 8)

Negative mood states, such as boredom and loneliness, are reasons that are commonly cited for relapse (Laudet, 2002). Clients report finding it essential to have structure and plans for day-to-day life, particularly in the early days of recovery, to begin to address the void left from removing substances. Leisure time also needs to be factored into this structure to create a balance between dealing with responsibilities and time for enjoyment.

Not everyone embraces the concept of leisure, since many of our clients perceive this as 'spare time' and therefore dangerous 'thinking about drinking' time. Prior to treatment, time will often be structured around getting and/or consuming drink or drugs. Boredom and the inability to fill time with meaning have been proposed as triggers to relapse in the cycle of addiction (Gordon, 2003; Wanigaratne, Wallace, Pullin, Keany, & Farmer, 1990).

Clients can often identify several activities they used to enjoy before the substance misuse became a priority. A helpful exercise might be to complete a timeline of the inverse link between increasing substance misuse and disengagement from enjoyable activities.

Thus, the aims for this group were to explore the:

- benefits of a balanced lifestyle
- impact of substance misuse on leisure activity
- changes required in leisure patterns as a relapse prevention strategy
- individual's interests and motivation
- secondary benefits of engaging in leisure activities—socializing, improving networks, self-esteem, and confidence.

Suggestion for group outline and content

The group might utilize three typologies of leisure, proposed by Passmore (1998), which classifies leisure according to the reasons that people are involved in them.

1   Achievement leisure: personally challenging pursuits that require an element of commitment, e.g., sports, learning languages/musical instruments.
2   Social leisure: emphasizes being with others, e.g., eating out, going to the cinema.
3   Time out leisure: undemanding and relaxing activities, e.g., listening to music, playing computer games.

The group might explore past, present, and future leisure interests and encourage clients to write one SMART goal in relation to engaging in this activity.

Pitfalls and hints

Facilitators should be aware that clients might feel that talking about leisure is indulgent and not a priority when basic needs may not be being met such as housing, financial, and benefit concerns. We emphasize that identifying pleasurable, meaningful, and purposeful activities is not a denial of the other work that needs to go on within recovery, it rather plays an important role in introducing an element of balance to recovery. The group can be encouraged to think about balancing the responsibilities that they have against allowing for fun and flow in recovery.

Facilitators may also come across staff who co-facilitate group sessions who do not value the opportunity to discuss leisure activities and consider leisure a distraction from the 'real work' that needs to go on within recovery. We have found it helpful to be able to explain the rationale for focusing on leisure and to have supporting literature available for staff to read.

It is useful to bear in mind that what one client might identify as a leisure occupation may well be considered a work occupation by another client. For example, a chef cooking for paid employment will attach different values to cooking compared with a grandmother who enjoys cooking for her grandchildren.

A discussion on barriers to engaging in leisure activities is another helpful component to the group. We have found it useful to develop a resource pack that lists local free or nearly free (under £5 for example) activities/events to highlight that money is not always a necessary resource for leisure activities.

Building life enjoyment group

'Recovery has got to feel like it's worthwhile to you, to the individual, you have got to find something enjoyable . . . that makes you stick at it and it makes you feel good.'

(Roy)

There is a growing body of evidence documenting the importance of positive social networks in achieving and sustaining abstinence (Copello, Orford, Hodgson, Tober, & Barrett, 2002; Waldorf, 1983). The key aspects of networks include moving away from other substance misusers and taking steps to create new interests, relationships, and social networks. Kielhofner states 'the enjoyment of doing things ranges from the simple satisfaction derived from small daily rituals to the intense pleasure people feel in pursuing their driving passions' (2008, p. 43).

Thus, the aims of the group were:

- To identify activities to build life enjoyment.
- To identify important relationships to build life enjoyment.
- To focus on essential resources required in early recovery.
- To identify a satisfying and balanced lifestyle.

Building life enjoyment is linked to the other two groups and takes a larger, overall picture of enjoyment and priorities in recovery.

This group uses the circular grid in Figure 5.1 to help clients identify what personal resources they may need, with a particular focus on enjoy-

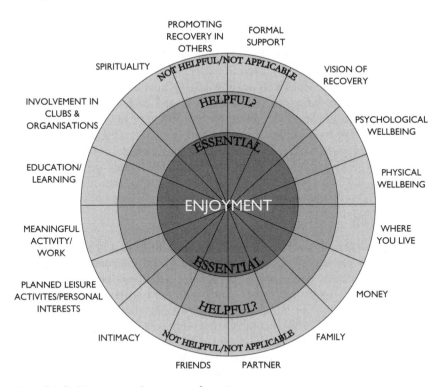

Figure 5.1 Building personal resources for enjoyment.

ment in their recovery. Clients indicate whether a resource (named and located around the circle) is essential to their recovery, may or may not be helpful at this point, or not helpful/not applicable. Clients are then encouraged to think about how they incorporate the essential resources in to their recovery in a more detailed manner (for further details see Hill, 2010).

Pitfalls and hints

This group has had very positive feedback from clients, because it breaks down what is important (and not so important) in a pictorial format. Using highlighters to indicate whether a resource is essential/may be/not helpful has worked well.

As with most of these groups, items identified as 'essential' will change as time goes on and clients change. We encourage clients to complete the grid as they view life on the current day and over the coming week. Some people like to take an extra copy away with them to complete at a later date.

One difficulty that may occur in any group looking at recovery is when members of the group are in different places in terms of their recovery. For example, some clients may view the inpatient experience as respite, a temporary reprieve from the day-in and day-out of substance misuse, and have difficulties taking groups seriously and thinking about changes they may need to make. This throws up a difficult dynamic in the group when others are at a point where they are motivated to think about a different future and changes that they need to make. What we have found helpful is to discuss where people are at, acknowledging how difficult it must be in a unit where the programme is abstinence-based and for people to seek support outside of the group. Naming the difficulty has proven to be an effective strategy to open up discussion rather than 'telling clients off' and getting into a power struggle, which ultimately is not helpful to anyone. The use of motivational interviewing techniques in this group has been invaluable.

Conclusion

Addiction services and commissioners in the UK have a challenging road ahead if they are to truly provide recovery-focused intervention to clients. Changes to service philosophies, practices, relationships, and financial investment have to be addressed. Staff will need to be trained to work alongside clients on their individual recovery goals, and services review how they provide treatment to encompass recovery-based practice.

In the meantime, we have attempted to provide groups that take a broader view on recovery, that embrace the guiding principles of hope, positive identity, building a meaningful life, and restoring control and responsibility back to the client. Although these groups and ideas have worked on an inpatient unit, they could be adapted to suit specific service needs, client populations, and available resources. We have drawn on our experiences of setting up and running these groups and reflected on common themes that emerge when discussing these areas. It has been a rewarding experience to be a part of group work that reflects our occupational therapy roots, embraces client-centred practice, and focuses on the strengths and aspirations of clients. We would like to thank the many clients that have contributed to the groups and allowed us to be part of their recovery stories.

Suggested further reading and resources

Hill, R. G. (2010). *What's your reason? A practical guide to recovery*. London: Hunter-Lodge.

National Institute for Mental Health in England (2004). *The ten essential shared capabilities: A framework for the whole of the mental health workforce*. London: Department of Health.

Recovery Academy (www.recoveryacademy.org).

Shepherd, G., Boardman, J., & Slade, M. (2008). *Making recovery a reality*. London: Sainsbury Centre for Mental Health.

Social Exclusion Unit (2004). *Mental health and social exclusion*. London: Office of the Deputy Prime Minister.

Further details of a suggested group outline and content are available at the National Treatment Agency (http://www.nta.nhs.uk).

References

Andresen, R., Oades, L., & Caputi, P. (2003). The experience of recovery from schizophrenia: Towards an empirically validated stage model. *Australian and New Zealand Journal of Psychiatry, 37*, 586–594.

Anthony, W. A. (1993). Recovery from mental illness: The guiding vision of the mental health service system in the 1990s. *Psychosocial Rehabilitation Journal, 16*, 11–24.

Biernacki, P. (1986). *Pathways from heroin addiction: Recovery without treatment*. Philadelphia: Temple University Press.

Campbell, A., Finch, E., Brotchie, J., & Davis, P. (2007). *The international treatment effectiveness project: Implementing psychosocial interventions for adult drug misusers*. London: National Treatment Agency for Substance Misuse. Retrieved May 25, 2010, from http://www.nta.nhs.uk/uploads/nta_itep_implementing_psychosocial_interventions_for_adult_drug_misusers_rb34.pdf

Chacksfield, J. D., & Lancaster, J. (2008). Substance misuse. In J. Creek & L. Lougher (Eds.), *Occupational therapy and mental health* (4th ed., pp. 534–554). Edinburgh: Churchill Livingstone.

Copello, A., Orford, J., Hodgson, R., Tober, G., Barrett, C. on behalf of the United Kingdom Alcohol Treatment Trial research team (2002). Social behaviour and network therapy: Basic principles and early experiences. *Addict Behaviour, 27,* 345–366.

Department of Health (2001). *The expert patient.* London: Department of Health.

Department of Health (2006). *Our health, our care, our say.* London: Department of Health.

Department of Health (2008). *'Drugs: protecting families and communities: The 2008 Drug Strategy'.* London: Department of Health.

Drucker, P. F. (1954). *The practice of management.* New York: Harper Collins.

Drug Scope and Adfam (2009). *Recovery and drug dependency: A new deal for families.* Retrieved November 31, 2010, from http://www.adfam.org.uk/docs/recovery_dependency.pdf

Gordon, S. (2003). *Relapse and recovery: Behavioural strategies for change.* Wernersville, PA: Caron Foundation.

Hill, R. G. (2010). *What's your reason? A practical guide to recovery.* London: Hunter-Lodge.

Kielhofner, G. (2008). *A model of human occupation: Theory and application* (4th ed.). Baltimore: Lippincott Williams & Wilkins.

Laudet, A. (2002). *Reasons for initiation and maintenance of drug use and alcohol use among dually-diagnosed individuals.* National Development and Research Institutes. Retrieved May 20, 2010, from http://www.ndri.org

McIntosh, J., & McKeganey, N. (2001). Identity and recovery from dependent drug use: The addict's perspective. *Drugs: Education, Prevention and Policy,* 8, 47–59.

Miller, S. D., & Berg, I. K. (1995). *The miracle method: A radically new approach to problem drinking.* New York: W & W Norton and Co.

O'Brien, C. P., & McLellan, A. T. (1996). Myths about the treatment of addiction. *The Lancet, 347,* 237–240.

Passmore, A. (1998). Does leisure support and underpin adolescents' developing worker role? *Journal of Occupational Science,* 5, 161–165.

Stall, R., & Biernacki, P. (1986). Spontaneous remission from the problematic use of substances: An inductive model derived from a comparative analysis of the alcohol, opiate, tobacco and food/obesity literatures. *The International Journal of the Addictions, 21,* 1–23.

UK Drug Policy Commission Recovery Consensus Group (2008). *A vision of recovery.* Retrieved May 31, 2010, from http://www.ukdpc.org.uk/resources/A%20Vision%20of%20Recovery.pdf

Waldorf, D. (1983). Natural recovery from opiate addiction: Some social-psychological processes of untreated recovery. *Journal of Drug Issues, 13,* 237–247.

Wanigaratne, S., Wallace, W., Pullin, J., Keaney, F., & Farmer, R. (1990). *Relapse prevention for addictive behaviours: A manual for therapists.* Oxford: Blackwell Science.

Chapter 6

Mindfulness-based approaches to addiction

Robert Hill, Jane Hutton, Marcus Koch, and Ann McDonnell

> If we are prepared for thinking, there is no need to make an effort to
> think. This is called mindfulness.
>
> (Suzuki, 1979, p. 113)

In this chapter we examine mindfulness-based approaches to addiction. To
begin with, we give some background to the approach of mindfulness both
in the East and West, before moving on to discuss ways of practising
mindfulness. We discuss some of the issues that have arisen when introducing mindfulness to clients in an addiction centre, before concluding with
suggestions as to how you might go about and incorporating mindfulness
into your own work with clients.

Mindfulness: East and West

Mindfulness is about present moment awareness. It can be thought of as
moving away from a 'doing' mode into a 'being' mode, in which we focus
on accepting and allowing what is in our current experience to emerge, with
no need to suppress, judge, or immediately change it. Rather than focusing
on the past (maybe regrets of things that we have or have not done) or the
future (things that we want to happen or not happen), we fully experience
and live in the *present* moment, in its full richness. Jon Kabat-Zinn talks of
mindfulness as 'paying attention in a particular way: on purpose, in the
present moment, and non-judgementally' (1994, p. 4).

Mindfulness is by no means new, and the formal practice of mindfulness
meditation has always been central to Buddhism. Mindfulness based on
'Vipassana' (the gradual and direct cultivation of awareness) resides in the
core teachings of the Buddha, the 'Dharma'.

Buddhism recognizes that:

- We categorize our experiences into qualitative description—good, bad,
  or neutral, and then react with a set of fixed pre-programmed habitual
  responses.

- Because our attention is fixed on seeking out experiences that are good and seeking to avoid those that we see as bad, we are caught in endless cycles of desire and aversion.
- While we all seek happiness and peace, this can only be attained if we free our mind from this cycle of aversion and desire.
- Moment by moment life flies past and we miss the vividness of the present moment by being somewhere else or in the 'doing' mode.
- The essence of human experience and the way of the universe is impermanence.
- If we live in the present moment, then changes will flow naturally.

The cultivation of mindfulness is taught through various formal meditation practices and discussion of what arises in experience during these practices. The teacher engages in the practice while guiding the meditation. Mindfulness also encourages one to take a mindful moment-to-moment approach to daily life. Thus, one can walk mindfully, eat mindfully, indeed undertake any activity in a mindful way, simply by bringing a gentle, non-judgemental awareness to one's actions and experiences.

There are a number of inter-related facets of mindfulness:

- non-judging
- patience
- beginner's mind
- trust
- non-striving
- acceptance
- letting go.

Non-judging

This is about assuming the stance of an impartial witness, developing awareness of the constant stream of judging and reacting that we are normally caught up in, learning to take a step back from it and simply observing whatever comes up. As Jon Kabat-Zinn states, 'It is remarkable how liberating it feels to be able to see that your thoughts are just thoughts and that they are not 'you' or 'reality' . . . the simple act of recognising your thoughts as thoughts can free you from the distorted reality that they often create and allow for more clear-sightedness and a greater sense of manage-ability in your life' (1990, p. 69).

Patience

This means developing a perspective that views difficulties with calmness and without 'knee-jerk' reactions, remembering that sometimes things must unfold in their own time.

Beginner's mind

'See everything as if for the first time.' The next time that you see something that is familiar to you, ask yourself if you are really seeing it as it is; are you looking at it, or are you simply seeing the reflection of your own thoughts?

Trust

Trust in your own ability. There is no right or wrong way to approach mindfulness. The intention is not to become more like somebody else, but to become more fully oneself.

Non-striving

Mindfulness is not about trying to achieve something specific through meditation, or to 'get it right'. The practice of mindfulness involves simply paying attention, without judgement, to whatever is happening. It is about 'being' in the present moment and not 'doing' anything.

Acceptance

Acceptance means willingness to see things exactly as they are in the present moment. This attitude sets the stage for acting wisely; for being aware of what is going on, neither suppressing fears and prejudices nor allowing them to cloud awareness and lead to mindless reaction.

Letting go

This is the other side of acceptance. Often we cling on to ideas, thoughts, desires, and resentments, which prevents us from 'living in the moment' and from which we can learn to let go.

Mindfulness, by focusing on the present moment, reminds us that all things in life are changing from moment to moment, and attempting to deny change is as exhausting and futile as trying to cling to a slippery rock. Contemplating the impermanence of all things may sound dispiriting, but can lead to liberation from this fruitless effort. There is a paradox here for, although mindfulness can bring tremendous benefits, focusing on attempting to achieve or gain something inevitably detracts from being with things as they are *here-and-now*. As Jon Kabat-Zinn states in his guidance for practising sitting meditation, the invitation of mindfulness is towards 'reminding yourself from time to time that you are not trying to get anywhere or feel anything special, even relaxation, you are simply allowing yourself to be where you already are and to feel whatever is here to be felt in this moment.

Observing and accepting whatever is here, simply because it is already here, a part of your experience in this moment, regardless of whether it feels pleasant, unpleasant or neutral' (2002, np).

Despite this paradox, mindfulness has been successfully adapted for use in western medicine for people facing a wide variety of problems including stress, anxiety, depression, and chronic illnesses. It has also been shown to be beneficial for people who do not have problems that meet clinical criteria. The Mindfulness Based Stress Reduction (MBSR) programme is one such successful adaptation that has been used extensively since 1982, most notably by Jon Kabat-Zinn, whose writings and teaching have done much to make mindfulness accessible to a Western population. While originally developed for chronic pain and anxiety, MBSR has been successfully used for many physical and mental health conditions and, more recently, has been adapted for use in relapse prevention of the addictions.

MBSR (Kabat-Zinn, 1982) is taught in 8–10 weekly group sessions lasting up to two and a half hours for approximately 20–30 participants. This is supplemented with one full day of practice and daily home meditation practice guided by CDs (lasting 45 minutes). Evidence appears to suggest effectiveness for chronic pain (Kabat-Zinn, Lipworth, & Burney, 1985; Randolph, Caldera, Tacone, & Greak, 1999) and generalized anxiety (Kabat-Zinn et al., 1992), with gains being maintained years later (Miller, Fletcher, & Kabat-Zinn, 1995).

In the UK, Mindfulness Based Cognitive Therapy (MBCT) has been shown to be very effective with depression, particularly recurrent depression (Segal, Williams, & Teasdale, 2002). MBCT is taught in eight weekly group sessions, usually lasting 2 hours, for approximately 10–15 participants, supplemented with 45 minutes daily home meditation practice. The principle of mindful awareness has also been used successfully as a key tenet of Dialectical Behaviour Therapy for Borderline Personality Disorder (Linehan, 1993), and Acceptance and Commitment Therapy (Hayes, Strosahl, & Wilson, 2004).

Mindfulness has been shown to produce actual physiological changes in those who practise it regularly (Davidson, 2003; Varela, 2003). In particular, MRI scans have found left-sided activation of the anterior cortical areas in a mindfulness group compared with waiting-list controls (Davidson et al., 2003). Davidson *et al.* conclude that 'meditation may change brain and immune functions in positive ways, although they underscore the need for further research' (2003, p. 504).

Some of the qualitative changes that people note when they are experienced in mindfulness include:

- Responding to stimuli with increased calmness and clarity.
- A shift in relation to thoughts/feelings, which become just passing events in the mind ('Mental states come and go').

- A reduction in the amount of time spent in goal-directed activity.
- A more 'welcoming' and 'allowing' attitude to our thoughts and experiences rather than a 'need to solve' stance.
- An increased acceptance of ourselves and other people.
- Decreased tension, fear, and worry.
- Increased concentration and knowledge of reality.
- Increased self-discipline.
- Decreased impulses/urges.
- Increased relaxation.
- Decreased stress.
- Awareness that we can be responsible for perpetuating our own mental suffering.

Mindfulness and addiction

For many clients with substance-dependence problems, staying with one's own emotions is a particular difficulty, and exposure to unpleasant emotions can be a trigger to substance use. Moreover, many clients use substances in order to ensure that such emotions are not experienced in the first place. Staying in the *here-and-now* without changing one's response to it is a key skill that is often taught to clients undergoing therapy for their addiction. Mindfulness can play a key role in helping to develop awareness and this is particularly important in addictions, for as Kabat-Zinn notes 'in the case of alcohol and drug abuse or habits such as workaholism, our tendency toward unawareness may also be lethal, either rapidly or slowly' (1990, p. 25). When offering mindfulness to clients it is important to be aware that some clients may have other concerns or preoccupations, be they internal (mood states) or external (financial or social challenges). Mindfulness does not deny the reality of such concerns, but rather provides an opportunity to take time out from them.

We have offered guidance in mindfulness practice as part of an inpatient daily community group for a number of years, and in the next section we describe some of the issues and challenges that have arisen while doing this work and suggest some strategies for working with such difficulties.

Introducing the group

Mindfulness is, for many clients, an entirely new experience and the word itself may be totally unfamiliar. Therefore staff members introducing it need to be confident in explaining the rationale for mindfulness and running the group, as well as its practice. Both of these things develop through experience and knowledge, so building confidence through practice is essential. There is a danger that reading out loud a written script on a daily basis can sound repetitive, and we have found it helpful for facilitators to find a way to offer a personalized, perhaps less formal, overview of the group. We have included some suggestions here that you could tailor for your particular group.

'We are now going to do a mindfulness exercise.'

'Could anybody explain why these types of exercise may offer some benefit? Perhaps those of you who have been here some time could enlighten the newer patients.'

Typical responses may include 'It's meditation', 'Not thinking', 'A load of hippy crap'. Instead of directly challenging such views, it is useful to give some alternative suggestions and explanations for introducing mindfulness:

'Often, when people explain why they were drinking or using drugs, they talk about 'blanking-out the past' and/or 'forgetting about the future', as these can often be sources of stress and pain. Mindfulness exercises can help a person focus on the *here-and-now*, but without the downside of drugs.'

'Mindfulness is about using your own skills to maintain your focus of thought and not allowing distractions to take your thinking down negative or destructive paths.'

'It's boring', 'I'm clucking and my legs hurt', 'I have bad thoughts'
When such views are expressed, clients are really communicating about how they are feeling rather than commenting on mindfulness itself, and it is therefore worthwhile acknowledging such difficulties without getting caught up in them. This is exactly the kind of 'grist for the mill' that can be discussed in enquiry after practice.

'Many people mention negative thoughts as being the most difficult aspect of these exercises as there can sometimes be a lot of regret or guilt associated with the past, and a lot of worry, fear, and uncertainty associated with the future. These thoughts, which often lead to craving (and potentially relapse), can be controlled, and mindfulness can be a very useful tool in helping to do so.'

'Mindfulness can offer you the chance to respond differently to stress-ful situations.'

'It may work for some of you, and others may not feel much benefit at this time. However, I would ask that you all respect the exercise and one another, so as to allow those who are benefiting to remain focused.'

'Sometimes, just sitting quietly can be very difficult, especially when you are coming off a substance.'

'So, if you could all get comfortable in your seats. . .'

Selecting the mindfulness exercise

If working with a selection of exercises, groups will often 'get to know' the different versions, and will respond well when asked to choose which they would prefer on any given day. This selection should be done towards the end of the introduction.

Reported benefits of mindfulness

Those clients for whom the exercises prove beneficial often report both intense relaxation during the group practice and an increased ability to de-escalate and control cravings throughout the day. Clients often become increasingly confident and able to communicate with staff and peers in a more structured and creative way, in turn leading to a more constructive and supportive atmosphere on the unit. Certainly, even those clients who may initially appear sceptical about the benefits eventually seem able to gain at least a period of relaxation and also develop a respect for their peers and the exercise.

Dealing with disruptions in a group

Generally, a well-introduced group will engage the clients and minimize mid-exercise disruptions. However, occasionally certain clients may have problems remaining focused. Clients often respond positively to a simple visual cue from the facilitator. In cases of more extreme disruption it should be the facilitator's choice as to the intervention. A client could be asked to leave the group to allow for the continuing of the exercise with the remaining members. In more extreme cases, the mindfulness exercise could be halted to allow all group members to feed back how the disruption has impacted on them. However, disruptions are rare once the exercise is under way.

Should facilitators practise mindfulness themselves?

The developers of MBCT make a clear recommendation that intellectual knowledge alone is not enough, and that facilitators should use mindfulness in their own lives in order to embody the attitudes they invite participants to cultivate and adopt. In our clinical area, however, not all facilitators did practise mindfulness themselves and they did vary in their ability and confidence to facilitate the mindfulness group. Those who did practise mindfulness generally seemed more positive in engaging the clients with the exercise, and were more able to reassure clients who expressed doubts. It also seemed that having a sound understanding of the theory behind mindfulness (whether based on personal practice or not) allowed facilitators to offer a comprehensive introduction to the group and reassure clients that this was a safe and beneficial exercise to take part in before they spent 5–10 minutes in a group with their eyes shut.

Next steps

If you have been interested or intrigued by some of the ideas expressed in this chapter and want either to practise for yourself or to practise so that you can introduce it to your clients, then you will want to follow up what you have read here.

As the essence of mindfulness is in its practice, we strongly recommend that you gain some exposure to this, ideally through a teacher in a group context. The benefits of this are the ability to meet others interested in the same approach, plus the opportunity to discuss your thoughts and experiences of mindfulness, while supported by an experienced teacher. There are an increasing number of courses run for healthcare professionals, including the long-standing courses at the Centre for Mindfulness at Bangor University in North Wales.

If you are not able to find or attend a suitable course, then there are a number of mindfulness CDs available, the main ones being by Jon Kabat-Zinn and the Oxford Mindfulness Centre. Jon Kabat-Zinn's books provide an accessible and stimulating guide to the area and Rebecca Crane (2008) provides a very good introduction to mindfulness-based cognitive therapy. Buddhist texts on mindfulness can be quite complex, however we would recommend *Mindfulness in plain English* (1992) by the Venerable H, Gunaratana Mahathera as an accessible and practical guide.

Given that the essence of mindfulness lies in its practice we have included two simple mindfulness exercises below.

Mindfulness of the breath

- Commit to devoting some time (perhaps 15–20 minutes) to daily practice.
- Find a quiet place to sit, with the spine upright but not stiff, and wear clothes that do not restrict the breath.
- Close your eyes and focus on your breath.

- Start with three deep breaths and then just allow the body to breathe normally, simply noticing the feeling of breathing.
- Focus attention on the breath and allow everything else to be just as it is. If your mind starts to wander, just bring it back to the breath. Minds will always wander and bringing them back to the breath is the practice.
- Understand that your mind is just a 'gatekeeper', notice thoughts as they appear and disappear, observing them as they come and go.

Eating a raisin mindfully

- Take a raisin and hold it in the palm of your hand. Look at it, as if you had never seen such a thing before, turn it over and see how the light shines on it, exploring its texture.
- Notice any thoughts that come into your mind, noting that they are simply thoughts, and bring awareness back to the raisin.
- Hold the raisin beneath your nostrils and notice the smell of it.
- Slowly bring the raisin to your lips, open your mouth, and gently place the raisin on your tongue.
- Notice the taste, and any impatience to bite into the raisin.
- Bite into it mindfully, and notice the tastes it releases.
- Slowly chew it, and notice how your body begins the process of digestion.
- Notice the intention to swallow as it arises.
- Notice the sensations of swallowing, and realize that your body is now one raisin heavier.

'In walking, just walk. In sitting, just sit. Above all, don't wobble'. (Yun-Men)

Resources

Jon Kabat-Zinn CDs: http://www.mindfulnesscds.com
Oxford Mindfulness Centre: http://www.oxfordmindfulness.org
The Centre for Mindfulness Research and Practice: http://www.bangor.ac.uk/mindfulness

References

Crane, R. (2008). *Mindfulness-based cognitive therapy*. London: Routledge.
Davidson, R. (2003). The protean brain. In The Dalai Lama & Daniel Goleman (Eds.), *Destructive emotions and how we can overcome them* (pp. 334–354). London: Bloomsbury.
Davidson, R. J., Kabat-Zinn, J., Schumacher, J., Rosenkranz, M., Muller, D.,

Santorelli, S. F., Urbanowski, F., Harrington, A., Bonus, K., & Sheridan, J. F. (2003). Alterations in brain and immune function produced by mindfulness meditation. *Psychosomatic Medicine*, *65*, 564–570.

Hayes, S. C., Strosahl, K. D., & Wilson, K. G. (2004). *Acceptance and commitment therapy. An experiential approach to behavior change: An experimental approach to behavior change*. London: Guildford Press.

Kabat-Zinn, J. (1982). An out-patient program in behavioral medicine for chronic pain patients based on the practice of mindfulness meditation: Theoretical considerations and preliminary results. *General Hospital Psychiatry*, *4*, 33–47.

Kabat-Zinn, J. (1990). *Full catastrophe living—How to cope with stress, pain and illness using mindfulness meditation*. London: Piatikus Books.

Kabat-Zinn, J. (2002). Sitting meditations in guided mindfulness meditation 4 practice CDs Series 2. Retrieved November 1, 2010, from http://www.mindfulnesscds.com

Kabat-Zinn, J. (1994). *Wherever you go there you are: Mindfulness meditation in everyday life*. London: Piatkus Books.

Kabat-Zinn, J., Lipworth, L., & Burney, R. (1985). The clinical use of mindfulness meditation for the self-regulation of chronic pain. *Journal of Behavioral Medicine*, *8*, 163–190.

Kabat-Zinn, J., Massion, A. O., Kristeller, J., Peterson, L. G., Fletcher, K. E., Pbert, L., Lenderking, L. R., & Santorelli, S. F. (1992). Effectiveness of a meditation-based stress reduction program in the treatment of anxiety disorders. *American Journal of Psychiatry*, *149*, 936–943.

Linehan, M. (1993). *Cognitive behavioural treatment of borderline personality disorder*. London: Guildford Press.

Miller, J., Fletcher, K., & Kabat-Zinn, J. (1995). Three-year follow-up and clinical implications of a mindfulness-based stress reduction intervention in the treatment of anxiety disorders. *General Hospital Psychiatry*, *17*, 192–200.

Randolph, P. D., Caldera, Y. M., Tacone, A. M., & Greak, B. L. (1999). The long-term combined effects of medical treatment and a mindfulness-based behavioral program for the multidisciplinary management of chronic pain in West Texas. *Pain Digest*, *9*, 103–112.

Segal, Z. V., Williams, J. M. G., & Teasdale, J. (2002). *Mindfulness-based cognitive therapy for depression: A new approach to preventing relapse*. Guildford Press: London.

Suzuki, S. (1979). *Zen mind, beginner's mind*. New York: Weatherhill.

Varela, F. (2003). The scientific study of consciousness. In The Dalai Lama & Daniel Goleman (Eds.), *Destructive emotions and how we can overcome them* (pp. 305–333). London: Bloomsbury.

Venerable H. Gunaratana Mahathera (1992). *Mindfulness in plain English*. Retrieved October 3, 2010, from http://www.budaedu.org.tw

Chapter 7

An introduction to group Twelve-Step facilitation

Breaking barriers and myth-busting

Andrew Parker

Introduction

Recent research has confirmed what has long been claimed—that participating in Alcoholics Anonymous (AA) or Narcotics Anonymous (NA) is associated with abstinence and improvements in psychosocial functioning. Many who might benefit from AA/NA do not go however, often because of negative perceptions or misunderstandings of how AA/NA operates.

This chapter aims to provide therapists with the motivation, knowledge, and tools to address this systematically through Twelve-Step facilitation, with an emphasis on group settings.

Alcoholics and Narcotics Anonymous: a brief synopsis

Alcoholics Anonymous (AA) is a worldwide fellowship providing regular group meetings for those who wish to recover from addiction. Since its beginnings in the 1930s, several variants of AA have developed, such as Narcotics Anonymous, Cocaine Anonymous, and Gamblers Anonymous. All of these groups are based on the same principles and practice, guided by the Twelve Steps. For brevity, I shall use the term AA/NA to refer to them all.

In 70 years AA/NA has grown exponentially to be the largest organization of mutual-help groups in the world. Meetings are free and widely available. They occur in over 120 countries, with over 3500 meetings per week in the UK and over 50,000 meetings per week in the USA. AA/NA has an abstinence-based philosophy, and an explicit focus on holistic recovery of the person.

Central to AA/NA's path for recovery are the Twelve Steps. These are a distillation of the attitudes adopted, commitments made, and tasks undertaken, by the first 100 members of AA, and have subsequently been adopted as a suggested recovery template. The content of the Twelve Steps could be summarized as promoting the following:

- Insight into the nature of addiction (Step 1).
- Hope and commitment (Steps 2–3).
- Openness and honesty (Steps 4–6).
- Humility and making amends (Steps 7–9).
- Self-monitoring and appraisal (Step 10).
- Nurturing a relationship with a 'higher power' (Step 11).
- Helping others (Step 12).

The Twelve Steps use the language of 'we/us' rather than 'I/me', emphasizing the fellowship aspects. This is further emphasized by the recommendation to work through the Twelve Steps with the help of a sponsor.

There have evolved many memorable slogans encapsulating important truths about recovery in the AA/NA community. One of these, 'AA/NA is a simple programme for complicated people', reminds us that the core of the Twelve-Step programme boils down to wisdom of a very common-sense kind:

- Fellowship: using the support and experience of others in recovery.
- Pragmatism: doing whatever works.
- Spirituality: regaining a sense of meaning and purpose.

Is AA/NA effective?

Research studies have demonstrated for decades that attendance at AA/NA is associated with long-term abstinence. However, the data on their own do not prove that AA/NA contributes significantly to the *cause* of high abstinence rates. This has been a controversial point, for critics of AA/NA have often argued that it is those individuals who are already highly motivated who then chose to attend AA/NA.

In the last 15 years the quality and quantity of research on AA/NA has increased substantially, and the results of this have led to a growing confidence in AA/NA's *causal* effectiveness (Kelly & McCrady, 2008; Humphreys, 2004). Evaluating this research is complex, however, because the nature of AA/NA makes it impractical to test its effectiveness directly in randomized controlled trials (RCTs). Thus we must take account of data from high-quality observational studies as well. Such studies have a well-recognized role in establishing treatment effectiveness alongside RCTs, or where high-quality RCTs are not possible (Ligthelm, Borzi, Gumprecht, Kawamori, Wenying, & Valensi, 2007).

Kaskutas (2009) has recently examined this evidence against six criteria required to establish a causal effect. Kaskutas demonstrated that the evidence for a causal relationship is highly suggestive on one criterion (specificity of effect) and strong on all of the other five:

- Rates of abstinence are approximately twice as high among those who attend AA (magnitude).
- Higher levels of attendance are related to higher rates of abstinence (dose-response).
- The relationships are found for different samples/groups and follow-up periods (consistency).
- Prior AA attendance is predictive of subsequent abstinence (temporal).
- Mechanisms of action predicted by theories of behaviour change are present in AA (plausibility).

Such appraisals of the evidence have led to a greater interest by professional services in how they can promote attendance at AA/NA.

Facilitation: why just telling people to go to AA/NA is not enough

Unfortunately, simple advice to attend AA/NA often does not work. Experience and research indicate that many do not go at all, some go very infrequently, and only a minority go regularly (Gossop, Stewart, & Marsden, 2008; Kaskutas, Ammon, Delucchi, Room, Bond, & Weisner, 2005).

Perceptions of AA/NA by those not involved are often negative, coloured by myths, misunderstandings, and stereotyped views. While it is important to remember that attending AA/NA is not the only way to recover from addiction, the clear effectiveness and cost-effectiveness of AA/NA means that professionals should assist help-seekers to overcome these barriers as much as possible, and encourage people to give it a go with an open mind.

Specific methods used to do this in a professional setting are often grouped under the term 'Twelve-Step facilitation' (TSF). There are now several versions of TSF that have been shown in randomized controlled trials to increase attendance and involvement in AA/NA, as well as increasing rates of abstinence (Donovan & Floyd, 2008). I will highlight some of these methods, and then describe a brief group-based TSF intervention ('Mind the Gap') that attempts to overcome many of the myths, misunderstandings, and anxieties about attending AA/NA, alongside giving practical advice on how to get to meetings. TSF interventions can be classified as in Table 7.1.

Twelve-Step residential treatment programmes, often referred to as Minnesota Model Rehabilitation, offer primarily group therapy based closely on the Twelve-Step philosophy. At the heart of the treatment is exposure to AA/NA groups, or groups that mimic AA/NA and a focus on Steps 1–3 of the Twelve Steps. There is evidence that such programmes lead to higher attendance at AA/NA and higher rates of abstinence than programmes based on cognitive behavioural therapy (CBT; Humphreys & Moos, 2001).

Table 7.1 Twelve-Step facilitation interventions

	Group	*Individual*
Complex/extended	• Twelve-Step residential programmes (e.g., Minnesota Model)	• Project Match TSF (Nowinski, Baker, & Carroll, 1995)
Brief	• Mind the Gap (see below) • MAAEZ (Kaskutas, Subbaraman, Witbrodt, & Zemore, 2009)	• Intensive Referral (Timko, DeBenedetti, & Billow, 2006)

Project MATCH—a large randomized controlled trial—employed a manual-based TSF intervention delivered on an individual basis over 12–15 sessions by a trained counsellor (Nowinski et al., 1995). The intervention aimed to facilitate progress through the first three steps of the Twelve Steps as well as promote attendance at AA. Compared with cognitive behavioural therapy or motivational enhancement, TSF produced superior abstinence outcomes in the outpatient arm of the study. Furthermore, this superior effect seemed to be related to TSF's effectiveness in promoting involvement in AA (Donovan & Floyd, 2008).

A much briefer form of TSF is 'Intensive referral' to AA/NA, consisting of three one-to-one sessions with a counsellor who gives detailed practical advice on getting to AA/NA meetings, and helps to facilitate this via an existing member of AA/NA, and goal-setting. This brief intervention was shown to produce greater involvement in AA/NA and better alcohol and drug use outcomes at 6 months compared with standard referral to AA/NA (Timko et al., 2006).

For public services on tight budgets it may still prove difficult to find the extra resources even for a three-session one-to-one intervention. Given the group nature of AA/NA meetings, and the fact that group interventions, *if effective*, are likely to be cost-effective, brief group-based TSF is an obvious recent development in the field. An example is 'Mind the Gap', a single group intervention added to an existing group programme in an inpatient setting.

Mind 'the gap'

The group title was chosen to highlight the need to maintain work on recovery following formal treatment ('the Gap'), with the suggested method being to attend AA/NA groups. This was a small service development that added no extra cost. Its effectiveness has not yet been evaluated, but general support is provided by positive findings from the other variants of TSF highlighted above.

The 'Mind the Gap' group was developed on the National Alcohol Unit, Bethlem Hospital, which is a 2–4-week-stay inpatient ward for people with severe alcohol dependence. The Unit already ran a successful manualized group CBT relapse-prevention programme delivered by nursing and psychology staff. However, systematic encouragement to attend AA/NA was minimal, and there was limited opportunity for people to discuss any misgivings or prior experiences of AA/NA. It was decided to add a TSF group to the existing programme, to occur once every 2 weeks.

Referring to the evidence of effectiveness for both TSF and AA/NA itself was crucial in gaining whole team and managerial support. Initially some staff had misgivings about AA/NA, and were sceptical about its effectiveness. Others felt that AA/NA had 'religious overtones' and that statutory services should not be promoting attendance because of this. However, after presenting the evidence and information about AA/NA, the development was fully supported.

The group format and content was devised by the present author in liaison with a nursing staff member from the ward. They co-facilitated the group initially. Both are in recovery and had found the AA/NA Twelve-Step path immensely helpful. The group was supported by other staff members who sat in to learn more about AA/NA and how to facilitate the group. It was felt that although ideally one of the two facilitators would know AA/NA through personal experience, this was not essential. Given the brief and structured nature of the intervention, we felt that staff with no personal experience of AA/NA could quickly learn to become very effective facilitators after learning about key aspects of AA/NA, such as those addressed in this chapter, and attending some AA/NA meetings as a visitor.

Each 'Mind the Gap' group lasted 60 minutes and consisted of the following format:

- WELCOME and round of names.
- INTRODUCTION to purpose of group by referring to 'the Gap' in their lives without alcohol following formal treatment, and the need for ongoing recovery work to prevent relapse. Suggest AA/NA as an effective resource.
- ACKNOWLEDGE that many people have misgivings about AA/NA—this group is about exploring them, and addressing barriers and myths.
- ASK who has been to AA/NA and approximately how many meetings in total—this gives an idea of the level of experience in the group.
- EVIDENCE BAR CHART—a simple bar chart is drawn on the board (taken from a scientific research paper). There are two bars, one half the height of the other, showing that 1 year after formal treatment, 50% have relapsed if they don't get involved in AA/NA, but only 25% relapse if they do get involved in AA/NA. Emphasize that these results are maintained at 3 years.

- DISCUSS the bar chart by drawing out group members' expectations and knowledge about rates of relapse and the effectiveness of AA/NA.
- EVIDENCE HANDOUT. Give each group member a sheet of paper highlighting what scientific studies have shown regarding involvement in AA/NA and drinking/drug-use outcomes.
- WHO HAS TRIED AA/NA? Encourage people to volunteer their experiences. Then focus the discussion on positive and negative experiences of AA/NA.
- POSITIVES AND NEGATIVES. Write these on the board in two columns. Where possible, encourage group members to respond to negative experiences with their own positive experience in the spirit of helping group members to reconsider AA/NA.
- BREAKING BARRIERS, MYTHS, AND MYTH-BUSTING. Drawing from the list of positives and negatives, highlight some common themes of how people have found AA/NA helpful, but also the common obstacles. Try to correct unbalanced views using the tips in the section below on breaking barriers and myth-busting. But where possible draw on the positive remarks of other group members.
- PRACTICAL TIPS on getting to AA/NA meetings. Suggest the following:
  - Research the website for meeting locations and times.
  - Carry the AA/NA booklet with you.
  - If there is a contact number, call to say that you are coming to that meeting for the first time—you may be greeted, and may even be offered a lift!
  - Plan meetings to attend to fit in with other journeys—e.g., to/from visiting a friend.
  - Talk to others at meetings—find out where the best meetings are.
  - Arrange to meet others at meetings and swap contact details to keep in touch.
  - Shop around—don't just go to one.
  - Arrange your journey so that you arrive in plenty of time.
  - Leave your judging self at the door and go in with an open mind.
  - Reward yourself for having attended—meet up with a sober friend, treat yourself.
- CLOSE THE GROUP by summarizing the main points, and ask if anyone has any final questions. Ask group members to raise their hands if they intend to give AA/NA a chance. Thank everyone for coming.

Common themes: breaking barriers and myth-busting

Some of the obstacles to trying AA/NA are simply about misinformation. However, often it is more complex. Minimization, which can lead to underestimating one's relapse risk, will tend to lower the motivation to go, and may manifest as negativity towards attending AA/NA. Fear takes many forms and is another potent obstacle: fear of speaking in groups, fear of having to be honest with oneself, and fear of the challenge or simply the unknown. Often much is made of the spiritual aspect of the Twelve-Step programme. People will often say 'AA/NA is not for me—I don't believe in God'. However, such statements misunderstand the nature of spirituality in AA/NA. Then there are statements such as 'AA is just another place to make drinking mates' or 'AA/NA is full of skid row addicts just retelling their misery stories'.

Below are offered some suggestions to facilitators in a TSF group on how to tackle some of these obstacles

Facilitator stance

Although it is important to correct views that are factually wrong about how AA/NA operates, it is important not to invalidate people's previous experiences. Generally it is more fruitful to focus on what AA/NA *is* about and what positive experiences group members may have in the future, rather than what it *isn't* or what negative experiences they have had in the past. Concentrating on the positive things AA/NA has to offer is essential. Often the best people to do this are active members of AA/NA in recovery. Reach out to them—they will be very willing to help—and invite them to meet members of the group. As in AA/NA itself, the facilitator's stance in a TSF group should be a 'soft sell' approach, collaborative, and not dogmatic or instructional.

Keep it simple

'Keep it simple' is a famous AA/NA saying, along with others such as 'one day at a time' and 'AA/NA is a simple programme for complicated people' or 'HOW? Honesty, Open-mindedness, Willingness'. Such sayings are worth becoming familiar with. They are often witty nuggets of truth that sink in far deeper than a string of sentences explaining the same—especially for those with poor attention.

'Keep it simple' reminds us of several things. Firstly, the *only* requirement for AA/NA membership is a desire to stop drinking/using drugs. Secondly, there are no dogmas that members must accept—all tenets and steps are mere suggestions. Thirdly, AA/NA is a pragmatic programme. Members are encouraged to try out suggestions, and to do what works for them.

Spirituality is about life meaning and purpose, not spirits

It is certainly true that AA/NA, through the Twelve Steps, offers a *spiritual* programme for recovery. However, this does not mean a religious one, nor does it require any belief in a supernatural being at all. The word 'God' features in several of the Twelve Steps, and is also prominent in the early AA/NA literature, such as the *Big Book*. However, even in the early days, the phrase '*as we understood him*' would follow, and always in italics to stress the importance of a *personal* understanding. Later the term 'God' often became 'higher power', broadening the concept further.

One might ask what such concepts have to do with recovery from addiction at all? The simple answer is that very often, although not always, a re-evaluation of one's spiritual compass is central to establishing recovery and living a meaningful life without alcohol or drugs. As well as being illustrated in the AA/NA literature, an increasing body of recent scientific research now highlights this as being true (Zemore, 2007; Pardini, Plante, Sherman, & Stump, 2000).

But what does 'spiritual' mean? Clearly for some people it can have a religious meaning and refer to a supernatural God. However, the term 'spiritual' is often used simply to indicate one's sense of life meaning and purpose. One could be agnostic or atheist and still proclaim to be 'spiritual', as people often do. For those with a religious faith, their core sense of meaning and purpose may come from the doctrine of their religion. However, this does not have to be the case. The AA/NA community clearly recognizes this, and the great diversity of positions among its membership. This has led to members redefining 'God' as 'Good Orderly Direction', or even 'Group Of Drunks'.

But one aspect of the AA/NA's references to 'higher power' is worth stressing. The message is that the conscious-self often fails if it tries to achieve recovery by itself. By referring to 'higher power', AA/NA members are suggesting that individuals look beyond themselves for the solutions—to something or someone with greater wisdom on the topic. An obvious place to look is at people who have already achieved some years of sobriety, or to the AA/NA group as a whole. Another suggestion is that it can mean to 'listen to one's heart'—essentially one's unconscious (wiser) self, rather than the Ego-self.

Discussing these points will help many to broaden their view of what the spiritual aspect of the programme is really about. However, for some, the language of 'spiritual' and 'higher power' will remain thorny and off-putting. For these people it is worth pointing out that research has shown that atheists involved in AA/NA do just as well as non-atheists. This is not at all surprising since AA/NA is many things to many people, and the pragmatic aspects are equally, if not more, important. Again, it can be suggested that they take what works for them, and leave the rest.

Shop around

Often people will say, 'I've tried AA/NA and I didn't like it'. It's worth asking how many meetings they went to, because often it is only one, or just a few. Given how easy it is to find reasons not to like AA/NA, it is not surprising that many make their judgements quickly. Try to encourage an open mind, however, and suggest that people shop around for different meetings. I often suggest that people try at least half a dozen *different* meetings and to attend a dozen times in total before making their mind up. Advise them to speak to others, and find out where the 'best' meetings are locally. It is very common to hear people describe how they were lukewarm about AA/NA initially, or even disliked it, only to find that in time it grew on them and became a cornerstone of their recovery.

Enlist specific help for social phobia

Anxiety in social settings and speaking to an audience does not necessarily make AA/NA inappropriate. In fact overcoming excessive social anxiety may be essential for preventing further alcohol/drug use, for isolation and loneliness are potent causes of relapse. Sensitivity is required, however, and the advice of a psychiatrist or psychologist may be useful.

Some specific tactics may help enormously in surmounting the hurdle of the first AA/NA meeting. For example, inviting an existing AA/NA member to meet with the individual for a chat, with a view to going to a meeting together; or helping to put the person in touch with others who could offer a lift to meetings.

Look for similarities not differences

In our highly individualist society we are used to judging everything: 'This suits me, this doesn't, . . . he's so *this*, she's so *that*. . .', and so on. Sometimes it seems that we have lost the art of being together as a community—accepting each other. This can be detrimental to getting on in AA/NA as there will be plenty of reasons to judge others in the room, and conclude: 'These are not my kind of people'. Such a stance is sometimes a projection of one's own self-dislike. However, whatever the cause, it is important to suggest that people look for the similarities and not the differences.

AA/NA works through people identifying with each other and sharing. If that can be allowed to happen, then it can quickly remove the sense of isolation and even reduce the shame. People should be encouraged to look particularly for the similarities in their stories of substance use. One person might be a banker, another a bin-man, but both may recognize how they neglected their family, began lying all the time, and needed to drink in the mornings simply to function. Such mutual recognition helps people to notice the difference between simply drinking a lot, and the disease of addiction.

A similarity shared by everyone in the room will be that they are each trying to make a positive change in their life. Acknowledging each other's courage and presence, even by simple words such as 'It's good to see you here, John', can bring unexpected increases in one's own sense of belonging. Simple gestures like this are at the very heart of AA/NA.

How to encourage people to attend AA/NA takes practice and trying out different ways. The tips (above) may help, but going along to some open meetings as a guest will also be invaluable experience.

Summary

Addiction can be a devastating condition and often a relapsing and remitting one. While AA/NA is not the only route to long-term abstinent recovery, it is a very good one, as emphasized by recent scientific evidence. As a free resource it has the potential to reduce healthcare costs significantly (Humphreys & Moos, 2001). However, it is under-utilized and often poorly understood by both professionals and members of the public. To address this, Twelve-Step facilitation (TSF) has evolved as an evidence-based intervention to encourage people to attend AA/NA and keep an open mind about how it can help them. Various forms of TSF have been devised, some of which have been outlined here. Group TSF is a relatively new innovation, and a brief form of this—'Mind the Gap'—has been described. Other, more extended forms of group TSF now exist in a manualized form, such as MAAEZ, which has demonstrated effectiveness in a recent trial (Kaskutas et al., 2009). At the heart of TSF is the need to portray a positive view of AA/NA, but also the need to overcome misunderstandings, myths, and barriers. Some suggestions have been offered here on how facilitators may approach these issues, either in a group setting or one-to-one. The key points are for the facilitator to become very familiar with the workings of AA/NA, and to adopt a 'soft sell' approach in collaboration with the individual.

References

Donovan, D. M., & Floyd, A. S. (2008). Facilitating involvement in twelve-step programs. *Recent Developments in Alcoholism, 18*, 303–320.

Gossop, M., Stewart, D., & Marsden, J. (2008). Attendance at Narcotics Anonymous and Alcoholics Anonymous meetings, frequency of attendance and substance use outcomes after residential treatment for drug dependence: A 5-year follow-up study. *Addiction, 103*, 119–125.

Humphreys, K. (2004). *Circles of recovery: Self-help organizations for addictions.* Cambridge: Cambridge University Press.

Humphreys, K., & Moos, R. (2001). Can encouraging substance abuse patients to participate in self-help groups reduce demand for health care? A quasi-experimental study. *Alcoholism: Clinical and Experimental Research, 25*, 711–716.

Kaskutas, L. A. (2009). Alcoholics Anonymous effectiveness: Faith meets science. *Journal of Addictive Diseases, 28*, 145–157.

Kaskutas, L. A., Ammon, L., Delucchi, K., Room, R., Bond, J., & Weisner, C. (2005). Alcoholics anonymous careers: Patterns of AA involvement five years after treatment entry. *Alcoholism: Clinical and Experimental Research, 29,* 1983–1990.

Kaskutas, L. A., Subbaraman, M. S., Witbrodt, J., & Zemore, S. E. (2009). Effectiveness of making Alcoholics Anonymous easier: A group format 12-step facilitation approach. *Journal of Substance Abuse Treatment, 37,* 228–239.

Kelly, J. F., & McCrady, B. S. (2008). Twelve-Step facilitation in non-specialty settings. *Recent Developments in Alcoholism, 18,* 321–348.

Ligthelm, R. J., Borzi, V., Gumprecht, J., Kawamori, R., Wenying, Y., & Valensi, P. (2007). Importance of observational studies in clinical practice. *Clinical Therapeutics, 29,* 1284–1292.

Nowinski, J., Baker, S., & Carroll, K. (1995). *Twelve-step facilitation therapy manual: A clinical research guide for therapists treating individuals with alcohol abuse and dependence.* Bethesda, MD: National Institute on Alcohol Abuse and Alcoholism.

Pardini, D. A., Plante, T. G., Sherman, A., & Stump, J. E. (2000). Religious faith and spirituality in substance abuse recovery: Determining the mental health benefits. *Journal of Substance Abuse Treatment, 19,* 347–354.

Timko, C., DeBenedetti, A., & Billow, R. (2006). Intensive referral to 12-step self-help groups and 6-month substance use disorder outcomes. *Addiction, 101,* 678–688.

Zemore, S. E. (2007). A role for spiritual change in the benefits of 12-step involvement. *Alcoholism: Clinical and Experimental Research, 31,* 76s–79s.

Practical considerations in addictions group work

Introduction to practical considerations

The second part of the book, 'Practical considerations in addictions group work', brings together some of the practical issues encountered in undertaking group work. We are mindful that all of these chapters have been informed by our experiences of group work within inpatient settings, but hope that they are broad enough and offer sufficient stimulation and guidance for those working in other settings.

Chapter 8, written by the editors with their colleague Laura Marshall, considers some of the core issues around how to plan and implement groups in addiction. The chapter provides a model of training and discussion of how groups evolve from initial idea to implementation. The Neurobiology of Alcohol Group that Laura was instrumental in writing and facilitating is used as a case example.

Chapter 9 is a personal narrative written by Catherine Atnas who worked as an assistant psychologist on an inpatient drug and alcohol ward. The brief that we gave Catherine was to write something that would be of help to all of those who have to run groups as part of their work and experience anxiety when doing so. As her chapter makes clear, a small amount of anxiety is not only normal but actually quite helpful, and for those whose anxiety is somewhat greater she provides some practical tips on how to reduce it.

The prospect of running a group can raise a range of feelings in both new and more experienced clinicians. While facilitators can prepare for the content of structured groups, group processes can feel less predictable and understandably raise levels of anxiety, fear, and apprehension. Some of the most common concerns and problems staff experience when running groups are examined in Chapter 10. The editors explore ways of dealing with difficult behaviours that can distract the group, the client, or the facilitator away from the group topic.

Chapter 11, also written by the editors and their colleague Megan Underhill, examines the issue of group effectiveness, both in terms of formal evaluation methods and more process-focused approaches. We argue that evaluation is an intrinsic part of all groups rather than an optional add-on, and in this chapter both formal evaluation methods and reflective evaluation approaches are explored. The chapter concludes by considering what to do with the data once it has been collected.

Chapter 12, written by Robert Hill and Peter Ryan, looks at the issue of staff stress and burnout. Building on a large-scale research project that they undertook in Denmark, Finland, Norway, Poland and the UK, they highlight what it is in particular that is so stressful about running groups. A method of working with staff to deal with stress and burnout is reviewed with particular emphasis on the role of the group within the wider system of demands.

From idea to implementation

Planning and training strategies for establishing groups in addictions

Robert Hill, Laura Marshall, and Jennifer Harris

Introduction

There are many books and specialized texts in the field of education and human resources that usefully discuss the setting up and designing of groups. The literature focusing on health-related groups is somewhat smaller and that which specifically looks at substance related groups smaller still. When such work exists, it often neglects to address factors surrounding the initial construction of groups. In this chapter we will seek to redress this imbalance and explore how substance-use groups come about and the issues to consider when moving from idea to implementation.

As we have seen in the introduction to this book, there are many reasons for wanting to set up a new group. Some readers may be interested in designing a very specific group such as anger management, others may be interested in adapting an already existing group and some, particularly those involved in new services, may want to design a complete group programme. The aim of this chapter is to highlight some of the ways you can develop initial ideas and train staff to implement groups. We conclude by briefly discussing issues pertinent to a substance-using population and providing a case example from our own work on an inpatient addictions ward.

Developing ideas for addictions groups

While these factors could be labelled in a number of ways, we believe there are eight key considerations that need to be considered when planning a new group. These are: (1) purpose; (2) structures; (3) role responsibilities; (4) location and resources; (5) membership and group size; (6) time-frame; (7) group rules and boundaries; and (8) evidence and evaluation.

Purpose

Before agreeing on the group's purpose, there is usually that moment of illumination when someone says 'I know, let's run a group on . . .'. This thought may emerge as a moment of inspiration, as the outcome of an identified service demand, as a request from another professional in the service, or because it seems to be the right time to change one of the groups that has been running for years. Groups within the substance misuse field often want to achieve multiple ends; for example, imparting information, motivating clients to change, creating a space for the expression and processing of feelings, and challenging distorted thinking. Because of the manifold nature of such aims it is clearly important to be clear about the difference between your primary aim and those that are secondary. Thus, it is helpful to be able to complete the following statements:

'Our primary reason for running this group on . . . is . . .'

'Our secondary aim for running this group on . . . is . . .'

These seemingly simple sentences are in fact deceptively complex and you may need to repeat this exercise a number of times before you are able to settle on clear objectives. Such clarity cascades down so that it will not only help when constructing the group, but also when facilitating the group. Such understanding helps the facilitator to: (1) remain focused; (2) clearly communicate the group's aims and objectives; (3) explain the group's relevance to participants; and (4) articulate how this particular group may differ from and/or complement other groups on offer.

In addition to the group's primary objective there may be a wide range of specific secondary objectives that might include maintaining group members' physical and emotional safety, encouraging participation, and encouraging the group to remain focused on the topic. As with the primary objective, secondary objectives must also be clearly thought through and stated as concisely and clearly as possible.

Structure

By structure we mean the specific shape and format of the group. In our own practice we have created detailed group guidelines for the facilitators and handouts for the clients, many of which can be found in the National Treatment Agency for Substance Misuse's (NTA) library of psychosocial resources. We have found that clearly communicating the group structure, as well as its aims and objectives, significantly reduces anxiety for both facilitators and group members. Structure also functions as an anchor point for the facilitator to guide the group and return to should the group become side-tracked.

Role responsibilities

Role responsibilities refer to the co-facilitators' roles before, during, and after the group, as well as the roles of the surrounding treatment system.

In setting up a group and before each group, it is important to consider a plan and be aware of specific policies and protocols for emergency situations such as violence, self-harm, seizures, and fire. Part of this planning will involve considering contingency plans for when a client prematurely leaves the group early due to distress, anger or intoxication, particularly what support might be available for them. It is essential to be aware of the location of panic buttons and to sit within reach of these, and to know where additional support can be accessed or which telephone to dial for emergency services. It is the facilitators' job to keep the group safe.

Pre-group preparation allows time for the facilitators to re-familiarize themselves with the group topic/materials, gather together group resources, allocate facilitation roles, and plan ahead for any group issues that may arise, and, when necessary, alert team members outside the group about where their support may be needed. Pre-group preparation is particularly helpful when facilitators are new to group work, new to a particular group, or have not worked together before.

Location and resources

In many wards and rehabs, most rooms are multifunctional, so having a protected room for your group may be a luxury. If you do have a choice, select a room that is not too big or small for the expected number in the group. It is also useful to be able to moderate the temperature and have natural light because this can enhance both attention and individual participation. It is helpful to have a room that is free from outside distractions and interruptions. Seating should be arranged in a circle so that all group members can see/hear others and be seen/heard. It is essential that resources such as whiteboard or flipchart, pens and paper, and handouts are available at the start of the group, and that facilitators are present to welcome group members to the room. Such preparation allows the group to maximize its time focusing on the task in hand.

Membership and group size

Defining your group membership is essential. Even so-called 'open groups' operate within an organizational structure and often make assumptions about who should and should not attend. There is everything to gain by being as clear and transparent as possible about such criteria. Membership might be defined by, for example, shared life experiences, life-stage, presenting problem, or based on demographics. There will be decisions to make about the referral and selection process, and whether prospective members will attend a pre-group consultation to ascertain acceptability/suitability for group work and individual goals. One might also ask important questions relating to compulsion versus free attendance, minimum attendance expectations, whether new members are able to join during the course of a group, whether clients who already have been in the group can or need to re-attend, and so forth.

Time-frame

A specified time-frame relates to the length of the group programme, the duration of each group session, and the date and time the group will take place. Depending on your service setting and group purpose, groups can vary according to how flexible or fixed they are with regard to these factors. However, there are benefits to deciding this strategically rather than responding to spontaneous management decisions. A specified time-frame can allow participants to engage with the group and make the most of their group time.

Ground rules and boundaries

Although you may need to think through exactly what rules and agreements are appropriate to your own setting, we have found it useful to ask group members to work within some agreed 'rules' ('group agreements') to make the group a safe and respectful place for all. On our inpatient wards these include: a focus on confidentiality; respect for different views; sharing time; not talking over each other; no glorification of drugs/alcohol; no eating, drinking, or smoking. We also display the group rules in the room and ask clients to read these out at the start of the group and reaffirm their agreement. When necessary these can be referred back to later on in the group and explored.

Confidentiality may deserve some further thought. The boundary between what is discussed 'within' versus 'outside' the group will vary according to the nature of the group. For example, some groups may be useful for their capacity to develop a supportive social network and so encourage meeting outside the groups. Other types of groups, such as a psycho-analytic group, might encourage no contact outside the group so that any psychological work remains in the group and is expressed with the whole group. Facilitators need to have a clear idea of what confidentiality means in their service setting and where the limits lie so that they can clearly communicate these to the group.

Evidence and evaluation

We would like to draw a distinction between 'evidence-based' and 'evidence awareness'. 'Evidence-based' implies that we only do things for which we can provide empirical support and, while this might be desirable, often within addictions we simply do not have the evidence for the effectiveness of one group approach over another. Therefore, when considering which interventions might be effective, we must turn to other sources of evidence, such as from individual therapy and the National Institute for Health and Clinical Excellence (NICE) recommendations. This can be helpful in highlighting things to avoid, as well as things we should definitely do. One would also find recommendations based on research and models of good practice from the NTA. It is also important whenever possible to collect your own evaluation data. Chapter 11 discusses the value of planning evaluation as part of the overall group design.

The process of training staff to facilitate groups

Training is central to the effective delivery of any group programme, and it would clearly be daunting for new staff to run a group without first knowing about the content of the group and observing an experienced practitioner running it. On our inpatient units we have adopted a process known as 'Knowledge, Observation, Co-facilitation'. All staff members are provided with a booklet to record their progress with this process for each group; this record can be used by the staff member and supervisor to identify developmental and training needs.

Knowledge ⟹ Observation ⟹ Co-facilitation

Group knowledge and group facilitation skills training

Knowledge of group content is essential and this is best provided by those experienced in the running of such groups. It is helpful if training covers the content of the group, key objectives, approaches and activities, group process and boundaries, pre-group planning, co-facilitator tasks and roles, evaluation, feedback, and de-briefing. The essential question that each new member of staff must be able to answer is:

- Do I know what this group is about?

Of course, if knowledge alone were sufficient to run groups successfully, then many of the anxieties associated with group facilitation would disappear. It is important to recognize that for some, concerns about facilitating groups can hinder their engagement with the knowledge components necessary to facilitate the group. Brown (2004) lists helpful group facilitator characteristics and skills, including: belief in the group process; confidence; courage to take risks; organization and planning ability; flexibility; and ability to manage ambiguity/challenging behaviour. Workshops can help promote belief in the group process through providing a clear rationale for the group and by clarifying the objectives and suggested methods by which information may be presented. In our experience, staff find activities such as role-play valuable methods through which their existing skills can be developed and 'tested out' in a simulated setting. Counselling expertise, including reflecting, summarizing, active listening, responding, clarifying, and supporting, can be incorporated when facilitating groups, and again can be learnt and reinforced through workshop activities.

Certain group skills such as linking, blocking and confronting can be difficult to 'train' people in, as in many respects, we need to facilitate groups in order to learn these. One might also develop these through observing more experienced facilitators and working with different facilitators in order to experience different styles. By making these skills a focus of debriefing, facilitators can reflect on how their skills are developing and obtain constructive feedback on how others receive their style of working. It may be helpful for new facilitators to be part of a staff group themselves, for example group supervision, reflection, or case discussion, as this may provide a forum for 'testing out' skills in an environment that may be perceived as safer or perhaps more forgiving than client groups.

Group process training may cover recognizing and fostering helpful group factors such as optimism, modelling, and social skills development. Additionally, the training should prepare facilitators to cope emotionally and psychologically with difficult group behaviours (which may be heightened due to the compulsory nature of groups in inpatient settings), e.g., over/under participation, attention-seeking, distracting, disengagement, and so forth. Facilitators should be encouraged to draw on clinical skills such as de-escalation, positive and constructive feedback, and boundary setting throughout the group. The post-group evaluation is a crucial tool for assessing the utility of the approaches used by facilitators and an important opportunity for reflection and development.

Ongoing support is also important, and this can be in the form of post-group evaluation between the co-facilitators following each group, group and individual supervision, personal reading, and a forum for reviewing groups and discussing their running. Individual supervision can feel a safe place to reflect on group processes and identify training needs. While supervision on a group or indeed group supervision has an ostensible educative aspect, it also offers an opportunity for co-facilitators' to gain personal experience of belonging to a group. We have found it effective to have a named 'link' person who communicates between front-line staff and managers; this helps to keep the group programme alive and developing so that it best meets the needs of the clients and also helps to support staff in this enjoyable but potentially demanding role.

Observation

On our inpatient ward we strongly encourage staff members to observe each group that they will be co-facilitating on a minimum of two occasions before co-facilitating themselves. Observation should be of experienced staff members with time set aside, preferably soon after the group, for the observer to ask any questions or raise any concerns that they may have had while observing.

The importance of observation is twofold. With experienced facilitators modelling the group, the observer is afforded the opportunity to see how the content is delivered in an appropriate manner, including how meaningful links are made between sections of the group and between other groups. The observer can also gain insight into the type of questions and challenges that may arise and indeed observe the techniques used to deal with these. Observation is the only chance to see skills in action working well, while not directly involved in the group process, and a valuable chance to enhance personal understanding of the potentially curious nature of being in a group.

Co-facilitation

Co-facilitation should occur once both the knowledge and observational components have been achieved. Co-facilitation is often misunderstood as merely meaning having two staff members in a group. However, it actually involves two staff members who are sharing the running of the group in an identified and agreed way. There are different models for facilitation; for example, one facilitator may take care of the structure and content, while the other is more mindful of process issues such as keeping the boundaries. Alternatively, facilitators might take particular stages of the group. Whatever the division, there needs to be absolute clarity and agreement before the group begins as to who is doing what. In other words:

- Do I know what my role is in this group?

Particular considerations for addictions groups

As a group, clients with substance misuse problems have often had difficulties with authority, experienced a significant amount of trauma, and led isolated, stigmatized, and often quite chaotic lives with similarly chaotic internal lives. Motivation is another issue for consideration, one cannot assume that all group members will have the same level of motivation even where they are all ostensibly at the same stage of recovery, for example, detoxification. We know that each individual's motivation will fluctuate across time. Since clients may experience poor attention and concentration, it may be helpful to adjust the length of the group accordingly and repeat the group's core message. Many group members will be skilled in avoiding their difficulties, and the very nature of attending a group can be an unsettling challenge to this well-versed coping strategy. Furthermore, some group members may well have been coerced into treatment, or may be experiencing numerous social stressors, physical health issues, and mental health issues.

In light of these needs, we have found that it is helpful to have an active, encouraging, empathic, supportive, and accepting manner that recognizes strengths and positive changes. This is also supported by other clinicians such as Khantzian, Halliday and McAuliffe (1990) and Flores (1996). For similar reasons, we have found that drug and alcohol users most benefit from groups that are motivational, optimistic, and positive in their approach, and also offer a practical, skills-based, and future-oriented perspective.

Case example: The Neurobiology of Alcohol Group

Clinical setting and context

Two separate inpatient detoxification wards were merging to form one large ward incorporating both opiate and alcohol clients. A new group programme was being developed to meet the needs of both client groups.

Identifying the need

While many of the groups were suitable for both sets of clients, it became apparent that the opiate clients required an overdose management/naloxone group that was not relevant for the alcohol clients. Furthermore, many alcohol clients expressed concerns about the neurobiological effects of alcohol. It was therefore thought that a group might be an appropriate way to provide psycho-education, offer an opportunity for clients to share their concerns, and receive realistic and practical suggestions.

Generating ideas

There were several key areas that were identified as being particularly relevant to alcohol clients undergoing detoxification. These included the short-term effects of alcohol, such as impaired inhibitory control, and longer-term effects on memory and executive functioning. Clients could be advised how medications and personal strategies could help to improve neurobiological recovery. We also wanted the group to engender optimism about neuropsychological recovery.

Background research

A review of recent literature was carried out and discussion occurred between the psychology team (who were writing the group) and other professionals in order to source ideas. Attendance at a conference created the opportunity to liaise with Dr David McCartney, clinical lead of LEAP (Lothian and Edinburgh Abstinence Project), a General Practitioner with a special interest in the neurobiology of addiction. He provided valuable reading lists and information on how the service he worked for incorporated the topic into a group for substance-misuse clients.

Writing the group

The group took approximately two days to write. It was made as interactive as possible, with several images used to illustrate brain areas and some basic brain chemistry. Careful consideration was given to the balance between psycho-education and group discussion, and a 'game' was incorporated to demonstrate the inhibitory functions of the frontal lobe. It was imperative to ensure that the level of complexity was appropriate for both clients and staff who would facilitate the group. We were mindful of the tone of the group material, aiming for a realistic yet optimistic perspective. A handout summarizing the group was designed, and space was left for clients to make notes and do further exercises if they wished.

Pilot phase: 'fine-tuning the content'

The group was piloted using two experienced facilitators, both of whom had been involved in the writing of the group. A third member of staff observed to give an objective viewpoint of the group process. Around six clients attended the group, which lasted about an hour. Feedback from clients was overall very positive, the main criticism being that some of the language was too complex at times and this was later amended. The observer was able to point out several areas of the group where links to other groups in the programme could be made and therefore the relevance of the topic reinforced. For example, when talking about how alcohol affects inhibitory control, we could link back to another group about coping with a lapse and how one drink may often lead to many.

Training the staff team

There were some understandable anxieties from staff around facilitating the group. Because of the subject, the group required an understanding of basic brain functions and the effects of detoxification medications. Training was carried out during a one-hour session and potential facilitators were given time to familiarize themselves and ask questions regarding the content. Staff were then timetabled to observe while experienced facilitators ran the group, and support was given afterwards to clarify any queries. New facilitators would then be paired with an experienced facilitator when they ran the group for the first time. This way, the sense of being 'thrown in at the deep end' was reduced and staff reported finding the group challenging yet rewarding to deliver.

Ongoing evaluation and support

The group has been running for several months and many different members of the team now facilitate its running, including doctors, nurses, support workers, and volunteers. Whenever possible, the writers of the group co-facilitate to ensure the content remains accessible and up to date. Importantly, the group is regularly evaluated and continues to receive positive and constructive feedback from clients. The client handout has been expanded to contain greater depth of information because of requests from the client group. Interestingly, after the group, clients often show an interest and request that a similar group be designed to cover the effects of alcohol on the liver and other body systems. Timetable allowing, this may then be the next new group we incorporate in our programme.

Conclusion

We hope you have found this chapter a useful resource for beginning to think about strategies for planning and training groups in the substance-misuse field. Perhaps the most time-consuming part of setting up a new group, or indeed a new programme, is generating ideas to meet the identified need. Once the ideas begin to flow, we have found that actually writing the group is a relatively brief process and that ongoing feedback and observations from others can help the group mould into its final form. Training staff to run groups can be a demanding task, especially if the system or the staff are new to group work. We have found that through brief, interactive workshops, many staff will discover that facilitating groups can be a hugely enjoyable and rewarding experience. Once the group is set up and the staff trained, the most important, and perhaps most daunting, task is to begin piloting it with clients. By accepting constructive criticism and exploring suggestions, staff can maximize the potential of the group and remain positive and motivated about facilitating. Remember, group facilitation skills are best developed through hands-on experience and ongoing reflection, and we trust you'll have some fun along the way too.

References

Brown, N. W. (2004). *Psychoeducational groups: Process and practice* (2nd ed.). Oxford: Routledge.

Flores, P. J. (1996). *Group psychotherapy with addicted populations: An integration of Twelve-Step and psychodynamic theory*. Oxford: Routledge.

Khantzian, E. J., Halliday, K. S., & McAuliffe, W. E. (1990). *Addiction and the vulnerable: Modified dynamic group therapy for substance abusers*. London: The Guilford Press.

Chapter 9

'Stop looking at me!'

How to make anxiety work for you and not against you

Catherine Atnas

'As they walk into the room, one by one, I can feel them staring expectantly at me . . . my heart beat fills the room, my face is hot . . . what's this group about again? They'll know I don't have a clue what I'm talking about, I'm going to look like an idiot, why did they make me do this group?!'

This chapter aims to offer some support and strategies to those individuals who have not had specific group training or lack facilitation experience. It considers some of the anxieties facilitators can experience before facilitating a group and also looks at ways of reducing such anxieties. Before sharing some of my own experiences and strategies for managing anxiety, I will briefly differentiate between two types of anxiety and describe some of the different types of groups that we may be expected to facilitate.

Firstly and most importantly, I think it is essential to normalize anxiety. Public speaking is universally acknowledged as one of the top-three fears among the general public, and participating within a group (whether as a facilitator or group member) essentially involves public speaking. In addition to this, group facilitators are also asked to keep the group safe and focused, while responding to any inevitable dynamics that arise. Indeed, one might consider it a little unusual not to feel some sort of anxiety before participating in a group.

Types of anxiety

I would like to differentiate between two kinds of anxiety that can be experienced by those asked to run groups, namely 'context anxiety' and 'process anxiety'.

Content anxiety

Content anxiety refers to the actual material presented in the group, namely the group topic. You may find yourself worrying about whether you know the group topic well enough, whether you will forget it when under pressure, and so forth. Perhaps one of the strongest underlying concerns relates to a fear of looking stupid, and believing that you, as the facilitator, are 'supposed to know it all'! You might expect such anxiety to subside once you become more practiced and/or knowledgeable about the particular group content, and indeed it does, although one never stands still in relation to this. Indeed, each patient and each group can be seen as an opportunity for further learning and development (Yalom, 1985).

Process anxiety

Process anxiety, on the other hand, is the fear of not being able to control the group or deal with certain behaviours that may arise in the group. When we experience process anxiety, we might recognize thoughts such as 'What if someone gets really angry or upset in the group?', or 'What will I do if someone asks me if I've ever used drugs?' There are a range of factors that are likely to influence your level of process anxiety, such as who might be attending the group, the general atmosphere of a ward, how well you know the clients in your group or your co-facilitator, and indeed, how you might be feeling on a certain day (e.g., tired or under the weather). I would say that it is genuinely more difficult to prepare for process anxiety.

Types of groups

Structured and unstructured groups

Whether working on an inpatient ward or in the community, groups can be structured or unstructured, with either compulsory or voluntary attendance; such differences are likely to raise different concerns for facilitators.

A structured group is a group in which the facilitator has a defined content to be delivered within a specific amount of time and in a certain way. Many relapse prevention groups fall within this category, with each group following a specific structure to address different aspects of relapse prevention, such as dealing with cravings or identifying high-risk situations. Unstructured groups, on the other hand, are more open in that the clients are invited to bring up any issues that may be pertinent to them, such as how they are feeling at the moment and any problems they are experiencing.

While structured groups are likely to provoke anxiety relating to the content of the information, many newer facilitators find unstructured groups more anxiety-provoking since it is harder to predict the themes or interactions that might arise. This may be especially true for unstructured groups in the context of an addiction service where some clients have difficulty expressing their feelings in an appropriate manner. To name a few scenarios, facilitators may fear silence, over-disclosure, acting out, or aggressive outbursts.

Compulsory and voluntary groups

Whether attendance at a group is considered to be voluntary or compulsory creates yet more food for thought for the facilitator. When groups are voluntary, the expectation is that clients are attending by their own free will and are motivated to attend groups. One might therefore expect voluntary groups to raise a lower level of process anxiety for the facilitator. However, when group attendance is compulsory, or clients have been coerced to attend for some secondary gain, we might understandably be concerned about how receptive clients are to attending our group. Indeed, clients who feel they are being 'forced' to attend can show resistance and attempt to gain control by rebelling in some way, for instance by deliberately trying to sabotage the group or generally having a negative attitude about participating. A significant number of substance-misuse clients have experienced abusive parenting, had difficult educational experiences or spent time in prison; they may subsequently project their feelings about authority figures onto the group facilitator. Anticipating issues such as these can obviously heighten your anxiety levels (particularly process anxiety) with worst-case scenarios of your losing control of an unruly group dominating your thoughts.

Top tips for beating anxiety

Below are some strategies that I have found helpful when facilitating groups to help manage both content and process anxiety. These are also generally good practice when facilitating any group.

Be prepared

I strongly suggest that before co-facilitating a group you receive training or teaching about the particular group, observe the group, and then co-facilitate with a more experienced facilitator (see Chapter 8). This will enable you to see the group 'in action' and give you useful information about the types of questions clients may ask in a particular group, as well as experience of facilitating the group while being supported by someone who knows the group well.

Any anxiety that relates to lack of knowledge can be significantly reduced by taking the time to thoroughly read the group material and make personal notes to aid your own understanding. Preparing in advance also gives you the time and opportunity to discuss the group content with a more experienced facilitator and to develop ideas about the possible questions that clients may ask.

In addition to preparing for the topic, it is also important to prepare for possible group issues (this helps reduce 'process anxiety'). In an inpatient setting for example, this would mean having a thorough handover to hear how group members have been that day, identifying current issues, hostilities between certain group members, reading and/or writing difficulties, and so forth. Roback (2000) suggests early identification of high-risk members, who he suggests may potentially become 'group deviants' and require more facilitator intervention. This enables the co-facilitators to be aware of possible difficulties that may arise in the group and also to plan ahead ways to respond should these arise.

It is essential to meet with your co-facilitator before the group to discuss these issues, and also to decide on who will facilitate which part of the group. Uncertainty due to the lack of a decisive treatment plan can in itself cause anxiety (Yalom, 1985). Failing to allocate different sections of the group before starting can therefore lead to a heightened sense of anxiety. Conversely, being organized and knowing what you are doing can reduce content anxiety and make you feel more in control. Additionally, this is a time when facilitators can think about how to adapt the group to meet that particular group's needs. For example, if several clients have reading and writing difficulties, it may be necessary to change a written exercise into a discussion-based one.

Take a team approach

There should always be two facilitators in a group. This enables you to share the work by allocating responsibility for different sections, thereby reducing the amount of information you have to remember at one time, which could help to reduce content anxiety. Additionally, when one facilitator is taking the lead, the other has the opportunity to observe group processes and to help maintain group boundaries. Having two facilitators, rather than one, creates greater safety within the group and enables you to back each other up and gain support from each other, particularly at times when group members are behaving in a challenging manner.

Co-facilitating allows you the opportunity to reflect on group issues after the session, discuss future strategies for similar situations, and thereby increase your confidence for the next group session.

Regular supervision is an essential part of co-facilitation and crucial for managing anxiety. If you have had a particularly difficult group, I would recommend seeking supervision with a more experienced facilitator. This can help you to explore different strategies for dealing with certain situations and also to discuss specific elements of the group that you find difficult.

Recognize and beat cognitive distortions

It can be helpful to become mindful of the sorts of thoughts that flash through your mind before a group and take some time to challenge any unhelpful thoughts you notice. Anxiety can be increased by thinking errors such as 'catastrophizing' (you think the worst will happen), 'emotional reasoning' (you think something must be true because you feel it so strongly), 'magnification' (unreasonably magnifying the negative), 'mind reading' (believing that you know what other people are thinking), 'personalization' (believing other people act negatively because of you), and 'labelling' (putting a fixed label on yourself). Take some time to look for evidence for and against these thoughts and find a more balanced thought. Sometimes it can help to talk about this with other people.

Don't try to be an expert

If you are asked a question and do not know the answer, I would recommend that you do not try to pretend that you do! Clients are very adept at seeing through attempts to pretend or cover up. It is far more helpful to be genuine and honest rather than give wrong information. I have found that groups are generally accepting when I admit that I do not have the answer to a question but will make a note of it and find out after the group. You can always open up the question to other group members. If you find that you are unable to understand some of the terminology that members are using, then ask them to explain what they mean.

Think 'group'

If you get stuck, reflect the question back to the group and ask them 'What do you think?' or 'What is your experience?' This is entirely acceptable; after all, the group is for them. Reflecting questions and dilemmas back to the group enables the facilitator to have some time to get back on track and also opens up the discussion, enabling the clients to talk about issues important to them. In my experience of facilitating groups in an addictions setting, clients are often far more accepting of their peers' suggestions than those of a staff member. Opening up one group member's question to the whole group allows the group to draw from others' experiences, whether in terms of treatment, aftercare, or ways of coping in specific situations. This empowers the group to feel knowledgeable and appreciated, and can also make you feel less like a target if you don't know the answer to a question.

Use OARS therapeutic skills (Open questions, Affirmations, Reflections, Summaries)

These therapeutic tools are interaction techniques that originate from Motivational Interviewing (Miller & Rollnick, 1991), a client-centred directive approach often used in addiction counselling to explore ambivalence and enhance motivation for change. I find the OARS skills really helpful to use during groups. Open questions enable more discussion to be generated, as they cannot be answered with just one word. By asking questions beginning with 'How. . .?' and 'In what ways. . .?', you enable the clients to explore their issues in more depth. Like anybody else, clients want to be appreciated for their hard work, so by affirming what they have said and thanking them for their contributions you can make group members feel valued as well as create a positive therapeutic relationship. Reflections and summaries are useful to make sure that you have understood what the client has said correctly, and also to summarize salient themes and change talk. These skills encourage us to really listen to our clients and allow them to feel understood, which helps develop rapport and trust.

Evaluate

Once the group is over, it is important for the facilitators to take some time to evaluate. This can be an important learning experience. During evaluation you have time to discuss the processes in the group, whether a client was appropriately challenged, what could be done differently next time, as well as what worked well. If you feel that a group has 'gone badly', it is important to get support and feedback from your co-facilitator as otherwise you may be even more anxious the next time you have to facilitate a group. This is also a time when you can reflect on your own practice and on how the group processes may have affected you. This is a broad overview but you can read more details about evaluation in Chapter 11.

Avoidance and safety behaviours

If you get particularly anxious by the prospect of facilitating a group, you may try to avoid doing the group. This can be through direct avoidance, such as finding excuses so you do not have to run the group, or more subtle avoidance, such as not taking an active role in the group. Additionally, you may develop other strategies for dealing with the situation, such as finishing the group early, not challenging clients if they are inappropriate, or allowing the clients to talk about what they want to rather than facilitating the group as it should be. In cognitive therapy, such behaviours are known as safety-seeking behaviours. While they are used to try to reduce anxiety, they actually play a large part in maintaining anxiety. If you avoid the situation altogether, or allow the clients to do what they like in the group, then you reduce the chances of disconfirming your (negative) beliefs about facilitating the group and keep your fears alive. I would recommend trying your best not to engage in avoidance or safety-seeking behaviours. Although it will be anxiety-provoking at first, over time with more exposure to the groups, your anxiety will eventually reduce and become more manageable.

Some final thoughts

Having worked in inpatient detoxification settings where the individual members of a group can change on a daily basis, I am very aware of my fluctuating levels of process anxiety. It tends to be highest if I have been on leave and do not know the members of my group, and lowest when I have been working with the majority of members for several groups, as I have a better idea of what to expect. Additionally, it is important to remember that experiencing some anxiety is actually beneficial to you. Although we know that too much anxiety is likely to hamper performance, some anxiety can actually improve performance by activating us and increasing our attention to focus on the task in hand. So, as uncomfortable as it may feel, some anxiety is good!

As facilitators we can put a great deal of pressure on ourselves about how we think a group may have been, however there are many factors that make up a group and it is important to remember that we are only a small part of the process. Even very experienced facilitators will sometimes feel de-skilled after a group in which members have shown challenging or unmotivated behaviour. This highlights the importance of supervision in dealing with our own feelings when working in groups.

Group facilitation, like any other skill, requires practice! It can be very anxiety-provoking, especially when we are not familiar with the group content or the client group. However, with experience, we develop our knowledge of the group content, a better understanding of the client group as a whole, and we begin to develop our own 'tricks' that can help us to pre-empt potentially difficult situations. Over time we also find a facilitation style that is compatible with our personality and this is likely to increase our effectiveness as a facilitator (Douglass, 1978). For most people, anxiety will decline with exposure. However, some people really do not enjoy being part of a group. If you find that your anxiety about facilitating groups remains high and you dread coming into work because of it, then it is important to remember that, for most people, groups are just one part of their job. It is important to focus on your strengths and not on the one part of your job that you find challenging.

> 'Phew, it's over, I managed to get through it!
> Actually, I feel pretty good, much better than I thought I would!'

References

Douglass, T. (1978). *Basic groupwork*. Oxford: Routledge.

Miller, W. R., & Rollnick, S. (1991). *Motivational interviewing: Preparing people for change*. New York: Guilford Press.

Roback, H. B. (2000). Adverse outcomes in group psychotherapy: Risk factors, prevention and research directions. *Journal of Psychotherapy Practice and Research*, *9*, 113–122.

Yalom, I. D. (1985). *The theory and practice of group psychotherapy*. New York: Basic Books.

Chapter 10

Preparing for and responding to challenging group behaviours

Jennifer Harris and Robert Hill

Introduction

The prospect of running a group can raise a range of feelings in both new and more experienced clinicians. While as facilitators we can prepare for the content of structured groups, group processes can feel less predictable and understandably raise levels of anxiety, fear, and apprehension. This chapter explores ways of thinking about and responding to behaviours that can distract the group, the client, or the facilitator away from the group topic or task. While some of these suggestions are informed by psycho-dynamic concepts, they are mainly based on experiences of working in shorter-term structured groups within an inpatient detoxification unit.

Before we discuss a number of common difficulties that facilitators can experience within groups, along with some suggestions of how to respond to these, we would like to make a few general points about running groups with substances misusers. Individuals seeking treatment or support with substance misuse often share a common set of underlying difficulties with low self-esteem, managing feelings, and maintaining healthy interpersonal relationships. We also know that many clients use substances in an attempt to cope with and avoid such difficulties, and it is understandable that clients may then struggle to 'be with themselves' without the familiar safety of substances. This struggle is likely to be compounded within a group setting and the client's attempts to make the group feel 'safer', more familiar or more tolerable can manifest as behaviours that a facilitator may find challenging. Paradoxically it is this very discomfort that, if worked with therapeutically, allows clients insight and alternative ways to deal with emotional and interpersonal difficulties. This does not of course remove the facilitator's responsibility to respond appropriately to those behaviours that are not conducive to a safe or productive group atmosphere.

What then is the role of the facilitator? We need to keep a clear sense of what we are trying to achieve in the group and make the group sufficiently safe, constructive, and therapeutic. In order that members may benefit from the group experience, we also want to encourage group members to interact with each other. How does one create a safe place? In addition to those aspects covered in earlier chapters, safety can be promoted through setting group rules, paying close attention to the group dynamics, rewarding effort and involvement, responding to feelings, keeping the group on track, summarizing and pulling discussions together, balancing levels of participation within the group, confronting discrepancies between words and actions, modelling positive behaviours, and mediating conflicts (Bertcher, 1979). It is also about acknowledging that as group facilitators we may hold dual roles. Thus, one role will be as a group facilitator and another as therapist, key worker, doctor, or nurse, and it can be helpful to let the client know ahead of time that you will be meeting in a different capacity. However, safety is also promoted through our non-verbal actions, being mindful of our body language, facial expressions, gestures, tone of voice, and so forth.

We would encourage facilitators to take up Patrick Casement's (1985) idea of the therapist's 'internal supervisor'. This means noticing and trying to make sense of what is happening for individuals in the group, the group as a whole, and inside of oneself (Whitaker, 1985). When you notice behaviours, internally reflect on what this behaviour may be communicating for the individual and for the group, and then find a way of encouraging the client (and/or the group) to put this into words rather than behaviour. Depending on the nature of the group and the stage of treatment, this might mean responding to some behaviours within the group and others outside the group. Our stance should always be as empathic as possible with transparent and consistent boundaries.

Recognizing and responding

The following section explores some of the ways in which 'difficult' group behaviours may be manifested and some suggestions that facilitators can personalize and build on in their own group work.

Non-attendance, late-coming, and early-leaving

One's response to non-attendance, lateness, and premature departure may vary according to whether these behaviours happen on a one-off or regular basis. With regard to non-attendance, outpatient settings often have a 'three strikes and out' strategy, unless there are exceptional circumstances. Regular avoidance, lateness, or leaving of groups within an inpatient setting may be addressed by developing an agreed plan with the client about how to support group attendance/participation and how this may relate to their treatment contract.

Facilitators will need to agree their stance on late-comers and whether there is a cut-off time for allowing them to join the group. Yalom (1983) suggests that not allowing late-comers into a group that has already started will enhance the value of the group. When clients prefer not to attend groups and use this to their advantage, an individual meeting will be necessary to explore their reluctance and develop an agreed plan of support. How long facilitators wait for group members before starting the group also needs to be considered because this communicates an important message to the group about the value of punctuality.

Professionals cannot physically or ethically stop a group member from leaving the group, however we can express the hope that they can stay longer. We can acknowledge the group member's situation, encourage them to stay a little longer and ask if anyone in the group can suggest something helpful. You can invite them to stay and listen and only talk when they feel ready, or invite them to take a five minute break and then come back when they feel ready. Asking to go to the toilet is a not infrequent request, and one which needs to be accepted at face value. However, frequent requests either by the same person or by a number of different people may need to be reflected on by the facilitators.

Drug and alcohol use

When running groups for clients with alcohol and drug problems, it is not unlikely that clients will attend when having used drugs or consumed alcohol. For some groups this will be an accepted part of treatment and recovery, while for others such use will be a definite exclusion criterion and clients should be clearly informed of this before attending. When use is a definite exclusion criterion, it is worth considering the most therapeutic way to work with any clients who attend under the influence. It will almost certainly necessitate asking the client not to participate in this particular group session, while recognizing the need to offer appropriate support to the client before the next group. When there is no absolute ban on clients using substances, arguably the most important factors to consider are: (1) the impact of such use on the client's own participation; (2) the effect of such behaviour on other group members; and (3) whether the drug and alcohol use is disruptive to the group process as a whole. We have summarized some of our own thoughts about how one might deal with these issues in Figure 10.1.

1   no evident drug and alcohol use and no disruptive behaviours
2   no evident drug and alcohol use and some disruptive behaviours
3   drug and alcohol use but no disruptive behaviours and
4   drug and alcohol use and disruptive behaviour.

Reluctance

Reluctance can be shown through many behaviours, for example the client could arrive late, ask to leave the group, not participate, fall asleep, stare

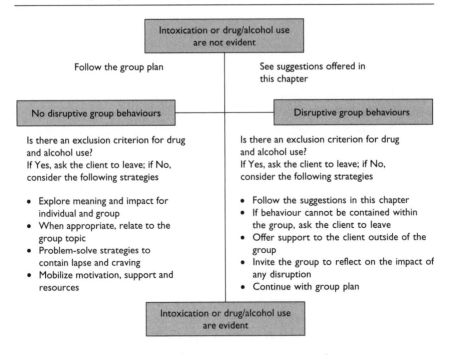

Figure 10.1 Grid to consider impact of substance use on group functioning.

out the window, or ask irrelevant questions. Similarly, reluctance can be an expression of other unmet needs and the client may benefit from individual support to express these feelings outside of the group context. It can sometimes help to present group attendance and participation as an opportunity to act differently, namely by facing difficulties and learning new skills rather than avoiding them. Whenever possible, you could use your knowledge of the client's goals to link these with what the group has to offer.

When a group member is feeling uncomfortable with withdrawal symptoms, or because of other factors such as illness or having heard difficult news, consider what allowances you will make with regard to attendance and participation. When it is agreed the client will stay, ensure that the room and seating is comfortable and consider whether you can use attendance as a form of behavioural experiment for the client (see Mitcheson, Maslin, Meynen, Morrison, Hill, & Wanigaratne, 2010). One way of doing this is to enlist the group member's interest by presenting the group as an opportunity to learn new ways of coping and distracting from the discomfort. Additionally, you could challenge the member to participate as much as possible and see what happens to their discomfort—the idea being that they test out what happens to their thoughts and feelings.

Silence

As with all group behaviours, there can be many reasons for silence and it is important to consider what is not being said by the individual or the group by their silence. Yet, there is also a distinction to be made between non-involvement versus someone who is not talking but clearly observed to be paying attention to the group. Thus, it is important to remember that group members can gain something useful from a group's content and process even when they do not speak. Be mindful that some members may be socially anxious and it is not helpful to press them further in a group setting before negotiating some goals and support with them.

Before responding to silence, it can help to consider whether this person is new to the group or treatment setting and do the best you can to make the group a safe place to talk. Keep any silent members involved in the group with regular eye-contact, and open up opportunities for quieter group members to contribute. You could ask questions such as 'What do other people think about this?' or 'Some people haven't spoken yet and I'm interested in what sort of ways they've coped with craving in the past?' If it looks like the 'silent' person is ready to talk, you could ask them directly something like, 'I'm wondering what you think about this?' and 'You seem to agree with what David was saying, what would you like to add?'

Facilitators should, whenever possible, affirm responses and give positive feedback. However, they also need to be mindful of whether talkative people are being allowed to dominate and if this is the case, open up the discussion to the group. If someone does not appear to be attending to the group, you can choose to ask in a gentle way (either within or outside the group) 'I notice that you're not really taking part in the group, what's going on for you today?'

Facilitators should take active steps to break a prolonged group silence, particularly if there are signs of increasing anxiety—there is a danger that levels of anxiety will become unbearable and group members will leave the group. Facilitators can explore what may be making it hard for the group to talk, offer a shift of focus, or offer a range of appropriate topics to open the discussion. Facilitators can internally reflect on whether they have said something to raise anxiety and if this is the case, acknowledge the error and find a way of continuing on a safer topic.

Social anxiety

Reluctance and silence can sometimes be the result of a very specific difficulty, namely speaking in front of other people. Public speaking, whether in a small or large group, is one of the most common fears among the population at large, and it would be surprising if this was not also present among those seeking treatment. Indeed, there is some evidence to suggest that rates of social anxiety are actually higher among alcohol-using clients and that stopping drinking will bring these difficulties to the fore again. If one has suspicions that social anxiety is the core problem, then work outside the session may be useful, in particular beginning to work on client's cognitions about being evaluated negatively. It is important to resist attempts to put the socially anxious group member on the spot believing this to be helpful. Even if the individual is able to respond, they may become very uncomfortable and it is likely to activate and feed into negative cognitions. It is important to find a way that the client can participate in the group without being so overwhelmed by fear or anticipatory anxiety that the message or focus of the group is lost on them. This might involve negotiating a graded hierarchy of participation with positive affirmation within the group and support outside the group to evaluate the experience and update cognitions accordingly.

Dominating behaviour

As with other behaviours, there are many possible reasons why an individual may dominate the group's time, space, or topic. In real terms dominating describes someone 'who talks a lot'. It can be helpful to internally reflect on what dominating behaviour may be about, both for the individual and for the group, in order to make a judgement of how best to respond so that the individual remains engaged, the group time is equally shared, and the group remains on topic.

In the context of medium- to longer-term groups, one person talking a lot is more common in the early stages before the group has become established (Whitaker, 1985), whereby the group supports the person in talking since they do not have to take risks in revealing themselves and they wait to see what the consequences of disclosure are. However, in a rolling group programme, in which new members can join the group at any point in the group's life (seen in inpatient detox treatments), monopolizing is more frequent. Some likely explanations are to do with defence against anxiety, treatment sabotage, sense of entitlement, direct challenging of authority, personality dimensions and/or disorders, ambivalence about treatment, avoidance of difficult material, gaining attention, and finally over-enthusiasm. Sometimes group members do not interrupt because they are fearful of the monopolizer. Neuropsychological difficulties with executive function can present themselves through difficulties with inhibition, turn-taking, understanding concepts, and monitoring behaviour (discussed more in Chapter 14).

One possible strategy for this behaviour would be to wait for a natural stopping point, summarize key motivational points shared, and invite other group members into the discussion with an open-ended question. Sometimes there does not appear to be a natural stopping point, with contributions linking into the next. When this happens, the facilitator will need to respectfully but firmly interrupt a group member before opening the discussion up to the group. You could say something like: 'Sharon, I'm going to stop you there.' If Sharon is making relevant comments, you could then invite other group members to add their thoughts, or you could summarize Sharon's contributions and link back to the group topic. However, if Sharon's comments have strayed away from the group focus, you could say something like: 'You are making some interesting points and I'm aware that now we need to get back to the group topic which is. . .'. Be ready with the next group topic or intervention. Use validation, open-ended questions, affirmation, reflective listening, and summaries to communicate that you value their contributions, but guide the group back to the topic. You can always offer to let the individual know that you are available to talk after the group.

Talking over each other

This is a common experience when there is a lot of energy in the group and several members want to have their say about the topic. Here we can say something like: 'It is hard to hear what everyone is saying at the moment and I don't want us to miss important ideas. Please could people talk one at a time? I'm going to ask each person in turn for their ideas. Sharon, what are your ideas about this? Thank you. What about you, David?' It helps for facilitators to mentally note who wished to contribute and invite each person to share, then open up a general discussion or move onto the next group topic.

Anger

Anger can stem from multiple sources involving the self or others, memories of the past, or interpretations of events happening in the *'here-and-now'*. Anger can manifest itself in both obvious and subtle ways. Ideally, the group facilitator may have some knowledge about the individual, their history, and current issues, or about the current group dynamics that may forewarn them about the possibility of anger issues arising within the group; at other times the facilitator will have no forewarning of possible tensions. Whatever the cause or manifestation, the group facilitator's role is to keep the individual and group safe (as well as themselves), and once this has been achieved, continue on the group topic and whenever possible use the 'incident' as an opportunity for the group to learn about managing difficult feelings. Whenever possible, it is best to avoid eliciting angry outbursts (even in an anger management group), although it is helpful to talk about the anger and ways to express or regulate associated feelings.

Yalom (1983) advises facilitators to be watchful for the early signs of irritation/frustration ('young anger') and to endeavour to address these early on rather than ignoring or denying these feelings exist. We can encourage other group members to share how they cope with these feelings. This can be a helpful modelling of self-awareness and emotion management. When the group has identified with anger as a 'default' emotion that masks the wider range of human emotions, it can be useful learning to unpick the emotion and see whether another emotion such as sadness, frustration, excitement, or humiliation lies beneath the anger. Some members may use anger as a strategy to leave the group prematurely and this needs to be addressed outside the group. However, there are times when angry outbursts do occur and group members may confront a peer or facilitator in a negative or unhelpful way. When you can see conflict arising, do your best to intervene: 'I'd like to stop you there and remind you to comment on what Bob has said rather than on Bob himself and let him know how it made you feel.' You may need to remind the group that it's acceptable for people to have different opinions. However, if those concerned are unable to talk about the difference calmly or constructively, then suggest talking about it after the group or if anger is escalating, ask those concerned to leave the group (if there is back-up outside the group). Be aware of local policies and emergency procedures. As with all disruptive behaviours, acknowledge the diversion and the feelings this may have elicited and then encourage the group to re-focus on the group topic.

When anger is expressed, be aware of your body language—endeavour to speak in a gentle, calm voice, use open, non-defensive body language, keep both hands visible, avoid sudden movements and prolonged eye contact, and give the client adequate space. Find words to name and validate the group member's feelings (e.g., 'I can see that you feel really strongly about this'), show concern for the their frustration, and use reflection skills to let the them know that he/she is heard and understood. Use open-ended questions to ask about the facts of the situation (rather than the feelings), e.g., 'What was it that made you feel angry?' Avoid arguing with or confronting the group member, and when the group member appears calmer, you can try to find some solutions to the problem.

Distress

Distress can be shown through noticeable tearfulness, verbalizing strong feelings and pain, and emotional outbursts, but can also manifest itself in less obvious ways, such as physical agitation, irritation, anger, closed-off body language, non-participation, detachment/dissociation, or a desire to leave the group. A group member may enter the group distressed or later become distressed where a group discussion triggered a painful memory or current concern. In detoxification, it is important to remember that emotions are resurfacing and can be labile and not always attributable to an external trigger. Emotion management is a key area of difficulty for many of our clients, and sitting with themselves in a group for an hour can be an extremely important but steep learning curve.

The aims for the facilitators may depend on the focus and approach of the group. Within an unstructured group, the facilitator might encourage the distressed group member to put their feelings into words for others to understand and to enhance the individual's self-understanding. The facilitator might also encourage other group members to explore their responses and resonance, and offer support. Emotions are 'grist for the therapeutic mill' (Yalom, 1983).

There is a distinction to be made between processing (this happens in individual therapy) and exploring (appropriate for group therapy). On the whole, the group is not there to process individual issues, although if the group format allows, individual concerns can be explored when they are relevant to the group topic or the majority of the group members. The goal is to promote safe exploration of issues related to change, not to process individual issues thoroughly. Processing an individual's issues puts the rest of the group in a passive, bystander role; the individual may also be responding to group pressure to be the 'helped person', thereby reducing the group's anxiety. It will also jeopardize covering a more structured group's agenda.

However, in a more structured group, there may be less 'space' to explore an individual's distress and a facilitator may need to move more quickly in order to bring the group back to the group structure. This requires judgement about when to pull a discussion in, and finding an empathic way to summarize the importance of the issue for the individual and encouraging them to use resources outside the group for support. We can say something like: 'I can see how upsetting this is for you. It sounds very important to have some time to talk about this and unfortunately we can't do justice to this in this group. Can we spend some time talking about this after the group please?' When someone is noticeably aroused, you can suggest some deep breathing, relaxation, or distraction techniques to calm and soothe the individual. In extreme cases, when the distress cannot be contained within the group, you can offer the individual an opportunity to take a break from the group. The decision as to whether they return should be left with the client; however, it is essential that there is another staff member who is able to spend time with the client outside of the group.

Disruptive and/or bizarre behaviours

The list of potentially disruptive or bizarre behaviours is quite long, for example: fidgeting, humming, staring out the window, repetitive behaviours, talking under the breath to oneself, or responding to hallucinations. Obviously one of the most important things to do is to consider the behaviour in light of what you know about this particular client, in this setting; is this usual or unusual behaviour for the client? Use your 'internal supervisor' to reflect on what this behaviour might be indicating. Hypotheses might include the behaviour as reflecting some mental health issue, a way of distracting from physical or emotional discomfort, or a way of gaining other people's attention. Your hypothesis will guide your response, whether this takes place during or outside the group.

You may choose to discuss the behaviour outside the group and develop a support plan to assist the individual in group participation. When other group members are clearly distracted, you need to find a way of drawing the group's attention back and contain their anxieties or concerns. When someone is showing, for example, active hallucinations, one facilitator can leave the group with the client and hand over to another member of the team. The other facilitator should continue with the group as far as possible.

Certainly our response to this type of behaviour will depend on the exact behaviour, but keep in mind the safety of the individual and group. Chapter 15 on co-morbid mental health issues discusses this in more detail.

'Why should we listen to you?'

Group members can sometimes challenge the authority, knowledge, and experience of the facilitators. For instance, the question 'Have you ever used?' can really throw some facilitators, as can the comment 'You don't know what you're talking about, everything you say is out of a book!' There is no way that we can predict what the questions are about, only that they will happen! Personal questions might relate to where you live, go out, how you spend your own time, whether you feel angry about something that has been said; members may ask you about your drug/alcohol use or your qualifications.

What might be the hidden message behind such statements that appear to challenge the facilitators' skills? You can internally reflect on whether you have perhaps been too confrontational or not shown sufficient structure/ control. Also consider whether this is the individual or group's way of trying to create safety by diverting attention from group issues. Perhaps the group members are expressing some sense of helplessness about change, or are feeling insufficiently guided or supported by treatment. Take steps to remedy any errors or name any possible key emotions.

Should facilitators answer personal questions? Firstly, does the question relate to something said in the group? For example, in a small group discussion where you are asking the clients to think of meaningful activities, they might understandably ask you about how you spend your time. It is also important to remember that clients may naturally be curious about you. Given that many people who work in addiction services are in recovery themselves, the desire to find out information may be genuine. However, do remember that you will no longer have control over anything you disclose about yourself or how that information may be used or who will have access to it. Do not compromise your safety and only disclose information you're happy to have shared that is resolved and no longer an issue.

It is important to consider how disclosing personal information will help the client/group. You can ask the group 'How is this important or useful for you to know this? How will it help you to know that about me?' You can use stock answers such as 'This group is for you to discuss things that relate to you, let's move on'. 'You're asking me about my drug use, this group is about coping with difficult feelings and I do have some ideas about how to cope with difficult feelings or situations', and return to the group. You can express your hope that the ideas being talked about will stimulate their ideas of what will help in their own situations, and that the ideas in the group come from other people with drug/alcohol problems. Most importantly, say it calmly and clearly and move on to the next topic. Try not to show defensiveness, even if you feel your experience is being challenged— this will simply add to the interest and could fuel further distractions.

Remember that when you are not able to answer a question, it is perfectly okay to say 'I don't know, but I will try to find out for you. Does anyone here have an idea about it?'

'Talking about this makes me feel worse!'

Some groups can elicit very powerful emotions in some clients and when necessary the facilitator may need to warn the group of this potential at the outset. For instance, some clients report how talking about craving elicits high levels of craving and thus seek to avoid the craving group. It is helpful for the facilitator to be aware of the evidence base and theoretical arguments for focusing on a particular topic. Thus, in the case of craving, we know that while it may elicit cravings in some people, talking about it in a safe context and working with that emotion is actually more protective than not addressing it at all. It can sometimes help to reframe 'talking makes it worse' as an opportunity to sit with difficulties, increase tolerance, and open up new coping skills rather than continuing to avoid difficulties.

'I've done this before!'

'I've done this before' is generally not followed by 'and it was great!' but rather 'and it didn't work.' The client's presence in the group is testament to that subjective feeling. The client indeed may be rather embarrassed at being back in treatment. The facilitator's job here is not to be dismissive of the client's statement, but to think of what may not have worked. Was the previous group poorly presented, was it too theoretical, did the client not put it into practice, was it the wrong group at the wrong time? If the facilitator is able to give a number of general reasons to as to why groups don't always work, without focusing on the particular client, it can help to foster an attitude of curiosity and to show that groups are not simply to be experienced but to be worked with, and that there are many prerequisites for their becoming useful.

Side-tracking

Side-tracking occurs when an individual diverts the conversation away from the focus of the named group topic or current theme. Diversions can include story telling, jokes, personal questions about the facilitator, or talking about unconnected topics. It is helpful to internally reflect on what may be being communicated by the distraction. Is this an attempt to take control, gain attention, avoid discomfort, or does it reflect a neuropsychological difficulty? Is the individual acting out on behalf of the group? Sometimes apparently irrelevant topics can result in something positive; for example, they may lead into a meaningful area of exploration, be a way of 'forming' the group, be a way of creating safety between group members, or be a metaphor for shared issues or fears. The facilitator can use their judgement on how much time to allow for such conversations, but try to help by naming any psychological content, e.g., 'It sounds like some people are feeling a bit let down about treatment at the moment. Would you like to talk about this after the group, either with ourselves or your keyworker?' and when possible link this back to the group topic. Sometimes there may be a significant event that the group wish to discuss before they feel they can focus on the designated group topic.

When there is a clear group structure, you can say 'Let's stop there. Although this is an interesting discussion, it seems that we've got off the subject of craving. Let's get back to thinking about how to cope with craving.' You can offer to continue individual conversations after the group or encourage group member to access resources outside the group. If the group seem to be questioning the usefulness of the topic, ask them to generate their own ideas of how they can make this group useful: 'Can anyone think of how this group may be useful?' or 'How might talking about high-risk situations be useful?'

Understanding challenging behaviours

This next section explores both group-level and individual-level explanations of why challenging behaviour may arise. Each behaviour tells us something about that individual and the group they are part of; this information can present a rich learning opportunity for the individual and/ or group to maximize their self-discovery and treatment experience.

Group-level explanations

There is a wealth of literature dedicated to exploring the area of group phenomena and dynamics, and while we can hardly do justice to this within a couple of paragraphs, there are some useful concepts that we would like to highlight. Psychodynamic perspectives are usefully explored by Martin Weegmann in Chapter 19 and the Introduction discusses how the group can elicit powerful feelings by confronting individuals with the reality of their situations.

Whitaker (1985) helpfully talks of 'restrictive solutions' that can be expected in the beginning phases of a group: these are ways in which group members make the group safe enough to remain in the group to do the necessary work. This can mean group members filling the group time by challenging the point of the group or the facilitator, interacting only with the facilitator, remaining silent, talking about superficial concerns, intellectualizing or focusing on one person. Within a longer-term group, once safety has been established, the group will typically move into using 'enabling solutions' where they speak freely and frankly, and try out new behaviours (Whitaker, 1985). It is likely that we will see more 'restrictive solutions' in short-term groups, especially those with a rolling programme, since the group is perpetually 'forming'. The challenge here is to create as much safety as possible with the structure of the group and through active facilitation. It can help to try to understand the fear underlying the 'restrictive solution' and alleviate this in some way.

A commonly used term is 'transference', and this is one way in which the past colours our present interpretation. Within a group setting, an individual can respond to another as if they were a significant figure from their past; something about that other person resembles the past person and they respond on the basis of that past relationship rather than the 'here and now' reality. Another useful concept to be aware of is the 'mirror reaction', when group members consciously respond to something they see in others that they unconsciously hate in themselves.

Individual-level explanations

There are many other potential explanations as to why individuals may experience difficulties within groups that do not relate solely to group dynamics.

Does the client have neuropsychological or cognitive difficulties?

Individuals can have neuropsychological difficulties in overall cognitive functioning, memory, or executive functioning, and these can manifest in many different ways. Individuals who do not follow the group may have poor time-keeping, remain silent, become distressed or angry, or dominate the group. Sometimes such behaviours are context-specific in that the individual may appear to function better outside the group context. Chapter 14 suggests ways of assessing and dealing with common neuropsychological problems.

Does the client have particular personality traits/disorders?

We all have different personality traits and some people have a specific personality disorder. It may be worth considering whether the behaviour within the group is consistent with the underlying personality disorder and whether it is unique to the group situation. This will help determine how much the group is a contributory factor in that person's response and what support may be helpful. It is vital to remember that personality traits and disorders are rarely chosen and that clients are expressing themselves in ways that feel safe and habitual. Longer-term psychotherapy groups and Dialectical Behavioural Therapy groups (Linehan, 1993) may address personality issues through the building up of emotional regulation and mindfulness skills.

Does this person have anger issues?

Underlying anger issues may present in a number of different ways. While it is possible to be passively aggressive through lateness and/or silence within the group, more common behaviours include: irritability with the group content, facilitators, or peers; side-tracking; direct challenges; and over-domination. Many of these factors can seem to stem from a sense of entitlement and the client's belief that they should be exempt from common rules and behaviours. Anger can also stem from unresolved bereavement or trauma issues that may be triggered by the group topic or process, or indeed specific events in the 'here and now'. While the group is not the place to deal with such underlying issues, knowing a client's history can help the facilitator to work with them within and outside the group.

Is this behaviour a defence against anxiety?

Anxiety can manifest in a number of ways, from lateness or silence to dominating behaviour. The most typical response can be shown by clients' attempts to avoid the limelight and by not fully participating in activities that draw attention to themselves. However, some people appear to over-compensate and can become quite dominating and/or can be quite rigid in their responses by controlling the topic or not allowing others to comment.

What is this person avoiding?

Sometimes avoidance can be very obvious, such as by non-attendance; however, it can also manifest as dominating behaviour, side-tracking, silence, or disruptive behaviour. The very nature of addiction can be viewed as avoidance, particularly in a population with high levels of emotional dysregulation and trauma. While treatment and group participation is an opportunity to face difficulties and learn new behaviours, this can understandably be very difficult for some clients. It is important for the facilitators to remember that even though the group topic may appear innocuous, it may be triggering painful memories or intense emotions.

Does this person have difficulties with authority?

Many groups are by their very nature hierarchical, with the facilitators taking the lead both in terms of structure and content. Groups can also bring up powerful transference from early family relationships. Some individuals can react against this by challenging the facilitator's authority. Early childhood experiences both in the home and in the school may be contributory factors, particularly if there is a history of abuse or trauma. Older clients may have had difficulties in employment and may react against those in authority, particularly if they are much younger than themselves. For some clients, challenges to authority can be an attempt at assertiveness or at questioning their relationship to the world.

What is this person's motivation?

Motivation is the key to change for those with a substance-dependence problem and we know that ambivalence during treatment is normal. Many different group behaviours can express a lack of motivation or ambivalence, and clients often fear talking about this openly for fear of being perceived as uncommitted. Part of the group facilitator's job is to understand the fluctuating nature of motivation and to help clients express this constructively and openly. Chapter 2 discusses this in more detail.

Is this person intentionally sabotaging treatment?

Sometimes a client is not ready or able to deal with the demands that group therapy or group work can bring. This may be related to specific groups or to treatment as a whole. Being able to acknowledge this openly and take responsibility for this can be difficult and therefore clients may engage in behaviour that puts their treatment in jeopardy. Understanding that not every treatment episode is going to be effective can be a very helpful conversation to have with clients and may help to dissipate unwanted or disruptive group behaviours.

Is this person over-enthusiastic?

Enthusiasm can sometimes become too much or be expressed in the wrong way. Understanding what is happening when over-enthusiasm occurs is extremely important. At one level, over-enthusiasm may simply be a running away with possibilities of what could be. However, it can also be a form of immediate gratification that the client is unable to control or monitor, and as such needs to be worked with as part of their overall treatment and ultimately to enhance social inclusion.

Does the person have another clinical disorder?

Many clients have a co-morbid clinical disorder alongside their substance dependence. Such disorders exist independently of the substance dependence and require staff to have knowledge of the disorder and understanding of how to work with this within a group context. For example, a client who finds it difficult to pay attention, sit still, and stay on task may in fact have ADHD. Similarly, a client who remains silent and avoids all eye contact with other group members may be suffering from clinical depression (see Chapter 15 for more details).

Does this person have a medical condition or pain issues?

Poor health and disease are not uncommon features of drug and alcohol dependence, and it is important to consider whether an individual may be in distress or pain, or may be worried about what's going on with their body. When clients are undergoing detoxification, this may be a time when health issues and pain come to the forefront and clients may understandably focus on physical pain or discomfort. Many of the behaviours we have discussed can be understood in the light of pain or health-related concerns.

Is the client withdrawing?

There is no doubt that withdrawal symptoms can affect the mind, body, and behaviour. How the client responds and deals with this experience is variable. In a group context it can shift the client's focus away from the group topic, affect motivation to attend or participate in the group, or trigger anger or distress.

Summary

While this chapter necessarily focuses on the more challenging aspects of group behaviour, it is important to remember that groups are often enjoyable and go well! The more positive group processes can include the powerful effect of group members coming face-to-face with each other, recognizing similarities, and knowing that they are not alone in their difficulties or experiences. Groups can offer real understanding, hope of positive change, and practical suggestions of how to cope, and provide an opportunity to test out new ways of being with other people. Moreover, not only can clients receive useful feedback, they can also experience the value of offering something worthwhile to others for no other reason than it matters.

References

Bertcher, H. J. (1979). *Group participation techniques for leaders and members*. Sage Human Services Guide 10. Sage: London.

Casement, P. (1985). *On learning from the patient*. London: Routledge.

Linehan, M. (1993). *Skills training manual for treating borderline personality disorder*. Diagnosis & Treatment of Mental Disorders series. London: The Guilford Press.

Mitcheson, L., Maslin, J., Meynen, T., Morrison, T., Hill, R., & Wanigaratne, S. (2010). *Applied cognitive and behavioural approaches to the treatment of addiction: A practical treatment guide*. Oxford: Wiley-Blackwell.

Whitaker, D. S. (1985). *Using groups to help people*. London: Routledge.

Yalom, I. D. (1983). *Inpatient group psychotherapy*. New York: Basic Books.

Chapter 11

How do we know the group has worked?

Jennifer Harris, Megan Underhill, and Robert Hill

Introduction

Wherever we work, whether in the National Health Service, the voluntary or private sector, we increasingly need to have evidence for the effectiveness of what we are doing. Within group work, this means showing that the group makes some difference to our clients or adds some value to the service. Having such evidence also helps us to value our own contributions to the process of facilitating groups, something that can be easily over-looked. The information gathered from evaluation can also help us to explore the 'how' of group work, to put forward explanations for beha-viours, changes or outcomes, and also provide material to develop theor-etical models. Often such evidence is lacking simply because we are not sure about what we want to measure, how best to go about doing it, or even whether we have sufficient time to gather evidence. However, we believe that evaluation is an intrinsic part of the group rather than an optional add-on, and in this chapter we explore both formal evaluation methods and reflective evaluation approaches, and conclude by considering ideas of what to do with your data.

What is evaluation?

- A new group programme was introduced on an inpatient detoxification unit; the team wished to know how satisfied the clients were with the groups.
- A drop-in centre was curious to know what benefits male clients gained from the men-only group sessions.
- A community team wanted to know whether group members felt more confident and able to cope with craving after attending three group sessions called 'coping with craving'.
- An outpatient clinic wanted to know whether those who attended the relapse prevention course showed more drug-free days than those who did not attend.

As you can see from the above examples, evaluation questions can be quite broad. Therefore, in order to ensure that evaluation is as meaningful as possible, it deserves careful consideration, ideally as part of the group's initial design. You can only measure whether the group is achieving what it set out to do if unambiguous group goals and objectives have been established. Group goals then need to be translated into specific operationally-defined outcomes (Benson, 2001). Without these, you might only be able to measure satisfaction with how the group is run, and possibly, interactive group processes.

There are a range of 'stakeholders' to consider when evaluating a group, each of whom may define a 'successful group' slightly differently. For instance, group members (and their social network) may be likely to value the group's personal impact on their lives, facilitators may focus more on their own role in facilitating group members' involvement, and funding bodies might well view success in terms of a cost-benefit analysis (Doel & Sawdon, 1999). Accordingly, one might gather data from a single or multiple viewpoint. The therapeutic model used within the group is also likely to influence the focus of the evaluation; for example, the evaluation of psychoanalytically-oriented groups might focus on insight and interaction, while that of cognitive behavioural or psychoeducational groups might measure knowledge or skills. Thus, the question of whether the group has worked will vary according to the perspective taken.

Formal evaluation methods

Standardized scales can offer greater statistical confidence in your findings. However, sometimes it may be necessary to design a scale to meet your particular circumstances. In this case, responses can be maximized by ensuring that your questions are relevant and useful, relatively few in number, worded unambiguously, and designed with the specific client group's level of understanding in mind. Involving group members in the initial design of your questionnaire will help ensure you cover the most salient aspects and also feed into a culture of collaboration.

Evaluation during the group

Direct group member feedback

One way of evaluating a group is to ask members for their thoughts while the group is running. It can be helpful to ask for specific feedback about what participants have learned or found most and least useful. This is best done immediately after a target activity or as a final activity before the group ends so that details are fresh and accessible. Facilitators can open the discussion by inviting members to give their opinions freely and therefore voluntarily, although this technique may miss the views of those who feel reticent about vocalizing these within a group context. Alternatively, facilitators can go round the group individually prompting everyone to speak. Group members might even rate the benefit of a specific activity or task on a scale from 0 to 10. While one facilitator focuses on following up on the feedback (this might mean summarizing, clarifying, affirming, or validating), the other might wish to record responses on a whiteboard or flipchart. Contributions can clearly be encouraged by the creation of an environment in which group members feel it is acceptable to have different views and comment constructively on aspects of the group.

Observations of changes

As well as eliciting verbal feedback from group members, facilitators (or indeed observers) may notice changes in language (e.g., applying concepts from the group), knowledge (e.g., overdose strategies), thinking (e.g., challenging thinking errors), or behaviour (e.g., offering support to peers). Such observations offer insight into how a group session may benefit an individual.

Evaluation after the individual group

Evaluating satisfaction

Brown (2004) highlights the advantage of specifically assessing participants' 'satisfaction' with the group. This might be assessed through a simple one-page questionnaire that group members complete at the end of the group or target activity. Questions might employ rating scales that ask clients to rate various dimensions such as the 'relevance of topic', 'presentation of material', 'usefulness of handouts', and 'amount of group discussion'. You might also wish to include some open-ended questions that ask for specific or additional comments about the group.

Example of question assessing usefulness of handouts from 'Coping With Craving' Group

Question 2: Please circle how useful you found the handout from today's group 'Coping With Craving'?

Not at all useful   Somewhat useful   Neutral   Fairly useful   Very useful

---

Evaluating specific events/activities

One might wish to evaluate how useful group members found a particular group activity, again with Likert scales or open-ended questions. For such ratings to be meaningful, they need to be completed by respondents as soon as possible after the activity. It is likely that respondents feel more able to be open and honest if they can complete questionnaires individually and so be free from the influence of group dynamics.

Example of question assessing usefulness of role-play during 'Refusal Skills' Group

Question 3: Please could you describe (a) what you found useful about the role-play 'refusing offers of a drink' and (b) what you did not find useful about the role-play:

(a) What did you find useful about the role-play?

(b) What did you not find useful?

Evaluating specific goals

If you wish to determine the effect of a particular group on selected outcome indicators, you can ask participants to complete a questionnaire before and after the group in order to ascertain change by comparing baseline and post-group ratings. Key outcomes might well relate to substance use, mental health, a skill, or group-level factors. Examples of some useful published standardized scales that measure domains of substance misuse are the High Risk Situations—Drinking Expectancies Questionnare and Drinking Refusal Self-Efficacy Questionnaire (Young & Oei, 1996); the Alcohol Craving Questionnaire (Singleton, Tiffany, & Henningfield, 1995) and the Readiness to Change Questionnaire (Rollnick, Heather, Gold, & Hall, 1992).

Evaluating group processes

We might also conceptualize benefit in terms of the processes that take place within the group, such as benefiting from a sense of belonging, from meeting with others in a similar situation, or increasing options for new behaviours through observing others within the group. Video recordings of the group session may complement questionnaire data and be analysed by trained raters to identify group processes. Below we have selected some published questionnaires that assess group processes, but interested readers can refer to Macgowan (2008) for further details.

- The Group Attitude Scale (Evans & Jarvis, 1986): this is a 20-item self-report measure of cohesion within the group.
- Group Engagement Measure (Macgowan & Newman, 2005): there are three versions with 37, 27, or 21 items. It is completed by a co-worker or observer.
- Group Climate Questionnaire (MacKenzie, 1983): this is a self-report scale consisting of 12 items that measures aspects of group atmosphere (positive working environment, tension, and avoidance).
- Curative Factors Scale—Revised (Stone, Lewis, & Beck, 1994): this measures the 12 therapeutic factors identified by Yalom (1975).
- 'Most important event' questionnaire (Bloch, Reibstein, Crouch, Holroyd, & Themen, 1979): this asks members to describe the event that was most important or significant to them during the group or over the series of groups. The written response is coded according to therapeutic factors.
- Impact of Today's Session (Kellett, Clarke, & Matthews, 2006): this is a self-report scale consisting of eight items; five items measure the impact of the group task and three measure interpersonal impact.

Evaluation across a number of group sessions

A review of the 'life of the group' might range from clinical reflection to a more formal systematic research endeavour. Questions might focus on how the individual or group as a whole developed across the life of the group; equally it might review whether the course of groups achieved the initial objectives and how to approach future group work. One can see that such evaluation might focus on process and/or outcome, and might use any of the methodology described previously.

Formal research requires ethical agreement; an application form for ethical approval for all research proposals involving participants who are NHS patients is downloadable at http://www.nres.npsa.nhs.uk/home. Audits usually require approval from a Trust Clinical Governance Committee.

One might collate data that already exist as part of clinical practice, namely the ratings and reflections from individual groups. Another way to generate feedback is through inviting clients to attend a focus group or an individual exit interview. These might be unstructured and follow the agenda of the group (or individual) or more structured with key open-ended questions (e.g., 'Can you describe what the group meant to your recovery?'). While focus groups may be subject to selective recall or influence by other members, they can offer valuable information about unexpected benefits, difficulties with the group programme, ideas for improvement, and so forth. Your data may be analysed using qualitative methods such as content analysis, interpretive phenomenological analysis, and discourse analysis (Willig, 2008).

You might choose to undertake a more formal evaluation, and this will benefit from thought and planning from the outset. To look at changes over time in key outcomes you will need to ask group members to complete measures before the first group and after the last group. If, for example, you wish to say something about what the group adds to individual treatment, then you will need to recruit two samples, one attending individual treatment and the other attending individual treatment and the group. This will require that you collect information about key characteristics, and control for confounding variables within your statistical analysis.

Reflective evaluation

During the group session: reflection 'in the moment'

In a group, 'a great deal happens all at once' (Whitaker, 1985, p. 194) and it is daunting for facilitators to know what to attend to and how to make meaning out of a wide range of events. The facilitator will be: focusing on the specific task or activity; monitoring time and participation; noting group processes that arise; generating meaning and hypotheses about individual's verbal and non-verbal behaviours, while also reflecting on their own thoughts and feelings and the impact of their interventions on the group's behaviour and discussion.

The information we gather from deliberate and mindful reflection can be used to make immediate modifications during the group session; this will help us to guide the group (and subsequent groups) so that it 'works well' and is a safe enough place to encourage growth and change for members. While our model of therapy and group objectives are likely to influence our reflections, these are likely to focus on both group and individual factors.

Group factors may arise from interactions between group members and interactions with facilitators. We might monitor the following:

* Group mood: being mindful of mood and how this changes.
* Themes: how themes arise and develop.
* Group cohesiveness: how this develops over the group's life.
* Group norms and belief systems: what is operating and for whom?
* Positions of power: what are the power dynamics in the room?
* Roles/alliances: are there subgroups or alliances forming?
* Defences: how are these emerging and why?

Typically our understanding of an individual group member is added to and emerges over a series of sessions. Particular attention might be paid to the following individual factors:

* Verbal and non-verbal self-presentation and participation.
* Response to group factors such as theme, norms, and mood.

- Acceptance/resistance to structure, named topic, and tasks.
- Participation in discussion.
- Attempts at new behaviours.
- Ability to apply learning to own experiences.
- Roles/alliances.
- Ability to offer and receive feedback.

It is also valuable to monitor our own feelings about the group process. Not only might this offer another way of understanding group dynamics, it also helps us be aware of maintaining our helping stance (Egan, 2002), thereby encouraging the group's exploration of issues.

'Reflection in the moment' can be a demanding task and develops through experience, supervision, personal reflection, reading, and attending courses. Those new to group facilitation can learn a lot by sitting in a group with no other role or purpose than to observe (Whitaker, 1985), followed by the opportunity to discuss observations and reflections with the facilitators and supervisor afterwards.

After the group: staff de-briefing/reflection

After the group, facilitators can use their recollections to engage in open discussion about the group. Whitaker (1985) suggests planning beforehand the issues that you may wish to examine in order to reduce selective recall. Brown (2004) also advocates advance planning to achieve systematic evaluation with minimal subjective reasoning. We find it beneficial to use a group evaluation form that covers the areas relevant to our model of group work on an inpatient unit; this helps to prompt and focus the areas identified for discussion. We also record seating arrangements on our form to assist consideration of member interaction. Using a form offers the additional advantage of focusing our attention towards the next group by identifying unfinished business and plans; such notes can also be useful memory aids for the next session and supervision (Tudor, 1999), and form the basis of clinical records.

Post-group reflection might consider the group as a whole, individual members, and the role of the facilitators.

The group as a whole

As well as using the group factors listed in 'reflection in the moment' to reflect more deeply about the group as a whole, you could also consider the following questions.

- To what extent were the initial objectives met?
- How would you describe the overall mood/atmosphere?
- What were the general themes that arose?

- What worked well?
- What did not work so well?

Individual group members

Here you might wish to reflect on the individual factors listed in 'reflection in the moment' in order to synthesize new and existing hypotheses about your group members. If you work in a setting where each individual has a personal contract identifying goals for their group participation, you may wish to evaluate how much the group helped them work towards these. You might also consider what information is pertinent to feed back to others involved in their care for overall treatment planning (particularly where this relates to concerns about risk), and identify any issues that might need following up with the individual(s) involved. This is a valuable time for you and your co-facilitator to think forward to the next group session and consider how you might approach anticipated issues.

Facilitators' input and role

This will serve several functions, namely an opportunity to ventilate, make sense of the group, receive and offer constructive feedback, and promote personal development. Putting your thoughts together can create a balanced sense of the group. Together you might consider whether you were able to keep to the group structure and topic, how you encouraged group members to participate, and how you promoted a sense of safety by what you said and how you behaved. Were there times when any of these felt jeopardized? You might discuss the timing, attunement, and impact of your interventions, particularly in what seemed distracted, distressed, or heated moments. How did you handle anything unexpected that happened or was said? It can be helpful to consider what sort of relationship you each held with the group (Tudor, 1999) and how these relationships are developing. You might wish to name the feelings that came up for you during the group and hypothesize about what this might tell you about the group or individuals at this time.

This is a valuable opportunity to offer and receive constructive feedback on each other's co-facilitation. You might appreciate how two facilitators notice and act on different aspects of the group process or structure. Such a discussion can also be an opportunity to plan what you could say or do differently next time, considering the relative merits of a range of verbal or behavioural interventions. Tudor (1999) emphasizes how such evaluation also helps you to prepare for your clinical supervision.

Benson (2001) recommends the use of a personal journal to record group-related thoughts, feelings, experiences, and insights. Such notes can often help to identify sources of anxiety or discomfort that might benefit from further exploration. One might also consider inviting your supervisor to observe your facilitation, or, where possible, consider the benefit of video-recording your facilitation.

After the group: staff supervision

Individual or group supervision can be used as a further resource for reflecting on or evaluating the group. Supervision will hopefully allow detailed exploration of content and process issues, specify areas and strategies for developing group facilitation skills, and promote understanding of the client and the role of groups within our clients' recovery. Ensuring time is set aside to specifically focus on the group can be particularly vital in busy and time-pressured work environments that demand staff to move on to other tasks directly after the group session. Reflection with our co-facilitators and supervisors also promotes a sense of support and value for this role, improves professional fulfilment, and buffers against stress and burnout.

Conclusions: how to make the most use of your data

To a certain extent, what you do with the results depends on the purpose of your evaluation/monitoring and subsequently the type of information gathered.

It can be easy for audit and study findings to remain filed away and not reach the attention of the clinical team or clients remaining in treatment. Think creatively about how this information can be displayed and disseminated, both locally and more widely. There is a wide range of possible audiences for findings to be circulated: within the immediate service, NHS Trust, stakeholders, clinical governance team, PCT/commissioners, non-statutory services, referrers, local Drug Action Team, National Treatment Agency, at conferences, and within professional journals.

We found very little literature relating to evaluating groups within addictions services, and while there is certainly a place for formal outcome studies, please do not overlook the value of simple evaluation techniques such as verbal feedback, one-page audits, or clinical reflections. They offer useful information and a basis to generate larger-scale studies or enquiries.

Headlines or bar charts of satisfaction ratings or outcome scores can be displayed in client and staff areas. While respecting the limits of confidentiality, it might be appropriate to publish group feedback or facilitators' reflections in a service newsletter or add this to group manuals or client handouts for prospective staff and clients to read ('testimonials' about the groups!). It also emphasizes the importance and value of the group work going on within a service, sometimes overlooked or minimized by the surrounding system.

Evaluation results can be used to directly inform development of the group format, whether in relation to the adjustment of individual group content or delivery style, or a group programme methodology. The impact of any changes made will then need to be evaluated further down the line, since evaluation is not just a one-off undertaking but a cyclical process. It needs to be incorporated as an essential element of group provision to ensure that group work is of maximum possible benefit to clients.

In summary, we hope that this chapter has raised your awareness of the benefits of evaluation and how this incorporates deliberate clinical reflection. We also hope that it has helped open up some ideas for evaluating your own group, and that you feel inspired to use some of the simple techniques suggested, Indeed, we hope that evaluation seems a less daunting and more exciting prospect than at the start of the chapter!

References

Benson, J. F. (2001). *Working more creatively with groups* (2nd ed.). Routledge: London.

Bloch, S., Reibstein, J., Crouch, E., Holroyd, P., & Themen, J. (1979). A method for the study of therapeutic factors in group psychotherapy. *The British Journal of Psychiatry, 134,* 257–263.

Brown, N. W. (2004). *Psychoeducational groups: Process and practice* (2nd ed.). New York: Brunner-Routledge.

Doel, M., & Sawdon, C. (1999). *The essential groupworker.* London: Jessica Kingsley.

Egan, G. (2002). *The skilled helper: A problem-management and opportunity-development approach to helping* (7th ed.). Pacific Grove, CA: Brooks/Cole & Thomas Learning.

Evans, N. J., & Jarvis, P. A. (1986). The group attitude scale: A measure of attraction to group. *Small Group Behavior, 17,* 203–216.

Kellett, S., Clarke, S., & Matthews, L. (2006). Session impact and outcome in group psychoeducative cognitive behavioural therapy. *Behavioural and Cognitive Psychotherapy, 35,* 335–342.

Macgowan, M. J. (2008). *A guide to evidence-based group work.* Oxford: Oxford University Press.

Macgowan, M. J., & Newman, F. L. (2005). The factor structure of the Group Engagement Measure. *Social Work Research, 29,* 107–118.

MacKenzie, K. R. (1983). The clinical application of a group climate measure. In R. R. Dies & K. R. MacKenzie (Eds.), *Advances in group psychotherapy: Integrating research and practice* (pp. 159–170). New York: International Universities Press.

Rollnick, S., Heather, N., Gold, R., & Hall, W. (1992). Development of a short 'readiness to change' questionnaire for use in brief, opportunistic interventions among excessive drinkers. *British Journal of Addiction, 87,* 743–754.

Singleton, E. G., Tiffany, S. T., & Henningfield, J. E. (1995). Development and validation of a new questionnaire to assess craving for alcohol. *NIDA Research Monographs, 153,* 289.

Stone, M. H., Lewis, C. M., & Beck, A. P. (1994). The structure of Yalom's curative factors scale. *International Journal of Group Psychotherapy, 44,* 239–245.

Tudor, K. (1999). *Group counselling*. Professional Skills for Counsellors series. London: Sage.

Whitaker, D. S. (1985). *Using groups to help people*. London: Routledge & Kegan Paul.

Willig, C. (2008). *Introducing qualitative research in psychology: Adventures in theory and method*. Milton Keynes: Open University Press.

Yalom, I. D. (1975). *The theory and practice of group psychotherapy* (2nd ed.). New York: Basic Books.

Young, R. M., & Oei, T. P.-S. (1996). *Drinking Expectancy Profile (DEP) test manual*. Queensland: Behaviour and Research Therapy Centre, The University of Queensland.

Chapter 12

Managing stress at work

Robert Hill and Peter Ryan

Introduction

Why include a chapter on stress in a book on group work in addictions? The answer is simple: running groups can be stressful. In this chapter, therefore, we look at the literature on stress in the workplace, outline a well-known model of stress, examine why group work can be particularly stressful, and conclude by looking at ways of tackling stress both in relation to groups and in the wider organization.

Occupational stress

Work-related stress is a significant impediment to job satisfaction and healthy psychosocial functioning. Over the last decade, the European Union (EU) has consistently identified work-related stress as one of the major workplace concerns—a challenge not only to the health of working people, but also to the productiveness of their organizations and the clients they serve.

Stress can be defined as a condition in which there is a marked discrepancy between the demands on an individual and the individual's ability to respond, the consequences of which may be detrimental to bio-psycho-social equilibrium and general wellbeing (Rabin, Feldman, & Kaplan, 1999). Stress can be acute or chronic. Acute stress refers to a short-lived episode (such as a violent incident) that may lead to acute or chronic strain according to how or whether it is resolved. Chronic stress refers to an ongoing condition or reaction, such as continued and prolonged overload.

The Demand-Control-Support (DCS) Model understands stress as an interaction of three factors: Demand, Control, and Support (Karasek & Theorell, 1990). A 'demand' can be defined as a situation in which the requirements of the work role exceed individual capacity. When overload is chronic, not an occasional emergency, then there is little opportunity to rest, recover, and restore balance. The high incidence of acute stressors such as violence exacerbates demand.

'Control' refers to the degree of involvement in decision-making that staff have with regard to the content of their job and their working conditions. Low control is when people are unable to influence their working conditions or job content, either because of autocratic management styles or because of chaotic job conditions. This prevents people from solving problems, making choices, and having input into outcomes for which they are responsible.

'Support' refers to the degree to which people feel connected to and part of a cohesive team. Lack of support occurs when people lose a sense of positive connection in the workplace, and where they may encounter a sense of isolation from colleagues, or chronic and unresolved conflict with others in the workplace.

Individual symptomatic responses to stress

The experience of stress can alter a person's cognitive, emotional, and behavioural response, and can also produce changes in their physiological functioning.

Common stress responses include:

- Emotional responses: anxiety, panic attacks; depression; mixed anxiety and depressive disorders; hypochondria; alienation and reduced emotional connection to both clients and the organization.
- Cognitive responses: difficulties in concentrating, remembering, learning new things, being creative, and making decisions.
- Physical responses: lowered immune system; raised blood pressure; headaches; muscle cramps and stiffness; skin rashes; fatigue; digestive difficulties; sleep disturbances; craving for sweet starchy food; psychosomatic physical illness.
- Behavioural responses: irritability; aggression; poor task focus; irrational acts; increased risk-taking behaviour; self-medication (smoking, drinking, prescription medication, illegal drugs).

While many of these represent fairly minor dysfunctions that are easily reversible once the threat or excessive pressure has passed, they are nevertheless damaging to the individual's quality of life at the time. However, under certain circumstances and for vulnerable individuals, such stress responses might translate into poor performance at work, other psychological and social problems, or poor physical health. Furthermore, in cases where the stress remains for extended periods, long-term psychological problems and more permanent ill-health can develop.

There is a growing body of evidence to suggest that mental health workers experience considerable stress in the course of their work, and further that stress affects their level of performance, success of interventions, job satisfaction, and ultimately their own health (Van der Klink, Blonk, Schene, & van Dijk, 2001). The structural costs in terms of absenteeism, loss of productivity, and use of health resources is high and increasing.

In their review of 19 papers focusing on stress and burnout among community mental health teams, Edwards, Burnard, Coyle, Fothergill, and Hannigan (2000) found evidence that all members of the multidisciplinary teams were experiencing increasing levels of stress and burnout. The major stress factors were divided into four areas: job-based, role-based, organizational stressors, and relationship stressors. These are briefly summarized below.

- Job-based: increases in workload and administration; time management problems; inappropriate referrals; and violent and suicidal clients.
- Role-based: role conflict; responsibility and role change; lack of time for personal study.
- Organizational stressors: those relating to organizational structure and climate, such as NHS and legislative reforms.
- Relationship stressors: those relating to relationships with others, such as inadequate supervision and dysfunctional community mental health teams.

One particularly significant stressor for mental health workers is the increasing intensity of work with more highly disturbed and potentially violent patients. Indeed, studies show that psychiatric workers experience greater relative risk of exposure to threat of violence than general nurses (Arnetz, Arnetz, & Petterson, 1996); 92% of Ryan and Poser's (1993) sample of psychiatric nurses reported at least one assault during their career. Rates of assaults range from one every 11 days (Whittington & Wykes, 1994) to one every 3.5 days (Gourney, 2001).

Stress in the context of group work

For the majority of people, even the most experienced and skilled, running groups can be a stressful business and there are a number of reasons for this. Staff working within inpatient and community settings are subject to multiple pressures, and so carrying out group work often has to compete against their 'statutory requirements'. This pressure is accentuated by the fact that, typically, group work is not part of the core training of any of the key occupational groups working in the drug or alcohol field. Staff can have an underlying anxiety that their group-work skills are not well developed, they may feel particularly exposed and 'observed' when facilitating groups, and further feel their performance may be negatively judged or found wanting by colleagues. When supervision and support are lacking, their perceptions may indeed be accurate. In addition, clients may be adept at picking up on and exploiting staff anxieties. For these reasons it can be particularly easy for group work to be delayed or postponed as other issues arise. Unfortunately, there is very little post-qualification training in group work outside the relatively specialized field of psychotherapy, and for those wanting to or needing to develop their skills further.

It is interesting to note that staff members who work in the field of addictions give many reasons for finding group work difficult, but that these can be broken down into three main areas. Firstly, there is the issue of overlapping and competing demands, so that fitting in groups where other activities need to be undertaken becomes difficult. This is particularly problematic on inpatient wards, where many other activities need to take place at the same time, such as ward rounds, management rounds, therapist appointments, and so forth. Secondly, some staff express concern regarding their ability or knowledge to run specific groups. While it may be the case that some staff do indeed lack the knowledge to run certain groups, it is more probable that they do not feel confident to explain their knowledge. Thirdly, staff speak about process anxiety (anxiety about running a group as opposed to anxiety about the knowledge component of the group), of being 'on show', of being judged both by clients and colleagues, and of experiencing nerves or fear more generally. This is a wide-ranging difficulty that clearly affects staff confidence and willingness to expose themselves to potentially difficult group situations.

Such difficulties can result in a disjointed group programme that some-times runs and sometimes does not, a sense from clients that their needs are not being met, and uncertainty and prolonged anxiety for individual staff members based on irregular exposure to groups. High levels of absenteeism can also occur on days when groups are run, or sometimes over-reliance on more junior staff running groups as they are less likely to be able to say no to this demand or to be able to find alternative activities to do instead. An intermittent, poorly run, group programme also has a negative impact for the organization delivering it, particularly if they are contracted to offer this as part of their treatment package or are using the group work programme as a primary reason for being commissioned. Non-delivery of such an important part of treatment could therefore result in contracts being can-celled or other sanctions being taken, such as a request that the cost of treatment be reduced if part of the treatment package is not being delivered.

Addressing stressors and increasing resources

Demands

There are a number of relatively obvious, but easily overlooked, require-ments that the organization can establish in order to ensure that the demands of group work can be successfully met. Firstly, it is important to establish and review whether group work is actually achievable within the existing organizational work pressures and demands. This is an ongoing exercise; our own work has made it clear to us that organizational reviews of the group programme are at least as important as client reviews. Even when this macro-level analysis has shown the feasibility of a group programme, the whole timetable can easily come unstuck if insufficient consideration is given to shift work schedules, annual leave entitlements, study leave, and projections of sick leave or other absences. Ideally, an organization should identify a contingency plan for such events. For instance, if your unit, ward, or rehab relies heavily on bank or temporary staff, is there any expectation of them running groups and, if there is no such expectation, can they undertake alternative activities to free up the permanent staff?

Another important consideration is the physical working environment and whether this supports group work. For example, is there enough space to run groups in an adequately ventilated and heated room with the necessary teaching aids. If staff members have to run around to find group material and aids before the group, this simply adds to their stress and indicates that the organization has not quite understood that it is the organization and not the individual who should control these factors. While such points are dazzlingly obvious on paper, they are easy to forget and their neglect can easily lead to both staff and clients feeling that somehow group work is just not prioritized or valued as much as other activities.

While it is primarily the role of the organization to problem solve around the issue of demands, the individual also has their part to play. Of particular importance is the need to be clear about individual capacities and communicating this clearly to others. This may be as simple as staff informing each other of their short- and long-term availability.

It is also imperative for the organization to provide protected time and adequate resources for training and supervision. The majority of organizations have very clear policies regarding these two factors, but poor implementation is often at the root of staff difficulties.

Knowledge

There is an important distinction between content knowledge (i.e., the group subject, the topic) and process knowledge (i.e., how group interactions occur, issues of power, leadership, and so forth), both of which can easily dissipate if not used regularly. The organization should provide initial teaching and training around particular group topics, followed up with refresher training and protected time to become familiar with the group content. Working with an experienced facilitator with time for evaluation allows individuals to translate knowledge into actual working practice. The issue of how to acquire process knowledge of group workings and practices is extremely difficult, particularly when the dominant treatment mode is cognitive-behavioural rather than psychodynamic. Indeed, while there are some good theoretical models available, translating these into practice is not always easy and understanding of ongoing group processes often only emerges through discussion and good clinical supervision. At the minimum, discussions should be had both pre-group and post-group among facilitators, and ideally a clinical supervision group set up to focus on group work. Both of these forums can help to deal with transference and counter-transference issues that are clearly of importance whatever the theoretical approach adopted. It is important that, for maximum effectiveness, discussions between staff members (including any external facilitators) are held in an atmosphere of learning and inquiry, so that staff members can be open with each other about their learning needs and any other concerns.

Anxiety

An individual leader's feelings about running a group may lie anywhere along a spectrum from no anxiety to phobic avoidance. These responses can be either fixed or situation-specific. A fixed response would occur whatever the situation (any form of group, any type of membership, any size etc.), whereas a situation-specific response would depend on various factors so that, for instance, running a group for medical professionals with substance-use problems may be more daunting than running a group for clients not in the medical profession. Charles Spielberger would refer to this as a difference between 'trait anxiety' (anxiety that is relatively fixed and part of you) and 'state anxiety' (anxiety related to the type of situation you find yourself in) (Spielberger, Gorsuch, & Lushene, 1970).

Generally, those who enter the helping professions and undertake professional training will not have severe trait anxiety problems. Firstly, the fact that it is a self-chosen profession high on face-to-face contact would deter very anxious individuals. Furthermore, those with high trait anxiety would either leave or find means of coping with their anxiety during training. For those who have been in treatment themselves and choose to enter the field as drug or alcohol workers, the same arguments would generally apply.

It is also important to note that everyone differs in terms of introversion and extraversion, and while there is some relationship with anxiety, it is not as simple as saying that introverts are more likely to be anxious. Moreover, there can be introverts who love doing groups (generally when they know their subject really well and are passionate about it) and extroverts who hate it because they may have to stick to one topic or follow group guidelines. For some staff groups, group work may be more anxiety-provoking because of the multiple roles that they hold, for example nurses, particularly on inpatient units, are far more likely to set boundaries outside group times than psychologists and therefore have to deal with clients' responses to such dual roles.

For the individual, perhaps the most important thing to acknowledge about groups is that a certain amount of anxiety is a normal response to any public-speaking situation. In the general population, public speaking ranks just below death on most surveys of what people fear the most. Being looked at and believing that you are going to be judged negatively is thus a pretty common experience. These feelings can be magnified in a group setting. There are a number of reasons for this. Firstly, group facilitation is more than 'just speaking' in front of people; it is about speaking and trying to manage a group at the same time. Secondly, clients with drug and alcohol problems can be quite incisive about their own and other people's weaknesses, and while the vast majority of clients are interested and attentive to what the group has to offer, a small minority can be quite vocal and critical of either the facilitator or the topic. This is compounded when the group is not optional and attendance is not necessarily because of any intrinsic motivation. However, on the positive side, a small amount of anxiety will help you to perform better once you learn to use it rather than fear it.

The most important point to make about performance anxiety is that it is highly unlikely to go away of its own accord. It is tempting to avoid groups until confidence increases, but the problem with this is that the problem may grow and avoidance has a habit of spreading from one situation to another. Gradual exposure to speaking in groups is the best possible means of combating any behavioural avoidance, plus focusing on the things that went well as opposed to anything that did not. Sharing concerns with other supportive staff can also be important, particularly as it is likely that colleagues will share similar concerns. Michael Motley (1997), an academic with a particular interest in public-speaking difficulties, suggests that reconceptualizing public speaking as a communication process rather than a performance can bring substantial relief to many anxious individuals.

Stress and the organizational response

Job stress has multiple causes, and so has to have multiple solutions. It is not always the case that stress is so circumscribed that it can be related to group work alone, and therefore it is important to consider strategies more broadly for combating stress in the organization. Interventions can occur at one of three levels: the individual, in small groups, and at the level of the organization. A well-designed stress-reduction programme addresses all three levels.

Personal intervention strategies are designed to help the individual employee cope more effectively with stress. Examples include:

- diet
- exercise
- cognitive techniques
- assertiveness training
- relaxation training.

Small group interventions are intended to help staff develop more social support at work. Examples include:

- supervisory training
- team building
- sensitivity training around drugs and alcohol misuse.

Strategies at the organizational level are directed towards improving the conditions of work. Examples include:

- modifying shifts
- reducing physical hazards
- improving career ladders
- job rotation and enrichment
- increasing skill levels
- increasing staff decision-making opportunities
- increasing staff sense of control and participation in the workplace.

More detailed information on how to run staff training for dealing with stress and violence at work can be found in Ryan, Dawson, and Hill (2008), *Managing stress and violence at work*. However, we have included some of the suggested workplace strategies here:

- Using staff meetings more effectively to encourage participation and input.
- Developing autonomous work groups.
- Setting up a Stress Management Committee.
- Providing in-house training in Stress Management.
- Increasing skill-based training by ensuring that Trust continuing professional development strategies include both effective stress management strategies and effective approaches to group work.
- Using career ladders to reward skill development by ensuring that the 'Knowledge Skills Framework' adopted in the NHS includes effective group work and stress management in promotion profiles.
- Using job rotations to expand skills by, for example, targeting senior registrar rotations into the development of core group work skills.
- Using job redesign to increase range of skill needed.

- Training in proactive supervision emphasizing positive feedback, employee growth and development, open lines of communication, and strong levels of support.
- Training in conflict resolution and team building.
- Appropriate use of staff away days.
- Organizing discussion groups on healthy stress reducers. The idea here is to encourage staff to share effective strategies with each other. An added benefit of this approach is that it also provides a mechanism for giving additional staff social support.

Case study

In 2005 the alcohol inpatient ward at South London and Maudsley NHS Foundation Trust participated in a two-day training programme designed to reduce levels of stress and burnout among staff. The training intervention was derived from a large-scale project that focused on inpatient and community mental health staff across five European countries. A research component was built into the work, with levels of staff burn-out being measured before the training intervention and one month afterwards. The team were able to identify four main sources of stress at work. These were: (1) group work; (2) dealing with complex clients; (3) effectively evaluating the shift; and (4) client aggression. A one-month follow-up showed that levels of emotional exhaustion and depersonalization had been reduced and feelings of personal accomplishment at work had risen (see Hill, Atnas, Ryan, Ashby, & Winnington, 2009).

While undertaking research is of course desirable, this is not always possible. However, it is still important to bear in mind ways in which you can judge whether an intervention has been successful or not. Thus, some pertinent questions to ask could include:

- Has social support (both co-workers and supervisory) increased?
- Have job demands decreased?
- Have employees' sense of autonomy and control increased?
- Has job satisfaction increased?
- Have level and use of skills increased?
- Have physical or psychological stress symptoms decreased?

Conclusion

A key aim of this chapter has been to highlight the important role that the organization can play in helping staff to reduce their levels of stress. There is a wealth of high quality data that support the view that workers with low levels of negative stress achieve far better outcomes than those who are either stressed or burnt out. The chapter has highlighted that working in mental health and addictions is a stressful business and that running groups can be a significant contributor to this. When stress occurs at work there is only so much the individual can do to reduce this and support is a key variable in reducing stress, irrespective of the level of demand in the workplace. Hopefully it provides some comfort to realize that it is normal to have a degree of anxiety when running groups. It is important to normalize feelings of anxiety and work with them instead of trying to push them away. Really knowing the material to be presented is crucial and this in and of itself can substantially reduce anxiety about performing. We hope that in reading this chapter you have come away with one or two ideas you can introduce in your team both in the short- and long-term, either in relation to group work or in relation to stress more generally. We believe that this will not only help each staff member to perform to their optimum ability, but also help serve our clients who look to us to help them to understand and explain their often self-defeating behaviours.

References

Arnetz, J., Arnetz, B., & Petterson, I. (1996). Violence in the nursing profession: Occupational and lifestyle risk factors in Swedish nurses. *Work and Stress, 10*, 119–127.

Edwards, D., Burnard, P., Coyle, D., Fothergill, A., & Hannigan, B. (2000). Stress and burnout in community mental health nursing: a review of the literature. *Journal of Psychiatric and Mental Health Nursing, 7*, 7–14.

Gourney, K. (2001). *The recognition, prevention and therapeutic management of violence in mental health care.* London: UKCC.

Hill, R. G., Ryan, P., Atnas, C. I., Ashby, K., & Winnington, J. (2009). Whole team training to reduce burn-out amongst staff on an in-patient ward. *Journal of Substance Use, 15*, 42–50.

Karasek, R., & Theorell, T. (1990). *Healthy work, stress, productivity and the reconstruction of working life.* New York: Basic Books.

Motley, M. T. (1997). *Overcoming your fear of public speaking: A proven method.* Boston: Houghton Mifflin Company.

Rabin, S., Feldman, D., & Kaplan, Z. (1999). Stress and intervention strategies in mental health professionals. *British Journal of Medical Psychology, 72*, 159–169.

Ryan, J., & Poser, E. (1993). Workplace violence. *Nursing Times, 89*, 38–41.

Ryan, P., Dawson, I., & Hill, R. G. (2008). *Managing stress and violence at work: A training programme for mental health services.* Brighton: Pavilion Publishing.

Spielberger, C., Gorsuch, R. L., & Lushene, R. E. (1970). *STAI manual.* Palo Alto, CA: Consulting Psychologists Press.

Van der Klink, J. J., Blonk, R., Schene, A., & van Dijk, F. (2001). The benefits of interventions for work-related stress. *American Journal of Public Health, 91*, 720–725.

Whittington, R., & Wykes, T. (1994). Violence in psychiatric hospitals: Are certain staff prone to being assaulted? *Journal of Advanced Nursing, 19*, 219–225.

Part III

Specific considerations in addictions group work

Introduction to specific considerations

The third and final part of the book, 'Specific considerations in addictions group work', focuses on a number of specific issues within the field of addictions. Chapter 13 explores diversity issues and how these can best be addressed within the group setting. Shamil Wanigaratne takes us on a journey exploring cultural issues within group work and describes a number of the complex issues that emerge when working with cultural diversity. He provides an interesting case study of working in the Middle East and introducing clients to sharing their experiences of addiction in a group context.

We know that substance misuse can lead to various types and degrees of neuropsychological dysfunction and, in Chapter 14, ways of working with people in groups who are dependent on substances and have additional cognitive impairment are explored. Monique Cloherty, a clinical neuropsychologist, and Robert Hill raise our awareness of neuropsychological issues among substance-using clients and how we might adapt groups to maximize participation.

Given the high prevalence of co-morbidity among clients with alcohol and drug problems, it is essential to be aware of how different diagnoses can affect the individual in a group context. Rachel Davies provides us with a practical chapter about this, pointing out firstly how to recognize common mental health issues and then how to work effectively with these within a group setting.

Chapter 16 examines particular issues when working with drug users in the criminal justice setting, in particular how to deal with clients who may be highly ambivalent about treatment. Tim Meynen and Nancy Akrasi give a good overview of the cognitive behavioural literature before sharing some of their own experiences in learning how to work with some of the common dilemmas that arise when working in partnership with the criminal justice system.

Elly Farmer and Deepti Shah-Armon cover the issue of personality disorder and describe two groups for clients who they have worked with in their substance misuse service. Firstly they discuss a group for female survivors of childhood sexual abuse and secondly a Dialectical Behaviour Therapy (DBT) group for those with borderline personality disorder. We are confident that many of the principles and techniques for dealing with difficult emotions outlined in the chapter can be used with the broader range of clients who come into contact with addictions services.

Chapters 18 provides a reflective account of the benefits and issues related to facilitating a women-only group. Ernestine Nhapi and Josephine Shaw provide their personal account of facilitating groups for women on an alcohol detoxification ward. The chapter explores the rationale for women-only groups, the role of the facilitator in running the group, as well as a number of common themes and issues.

The final chapter looks at ways of working with clients and staff from a psychodynamic perspective. Martin Weegmann admirably translates psychodynamic theory to offer readers a practical understanding of how psychodynamic concepts might illuminate our group work. While this is a specialized area of working and not widely available, its theoretical under-standing still affects many of the ways in which practitioners work in groups and it therefore seems an appropriate way to close the book.

Chapter 13

Cultural issues in group work

Shamil Wanigaratne

This chapter examines aspects of culture that may have an impact when conducting group work in the treatment of addictions. It highlights areas where it is possible to develop group interventions that are both culturally sensitive and culturally appropriate. An example of the author's work in the Middle East is used to highlight ways of using groups to work effectively in the field of addictions. The chapter concludes by examining how guidelines would help to address cultural issues when doing group work in multicultural societies, as well as within particular cultures.

Overview of culture and substance misuse

There are many texts and papers that deal with culture and substance misuse and an interested reader is guided to these (e.g., Cheung 1993; Johnson, 2007; Oetting, Donnermeyer, Trimble, & Beauvais, 1998; Rassool, 1998; Wanigaratne, Salas, & Strang, 2007). There are many definitions of culture available, however an enduring definition in the West is that from 1871 by Taylor, who defines culture as that: 'complex whole which includes knowledge, belief, art, morals, law, custom and any other capabilities and habits acquired by man as member of society' (cited in Helman, 2000, p. 2). While each of these aspects of culture has generated vast amounts of literature, 'belief' may be considered a significant aspect of addiction because of its undoubted role in the initiation of substance use, development of problematic use, and associated psychological interventions. Beliefs may be defined as 'systems of shared ideas, systems of concepts and rules and meanings that underlie and are expressed in the ways that human beings live' (Keesing & Stranthern, 1997, cited in Helman, 2000, p. 2). This implicit aspect of culture is arguably more powerful than explicit aspects, and indeed explains the transmission of culture from one generation to the next, yet is also the most difficult to pin down and describe. Approaches such as Cognitive Behavioural Therapy (CBT) place great emphasis on beliefs. While modern group interventions from a CBT perspective strive to encourage group members to be explicit about their beliefs and assumptions, and examine them in a rational way. Psychodynamic groups focus on the group process to help individuals become aware and subsequently understand their beliefs.

We know that substance use is part of most cultures and is as old as humanity itself (Wanigaratne et al., 2007). Accordingly, most cultures include the use of substances as part of their cultural beliefs, social customs, and in some cases religious rituals. In other cultures such as Islamic cultures substance misuse is seen as harmful and is not included in their systems, symbols, or canons. It is also important to consider issues such as dominant culture and subcultures when discussing substance use and misuse. Multicultural societies such as the United Kingdom, USA, and Canada are comprised of both a dominant culture and subcultures, each of which holds different value systems. Western majority cultures generally place a greater emphasis on the self, individuality, and autonomy, whereas minority cultures promote a more collectivist, community, and group approach (Sue & Sue, 2003; Blume & de la Cruz, 2005). Minority cultures define the 'self' more in terms of role in the community and service to others rather than individual achievement; such cultures also value 'interdependence' over 'independence' (Sue & Sue, 2003). Due to the collectivist nature of most minority communities and subcultures, group approaches may appear to offer a more natural and culturally congruent intervention. However, in practice, group therapy in the West is often based on the values and assumptions of the dominant culture. It is therefore generally geared towards serving the dominant culture and found wanting in terms of focus on and sensitivity to minority cultures.

While there is a common myth that substance misuse is greater among minority communities, this is not actually the case (Wanigaratne, Dar, Abdulrahim, & Strang, 2003). When the use of a substance or an addictive behaviour is not accepted by the dominant culture, this gives rise to subcultures with their own values, systems of beliefs, rituals, and customs. Intracultural behaviours and intercultural differences in attitudes and prejudices come to play a part in how and where substances are used. Subcultures also develop around a particular addiction, particular substance, or behaviour, e.g., injecting drugs. The subculture, with its shared set of norms, values, and beliefs, also becomes crucial for the individual's identity. The individual's role in the subculture, particularly if they are disenfranchised from the dominant culture, becomes crucial to their sense of self. This phenomenon is described in detail in *The street addict's role* (Stephens, 1991). In this subculture the addict is most likely to interact with other addicts, who not only reinforce the subculture but also make it difficult for a member to leave (Baklien & Samarasinghe, 2003).

Set and setting

Initiation into drug and alcohol use invariably takes place in a group setting. The role of the 'group' or the social context in the initiation and maintenance of substance use is cogently described by Zinberg (1984) in his text *Drug, set and setting*. The acceptability or unacceptability of a substance in a culture determines both the initiation and control of use; invariably, this is a group process. Alcohol, for example, is widely accepted as part of Western culture, but not in Islamic cultures. Chewing Khat is part of North African and some Arabic cultures yet, while imported to the West, it remains largely confined to the immigrant communities of those countries.

Harding and Zinberg (1997) argue that social controls, rituals, and sanctions apply to the use of all drugs, including alcohol. Small and larger social groups participating in cultural activities (such as weddings, festivals, parties, meeting friends, reunions, and family meals) all involve expectations, rituals, and sanctions. The set (i.e., the state of mind or the mood of the person using the substance) and the setting (i.e., the context in which the substance is being used) become part of the conditioning process and thus part of the experience of substance use itself. Sanctions are also very much part of the 'culture' and function to regulate the substance use; sanctions vary from culture to culture and from subculture to subculture. Nevertheless, Zinberg (1984) argues that sanctions become internalized within the members of the group or culture, and cites Edwards (1974) in describing how specific sanctions and rituals are developed and integrated by different groups. Within the context of group interventions in the addictions, we are primarily referring to individuals whose control and internal sanctions have either failed or been poorly developed. Group processes aim to instil control by developing sanctions and reinforcing them.

Case example of subculture, set, and setting: Twelve-Step groups

According to the available evidence the Twelve-Step approach can be seen as the most effective group intervention, if not the only intervention, to help an addicted individual move away from their addiction towards 'recovery' (e.g., Winters, Stinchfield, Opland, Weller, & Latimer, 2000; Kelly, 2003). The phenomenon of Twelve-Step groups such as Alcoholics Anonymous (AA) and Narcotics Anonymous (NA) can be understood as a subculture (or even a manufactured culture) that exists alongside a dominant culture where a system of beliefs, shared ideas, concepts, rules, and meanings have been set out. Groups based around the *Big book* (Alcoholics Anonymous, 2002), the Twelve Steps, and Traditions, meet to hear testimonies and experiences of individuals in order to align the participants' ideas and beliefs to that of the AA/NA philosophy. Hence members of the Twelve-Step movement and those who subscribe to its beliefs can be described as belonging to a group that fits the definition of a culture or subculture, albeit in a circular way.

In the case of Twelve-Step AA meetings, a new set and setting based on abstinence from substance use is created and reinforced through repeated ritual, custom, and normative behaviour. An individual who has given up an addiction to, for example, alcohol, is encouraged to attend as many meetings as possible in the immediate aftermath of their decision to change their substance use. This is summed up in the well-known Fellowship phrase of '90 meetings in 90 days', and acts to both reinforce the new culture and substitute the old. The aim is for the individual to gain a new set of beliefs, morals, and ways of behaving, all of which can be said to define a culture.

Culture and assumptions in Western group therapy

Group therapy currently practised in the West could be best described as broad and diverse, with a number of schools and traditions, but these can be broadly classified according to the main therapy types, namely Psychodynamic, Humanistic, Cognitive Behavioural, and Systemic. A fifth category of Integrative therapy could also be added to the list. Although the practice of group therapy uses diverse approaches, group therapy itself has its roots in psychodynamic psychotherapy.

Psychodynamic theory assumes 'universality' or culture blindness, and it is open to debate whether this is in fact true universality, given that psychotherapy originated from one culture, namely Eastern European Jewish culture. Littlewood (1992) notes this and observes that this is a worthwhile debate, since psychodynamic theory has had a profound influence on the development of all psychological therapies. He describes the context in which psychotherapy, and indeed group therapy, developed in Britain, and cites the British Medical Association's urgent report in the 1930s to the British government opposing the entry of Jewish doctors to Britain (Littlewood & Lipsedge, 1989). Amid this anti-Semitic fervour, emerging psychotherapy tended to ignore the social context in favour of the intra-psychic world, which was considered scientific and universal (Littlewood, 1992, 1989).

However, as the following example demonstrates, there are some difficulties with an assumption of universality. Islamic cultures, particularly Arabic cultures, hold the belief that it is not acceptable to talk about personal and family matters in public. It would therefore be expected that those who have been brought up in such cultures would find it difficult to engage in the group process. One can further expect that those who belong to cultures where values such as saving face, honour, shame, and guilt are strongly reinforced would be unlikely to engage in group work.

Although across the Atlantic Ocean in the USA there were parallel developments in therapy, the story of group therapy also begins in the same area of London alluded to by Littlewood (1992). The commonly cited history of Western group therapy starts with the work of Foulkes (1898–1976), who emphasized the social nature of human personality development, identifying groups as the matrix amid which the individual develops. He further argued that interpersonal and transpersonal factors continued to influence the individual throughout life (Brown & Zinkin, 2000). Thus, conducting therapy in groups enabled these factors to be elicited and worked on. The second major influence on group therapy was the work of Bion (1897–1979), another psychoanalyst working in North London. Bion (1961) described the basic assumptions behind the behaviour of members of a therapeutic group as 'dependency', 'flight–fight', and 'pairing'. 'Dependency' is based on the security needs of the members and refers to the emergence of a group leader. 'Flight–fight' is similar to avoidance behaviour, where the group achieves cohesion or bonding by finding a common enemy or issue to fight or run away from. 'Pairing' behaviour is where two people join to do the work of the group in helping others to avoid working; this is interpreted as representing reproduction. These assumptions essentially describe transference processes that interfere with the work of the group. The facilitator, through interpretation of the group dynamics, helps individuals gain insight into their problems. Following on from the work of these pioneers, therapy has developed in many directions. More recently, Irvin Yalom has added a significant contribution to psychodynamic and exploratory group therapy, particularly in his work on therapeutic factors. Like other writers in the field, Yalom (2005) describes in detail the process of developing a group culture, yet does not allude to the impact of cultural influences on group process.

Humanistic therapy developed from the pioneering work of Carl Rogers (1902–1987) and is perhaps the most commonly practised therapy modality in the field of addictions. However, early humanistic texts do not sufficiently explore the influence of culture on therapy process, and indeed group work. There is a similar lack of consideration of culture in the early work of Cognitive Behavioural Therapy. For example, Beck, Rush, Shaw, and Emery's (1979) seminal volume of *Cognitive therapy of depression* includes a chapter on group therapy for depression by Hallon and Shaw (1979) that can be seen as the forerunner of all CBT group work. However, even this chapter, and indeed the entire volume, neglects to consider cultural factors. Even now there is a limited amount of literature about CBT-based group work (e.g., Free, 1999; Bieling, McCabe, & Antony, 2009), and again this fails to deal with the issue of culture and its impact on the group process.

Over the last 20 years, 'Relapse prevention' (Marlatt & Gordon, 1985) and 'Motivational interviewing' (Miller & Rollnick, 2002) approaches have had the greatest impact on the addictions field (Wanigaratne, 2003), but until recently these approaches paid little attention to culture. Alan Marlatt has since taken on board this criticism and not only devotes an entire chapter to culture in the new edition of *Relapse prevention* (Marlatt & Donovan, 2005), but also incorporates cultural factors into the new model of relapse (Witkiewitz & Marlatt, 2004). While the new model awaits translation into group interventions and evaluation, it opens up the possibility of placing cultural factors at the heart of relapse-prevention work.

Approaches such as relapse prevention and CBT are based on teaching coping skills and it is likely that majority and minority cultures may show differences in coping skills. Clearly, outcomes from group work (and indeed individual work) would be enhanced if differences could be identified, suitable measurement instruments be developed, and ways to reduce barriers for uptake of skills be developed.

Cultural differences have also been found in the measurement of self-efficacy, a central construct in both relapse prevention and CBT (Earley, Gibson, & Chen, 1999; Sabogal, Otero-Sabagal, Perez-Stable, Martin, & Martin, 1989; Schaubroeck, Lam, & Xie, 2000). These differences seem to depend on whether individuals originate from a culture holding a 'collective' or 'individual' world-view. While awareness and sensitivity to these differences in itself would facilitate better therapy, measurement would allow group interventions to improve self-efficacy to be appropriately matched. Clearly more research is needed in this area, and the study of cultural difference in coping skills and self-efficacy should provide fertile grounds for future research.

Practical implications for group therapy

Cultural factors are important considerations in all addiction interventions, not just in group therapy, and many interventions may fail because of inadequate attention to cultural issues. The importance of 'identity shift' in motivating people to initiate and maintain change is emphasized by Robert West (2006) in his PRIME theory and by the recovery movement (White, 2007). A greater understanding of the process by which the 'identity' of a substance user is formed would undoubtedly be helpful in supporting a subsequent 'identity shift'. Since identity formation is essentially a group and an acculturation process, it could be argued that group interventions are more suited in supporting an 'identity shift'; this might help explain the success of the Twelve-Step movement.

Therapy groups may involve clashes of cultures and subcultures. It is unlikely that members of a group will all share the one cultural or subcultural group. Thus, the group becomes the setting for a 'clash of cultures' that in itself may be very useful for the change process. Encouraging group members to accept that not everyone in the group holds the same set of assumptions, beliefs, customs, rules, norms, and habits could be a first step in changing an individual's strongly held assumptions and beliefs. This process of interpersonal learning (Yalom, 2005) is a common and key feature of group work and is particularly relevant from a cultural perspective.

The selection or acceptance of individuals from different cultures and subcultures into a group setting might also be a useful step in helping individuals to acknowledge the role culture has played in acquiring and maintaining their addictive behaviour. Some people may drop out or prematurely exit a group because they cannot accept individuals from different cultures or subcultures being in the group. This is a challenge for facilitators to pick up and address early on in the group programme. In a CBT-orientated group, cultural values can be elicited and explored through a simple 'game' or brainstorming exercise that asks each member to list three assumptions or beliefs from the culture they identify with. In more psychodynamic or exploratory groups, this could be achieved through theme-led discussions.

Within multicultural societies such as the United Kingdom and the USA, one is likely to find therapy groups made up of therapists and participants from different cultural backgrounds. Issues of cultural sensitivity and principles of intercultural therapy therefore come into play. There are clearly many permutations that might arise within groups. The therapist and the recipient of therapy may belong to different cultures, giving rise to differing perceptions and dynamics (Kareem & Littlewood, 1992). The therapist might be from a minority group or different culture to that of the majority of group members, or the majority of the group and the facilitator might share one culture while an individual or a few members come from a different culture. For example, in the UK, a black therapist from a Caribbean background might run a group with majority middle-class white participants, thus highlighting what Littlewood (1992) describes as status contradiction.

Therapists and recipients of therapy are not immune to racism, prejudice, and ethnocentrism, although many therapists would like to believe that they are above such perceptions and feelings. Whether these are understood as transference issues, therapy-interfering factors, barriers, or simple 'blocks', they undoubtedly exist and need to be addressed. These issues will arise in both goal-orientated and process-orientated groups, but are likely to be more of a hindrance in the latter if left unaddressed.

Matching therapists and recipients in terms of their culture may seem ideal but is often impractical. Additionally cultures are never homogeneous, factors within the same culture such as subculture, status, community, caste, age and sexuality are likely to mediate the group process and group dynamics. Therapists must be alert to, for example, issues of honour or face in particular cultures, where disclosure of personal information that has the potential of leaking out to the community may inhibit group participation. When the group is mixed-gender from the same culture, gender issues may crop up as an inhibitory factor.

I would encourage group therapists to prepare to work with difference, enhance their awareness of possible dynamics associated with culture, and develop a sensitivity to address them. Examining one's own cultural background in terms of assumptions, attitudes, and core beliefs is a first step in this process. Having discussions with your colleagues from your own culture and from different cultures about your findings is the next step. This dialogue might be valuably continued with your clients. Some therapists might consider developing their awareness and sensitivity through further reading, study, and attending relevant training courses.

A training course in cultural issues might cover basic knowledge, skills, and competencies in the following areas:

- Definitions of culture and subcultures.
- Awareness of possible roles culture might play in the acquisition of an addiction.
- Issues of substance, set, and setting.
- Inter-cultural and intra-cultural therapy issues.
- Twelve-Step groups.
- How to address culture in group therapy—basic skills.

Case example: translating Western group therapy to the Middle East

The author, who is male and of Sri Lankan origin, was involved in providing consultation to a new residential addiction treatment centre in a Middle-East country that had no previous facilities for addiction treatment. His consultations have been mainly centred on the therapeutic programme and maintaining the quality of psychological assessment and therapy.

The therapeutic programme comprised structured groups based on the Relapse Prevention model (Marlatt & Gordon, 1985) and problem-solving work. Exploratory psychotherapy groups took place three times a week and were facilitated within an eclectic theoretical framework incorporating psychodynamic principles from Bion (1961) and Yalom (2005), as well as humanistic elements from Rogers (1961) and Maslow (1994). All group members were Muslim males and from the same culture; the group facilitator was from the same culture as the members, but not of the same nationality. Sometimes the groups were co-facilitated by female psychologists from the same culture. The group can be described as a slow open group. New members were introduced to the group; however, since there was a slow rate of new admissions to the centre, the group had quite a stable membership.

Although the Arab culture is fairly family- and group-orientated, there was considerable apprehension observed about participation in the group, which was most apparent when new members joined. Understandably, group work was a new experience and an evaluation showed that more than half reported feeling apprehensive about confidentiality.

All group members had grown up within a culture of not speaking about one's personal problems in public. However, a simple evaluation showed that they found the group useful and 80% reported positive outcomes that they attributed to the group. Over 60% agreed with the following statements: 'the group helped me: to be less shy, be more clear about what I want out of life, to take care of my psychological problems, understand the suffering of my family and friends, view myself positively, understand my addiction'. Perhaps most importantly, 84% of the participants thought that the groups were compatible with the Arab culture (Kafaji, 2007).

The facilitator observed that the group kept discussions at a superficial level and used a range of defences including splitting, regression, avoidance, denial, and projection. While the facilitator also observed the emergence of subgroups, ambiguity about 'group intention', and the formation of dependent relationships within the group, there was a sense of group cohesion and belonging (Kafaji, 2007).

This case example demonstrates the complexities of group work in addictions from a cultural perspective. The evaluation revealed paradoxical findings that both supported and criticized the universality assumptions of psychodynamic groups. The group members reported apprehension about the group and worries about confidentiality that were in keeping with cultural expectations, yet most rated the group highly and regarded it as helpful in their recovery. Similarly, while cultural aspects of 'keeping face', demonstrated by the superficiality of discussions and avoiding emotion in the group, were prevalent, group members reported positive group experiences. One must not underestimate from a cultural perspective how female co-facilitators may have contributed to the observed superficiality. It is also difficult to judge how the eclectic approach or facilitation style impacted on the group, and an evaluation of the group facilitated from a pure modality for a defined period might yield interesting findings. The therapist's orientation and adaptation of theoretical approaches to deal with addiction are also issues of interest.

Summary and conclusions

Addictions treatment can encompass exploratory groups, psychotherapy groups, support groups, motivational groups, Twelve-Step-based therapy groups, and relapse prevention groups. Cultural issues apply to all of these groups. There is very little published research on group work in the field of addictions, let alone the issue of culture within group work. Both process and outcome research relating to the issues raised in the previous sections are urgently needed, and the field is wide open for interested researchers. Both qualitative and quantitative research into the impact of various aspects of culture on group engagement would be useful and findings should be immediately translated into training programmes for clinicians and therapists in the field.

A great deal of group work in the addiction sector takes place in residential settings and typically staff have different levels of training and experience. Currently there is no baseline knowledge and skills framework for group work in the addictions field and a curriculum for basic competencies (knowledge and skills) is badly needed. This curriculum should contain a section on cultural competencies that addresses the issues raised in this chapter, supported by a mechanism whereby research studies can continuously feed into training. By enhancing workforce competencies and sensitivities to the cultural aspects of group work, treatment settings have much to gain, not only in better outcomes and patient experience, but also in staff satisfaction and morale.

References

Alcoholics Anonymous (2002). *Big book*. Hazelden: Hazelden Information and Education Service.

Baklien, B., & Samarasinghe, D. (2003). *Alcohol and poverty*. Colombo: Forut.

Beck, A. T., Rush, A. J., Shaw, B. F., & Emery, G. (1979). *Cognitive therapy of depression*. New York: Guilford Press.

Bieling, P. J., McCabe, R. E., & Antony, M. M. (2009). *Cognitive-behavioural therapy in groups*. London: The Guildford Press.

Bion, W. R. (1961). *Experiences in groups*. London: Tavistock.

Blume, A.W., & de la Cruz, B. G. (2005). Relapse prevention among diverse populations. In G. A. Marlatt & D. M. Donovan (Eds.), *Relapse prevention: maintenance strategies in the treatment of addictive behaviors*. New York: Guilford Press.

Brown, D., & Zinkin, L. (2000). *The psyche and the social world: Developments in group-analytic theory*. London: Jessica Kingsley.

Cheung, Y. W. (1993). Approaches to ethnicity: Clearing roadblocks in the study of ethnicity and substance use. *Substance Use & Misuse, 28*, 1209–1226.

Earley, P. C., Gibson, C. B., & Chen, C. C. (1999). 'How did I do' versus 'How did we do'? Cultural contrasts of performance feedback use and self-efficacy. *Journal of Cross-Cultural Psychology, 30*, 594–619.

Edwards, G. F. (1974). Drugs and drug dependence, and the concept of plasticity. *Quarterly Journal on the Studies on Alcohol, 35*, 176–195.

Free, M. L. (1999). *Cognitive therapy in groups: Guidelines and resources for practice.* Chichester: Wiley.

Hallon, S. D., & Shaw, B. F. (1979). Group cognitive therapy for depression. In A. T. Beck, A. J. Rush, B. F. Shaw, & G. Emery, *Cognitive therapy of depression.* New York: Guilford Press.

Harding, W., & Zinberg, N. E. (1997). The effectiveness of the subculture in developing rituals and social sanctions for controlled drug use. In B. M. Du Toit (Ed.), *Drugs, rituals and altered states of consciousness.* Rotterdam: A.A. Balkema.

Helman, C. G. (2000). *Culture, health and illness.* London: Hodder Arnold.

Johnson, T. P. (2007). Cultural-level influences on substance use & misuse. *Substance Use and Misuse, 42,* 305–316.

Kafaji, T. (2007). *Group therapy: Experience from the United Arab Emirates.* UEA International Conference on Addictions, Abu Dhabi.

Kareem, J., & Littlewood, R. (1992). *Intercultural therapy: Themes interpretations and practice.* Oxford: Blackwell Scientific.

Keesing, R. M., & Stranthern, A. (1997). *Cultural anthropology: Contemporary perspective.* New York: Harcourt Brace.

Kelly, J. F. (2003). Self-help for substance-use disorders: History, effectiveness, knowledge gaps and research opportunities. *Clinical Psychology Review, 23,* 639–663.

Littlewood, R. (1989). Glossary. In *Report Royal College of Psychiatrists Special (Ethnic) Issues Committee.* Royal College of Psychiatrists, London.

Littlewood, R. (1992). Towards an intercultural therapy. In J. Kareem & R. Littlewood (Eds.), *Intercultural therapy: Themes interpretations and practice.* Oxford: Blackwell Scientific.

Littlewood, R., & Lipsedge, M. (1989). *Aliens and alienists: Ethnic minorities and psychiatry* (2nd rev. ed.). London: Unwin Hyman.

Marlatt, G. A., & Donovan, D. M. (Eds.) (2005). *Relapse prevention: Maintenance strategies in the treatment of addictive behaviors.* New York: Guilford Press.

Marlatt, G. A., & Gordon, J. R. (1985). *Relapse prevention: Maintenance strategies in the treatment of addictive behaviors.* New York: Guildford Press.

Maslow, A. (1994). *Toward a psychology of being.* Chichester: John Wiley.

Miller, W. R., & Rollnick, S. (2002). *Motivational interviewing: Preparing people for change* (2nd ed.). New York: Guilford.

Oetting, E. R., Donnermeyer, J. F., Trimble, J. E., & Beauvais, F. (1998). Primary socialisation theory: Culture, ethnicity and cultural identification. The links between culture and substance use. *Substance Use and Misuse, 33,* 2075–2107.

Rassool, G. H. (1998). *Substance use and misuse: Nature, context and clinical interventions.* Oxford: Blackwell Science.

Rogers, C. R. (1961). *On becoming a person.* Boston: Houghton Mifflin.

Sabogal, F., Otero-Sabagal, R., Perez-Stable, E. J., Martin, B. V., & Martin, G. (1989). Perceived self-efficacy to avoid cigarette smoking and addiction: Differences between Hispanics and non-Hispanic Whites. *Hispanic Journal of Behavioral Science, 11,* 136–147.

Schaubroeck, J., Lam, S. S. K., & Xie, J. L. (2000). Collective efficacy versus self-efficacy in coping responses to stressors and control: A cross-cultural study. *Journal of Applied Psychology, 85,* 512–525.

Stephens, R. (1991). *The street addict role: A theory of heroin addiction*. Albany: State University of New York Press.

Sue, D. W., & Sue, D. (2003). *Counseling the culturally diverse: Theory and practice*. New York: Wiley.

Wanigaratne, S. (2003). Relapse prevention in practice. *The Drug and Alcohol Professional, 3*, 11–18.

Wanigaratne, S., Dar, K., Abdulrahim, D., & Strang, J. (2003). Ethnicity and drug use: Exploring the nature of particular relationships amongst diverse populations in the United Kingdom. *Drugs: Education, Prevention and Policy, 10*, 39–55.

Wanigaratne, S., Salas, S., & Strang, J. (2007). Substance misuse. In D. Bhugra & K. Bhui (Eds.), *Textbook of cultural psychiatry*. Cambridge: Cambridge University Press.

West, R. (2006). *Theory of addiction*. Oxford: Blackwell.

White, W. L. (2007). Addiction recovery: Its definition and conceptual boundaries. *Journal of Substance Abuse Treatment, 33*, 229–241.

Winters, K. C., Stinchfield, R. D., Opland, E., Weller, C., & Latimer, W. W. (2000). The effectiveness of the Minnesota Model approach in the treatment of adolescent drug abusers. *Addiction, 95*, 601–612.

Witkiewitz, K. A., & Marlatt, G. A. (2004). *Therapist's guide to evidence-based relapse prevention*. New York: Academic Press.

Yalom, I. D. (2005). *The theory and practice of group psychotherapy* (5th ed.) with M. Leszcz. New York: Basic Books.

Zinberg, N. (1984). *Drug, set and setting: The basics of controlled intoxicant use*. New York: Yale University Press.

Chapter 14

Working with cognitively impaired substance users

Monique Cloherty and Robert Hill

Groups can help clients to assist and challenge one another, and provide a microcosm from which to learn about and change behaviour. Groups can help improve socialization skills, decrease a sense of isolation, and build self-esteem. However, clients with cognitive impairments or deficits represent a special population that can pose particular challenges to the process of group therapy.

In this chapter we discuss ways of working within groups with individuals who are dependent on substances and also have cognitive impairments. We discuss the mechanisms for and common manifestations of cognitive impairment and how elements of group therapy can be modified to address the unique profiles of group members with cognitive impairment. The general stance taken in this chapter is that the majority of clients with a cognitive impairment will be in generic substance-focused rehabilitation or recovery groups and not in specific cognitive remediation groups.

Impairments directly associated with substance misuse

Substances can produce alterations in brain function and structure that can result in deficits in brain processes of varying degrees of severity and permanence. Substance misuse may have direct effects on central neurochemical systems subserving cognitive processes or psychomotor functioning, indirect effects via peripheral actions (i.e., sensory or motor functions), and chronic effects due to neuroadaptation or structural changes. Withdrawal from substances can also cause temporary cognitive changes, for example, the phenomenon of *delirium tremens.*

Alcohol

It is widely recognized that chronic alcohol dependence is associated with cognitive impairment (Knight & Longmore, 1994). Impairments tend to affect immediate learning and memory, often affecting visual memory (things that are seen) rather than verbal memory (memory for things heard or written). Visual search scanning and executive functioning processes also tend to be affected (Ryan & Butters, 1986). Following abstinence there is usually some improvement in cognitive functioning, including attention, memory, and executive functions (higher order processes such as reasoning, abstraction, planning, and organization), although the course of recovery is variable (Manning et al., 2008). Thus, improvements may be seen over a period of weeks, months, or even years (Brandt, Butters, Ryan, & Bayog, 1983).

Wernicke-Korsakoff's syndrome results in the loss of grey matter in memory and executive function structures (i.e., the orbito-frontal, mesio-temporal cortex, and diencephalic structures) and can lead to gross impairments of learning, memory, and executive functions, often with intact intellectual functioning. Clients are prone to confabulation and show additional specific cognitive deficits on speeded visuo-perceptual and spatial tasks. Moreover, such impairments are irreversible and the client often requires ongoing residential care.

Stimulants

Until recently there has been little evidence of the effects of stimulant use on cognitive functioning and a lack of convincing evidence for measurable significant impairments in cocaine users. However, research suggests that memory, followed by abstraction and attention, appear to be most vulnerable to chronic cocaine use (Ardila, Rosselli, & Strumwasser, 1991). Long-term dependent users may show impairments in attention, motivation, and executive function. It also seems that subtle impairments in higher cognitive functions such as executive functions may be more widespread than previously thought (Bechara, Dolan, Denburg, Hindes, Anderson, & Nathan, 2001). There is evidence for long-term neuroadaptations and changes in receptor densities (London, Ernst, Grant, Bonson, & Weinstein, 2000).

MDMA (also known as ecstasy) has been shown to produce small but significant effects in immediate and delayed verbal memory and abstinence has not been associated with recovery (Parrott & Lasky, 1998).

Opiates

Since opiate users almost always use alcohol and other drugs, it is difficult to identify the specific effects of opiates. That said, there is a lack of convincing evidence of the risk of cognitive impairment in opiate abusers, although it has been suggested that there may be subtle deficits involving the executive functions (Powell, 2004).

Cannabis

Early studies suggesting gross structural brain damage associated with heavy cannabis use have not been supported by later, better-controlled studies. It would appear that long-term heavy use of cannabis does not produce the severe or grossly debilitating impairment of memory, attention, and cognitive function that is found with chronic heavy alcohol use. There is, however, stronger evidence from electrophysiological and neuropsychological studies for more subtle impairments of memory, attention, and the organization and integration of complex information that heavily relies on executive functions (Pope & Yurgelun-Todd, 1996; Solowij, 1998). The longer cannabis has been used, the more pronounced the cognitive impairment (Pope & Yurgelun-Todd, 1996). However, it remains unclear how important these impairments are for everyday functioning, and indeed how or if they would manifest clearly in a group setting.

Impairments indirectly associated with substance misuse

The following section discusses a range of factors commonly found among substance users that can indirectly affect cognitive functioning. The areas covered do not lay claim to comprehensiveness and there are many additional conditions that are known to produce cognitive difficulties, including HIV, hepatitis C, pancreatitis, epilepsy, and heart disease. The interested reader can follow up a number of these areas in Tarter, Butters, and Beers (2001).

Premorbid neurological conditions

'Premorbid level of functioning' is a term used to describe an individual's general intellectual ability before any damage or change has occurred. For example, if a client had a head injury from a car crash, we may wish to compare their ability after the crash with their ability before the crash—to do this we need to know their premorbid level of functioning. From our years of working with dependent substance users, our impression is that a significant proportion of chronic substance users have lower than average premorbid levels of functioning. We suspect this may be due to a pre-existing learning difficulty, or because of poor educational opportunities, especially where clients report abusing substances from an early age.

Head injury

Head injuries and fractures are the two most common alcohol-related types of trauma (Jernigan, 1991). Alcohol abusers are also more likely to sustain a violent traumatic brain injury than other head-injured individuals, as well as show a poorer prognosis (Gerhart, Mellick, & Weintraub, 2003).

Impairment mediated by nutritional and metabolic disturbance

Nutritional deficiency is common in chronically dependent alcoholics. Thiamine deficiency is one factor related to cognitive deterioration and the development of Wernicke-Korsakoff's Syndrome. Thiamine deficiency results from inadequate dietary intake, damaged gastrointestinal absorption, and decreased hepatic storage (Charness, 1993).

Impairment via mood disturbance

Mood disorders can be associated with cognitive difficulties and frequently co-exist with substance misuse. Depression can be associated with impaired autobiographical memory (memory for events), and anxiety can manifest itself in poor attention and concentration. Apathy, which is a decrease in goal-related activity because of diminished motivation, is characteristic of clients with executive dysfunction. This may need to be differentiated from the loss of interest found in depression or difficulty engaging because of defensive factors.

Lack of skills acquisition and routine

Another area that deserves consideration is lack of coping skills and daily routine, both of which may affect cognitive functioning. Many clients with long histories of problematic substance use have not had the opportunity to develop appropriate coping skills, or lack practice in using these, and have led chaotic disorganized lives. Skills training can be used to teach coping behaviours not currently in a client's repertoire, to refresh or enhance cognitive skills that may aid recovery such as organization, planning, and response inhibition.

Delivering groups to cognitively impaired substance misusers

Cognitive impairments can complicate the group process. There is a great deal of evidence available showing an association between cognitive impairment and poor group attendance (Fals-Stewart, Schafrer, Lucente, Rustine, & Brown, 1994; Teichner, Horner, Roitzsch, Herron, & Thevos, 2002). This is obviously an important consideration when considering establishing a group in the first instance and the following section focuses on useful techniques that may aid the delivery of group therapy when some or all of the group members may have cognitive difficulties.

Assessment and formulation

A good understanding of a client's cognitive functioning and how this affects their behaviour will help to maximize their group participation. While neuropsychological assessment is likely to be the most comprehensive and useful way of achieving this, it is probable that this will only be available to a very small proportion of clients.

Many clients lack insight into their cognitive difficulties, particularly those with more subtle but nevertheless disabling cognitive and emotional changes. This can result in unrealistic expectations about their abilities. Hence a vital component of therapy is offering clients clear information about the physical, emotional, and behavioural consequences of their cognitive impairment. However, sometimes increased insight can lead to depression, similar to a grief reaction, as the client develops a more accurate view of their likely future, what they may have lost as a result of their substance misuse, and their chance of recovery (Rosenthal & Meyer, 1971). Understanding and managing clients' reactions to difficulties, and perceptions of the present and future, will be central to group approaches.

Attention and concentration impairments

Attention and concentration difficulties are common among dependent substance users, particularly during the early stages of recovery. Such difficulties may also be attributable to pre-morbid difficulties, such as attention deficit hyperactivity disorder (ADHD). Attention difficulties can often show themselves as restlessness, distractibility, impulsivity, poor listening skills, and complaints of feeling bored in the group.

If concentration and attention are particularly impaired, it may be beneficial to have breaks in the session or a change in style or technique that keeps clients interested and alert. For example, it can be helpful to alternate between small group work and large group discussion or between large group teaching of rehabilitation concepts and practical role plays. Therapeutic techniques such as summarizing, ordinarily used to show empathy, may be used to refocus the individual who is tangential or distractible. It can also be helpful to use visual aids such as a flipchart to act as an anchor point for the individual. Cueing the person's attention by saying their name or inviting their opinions or experiences can be another useful way to pull someone back into the room. For very key points in the group, the facilitator can ask everyone to focus more intently.

It is important to keep language 'short and sweet', using short sentences, simple language, and uncomplicated grammar. Key messages and concepts often need to be repeated. The group environment needs to be organized so that there are minimal distractions, i.e., keeping a 'do not disturb' sign outside the group, closing windows, and clearing any clutter. Alternating between different sensory ways of communicating (i.e., visual, auditory, tactile) can be useful in maintaining stimulation for clients who may get bored easily. Clients may also be encouraged to use self-instructional techniques during the group, i.e., 'Am I wandering?', 'What am I supposed to being doing now?' This can be pre-planned in one-to-one sessions with individual clients.

Memory impairments

Clients with memory impairment have residual learning capacities. For example, clients may have poor working memory (the ability to hold and manipulate information in the '*here and now*'), but intact delayed memory (memory for 30 minutes or more, often referred to as long-term memory). In these situations, using a strategy of 'by-passing' working memory through repetition and rehearsal can help get information into long-term memory. Another example is using visual means of relating information if the client has a poor verbal memory.

Memory problems can present in a number of different ways. For example, clients may be late to groups, be repetitive (and frustrate other group members), ask for information to be repeated, lose track of the group process, have difficulty applying what they have learnt to situations outside the group, or forget to undertake homework tasks. It is easy for this to be perceived as a lack of commitment to their recovery. If clients are unable to consolidate key recovery concepts, this can lead to difficulties in future group discussions that depend on this knowledge, and can result in clients gradually becoming isolated from other group members. Sadly, as subgroups form over time, these clients may feel forced out of the group process.

One effective strategy for improving memory for task instructions is frequent repetition of instructions and checking that the information has been encoded into memory. For tasks that take place over an extended time period, reminding clients of crucial information rather than repetition of the original instruction is likely to be most useful. Probably the best way to ensure that the client has encoded crucial information is to ask them to repeat back the information, rather than saying 'have you remembered that?'

Memory for group instructions will be enhanced by keeping the instructions as brief and linguistically simple as possible. Because instructions that are too lengthy will not be remembered, it is advisable to break them down into smaller parts if possible. This will also have the advantage of reducing task complexity.

Memory aids such as written summaries and cue cards can easily be incorporated into groups. It is sometimes advantageous to involve a group member to act as a memory prompter between sessions or to assist the client with memory problems to carry out homework tasks. Using external aids such as a diary, mobile phone alarm, palmtop organizer, or digital recorder can be useful to 'programme in' reminders for homework.

Getting the client to pay more attention to the information to be remembered and spending more time on encoding the information through a variety of means (e.g., through visualization) can be beneficial. Repeating a key message after initially presenting it at intervals of 30 seconds, 1 minute, 2 minutes, 5 minutes (also known as expanded rehearsal) can be very valuable in groups (see Wilson & Moffat, 1984).

Errorless learning is a technique that has been used for many years as a way of enhancing learning. It is particularly useful for psycho-educational groups where there is an educational component or facts that need to be remembered. Making mistakes often leads to discouragement, which results in a lack of motivation to even try the skill again. Often once a mistake is made, it can become very difficult to unlearn it, especially with clients with memory difficulties. Errorless learning is an excellent way to avoid discouragement, and to build success and self-confidence. Whenever a client is learning a new skill it is important to provide the person with all the help they need to accomplish the task and gradually take away support until the person can achieve the task independently. Studies of individuals with memory deficits resulting from acquired brain damage have consistently shown a substantial benefit from errorless learning (e.g., Baddeley & Wilson, 1994; Clare, Wilson, Carter, Roth, & Hodges, 2002; Parkin, Hunkin, & Squires, 1998). An example of using this principle would be a facilitator asking the group to summarize the main theme of the previous group. If, for example, the last group's theme was family support, the facilitator may say 'I am thinking of what we discussed last week. We discussed Family. What was the particular thing that we discussed? It began with the letter S'.

Executive functioning impairments

Executive functioning is a relatively new term in neuropsychology. Executive functions underpin reasoning, organizing and problem-solving, planning and decision-making; they are thought to be supported by the frontal lobes of the brain and their connections. They make up separate but integrated processes of initiation, set-shifting, inhibition, strategy generation, prospective memory (memory for events in the future), and working memory. Damage to these processes has been descriptively classified as 'the dysexecutive syndrome' (Burgess & Alderman, 2004). Everyday problems associated with the dysexecutive syndrome include planning problems, distractibility, impulsivity, poor decision-making and problem-solving, inappropriate social behaviour, aggression and emotional dysregulation, apathy, and difficulties with abstract reasoning.

Dysexecutive symptoms can present as non-cooperation, passivity (not participating), or taking over the group due to difficulties with self-monitoring. It can also be misconstrued as laziness or disinterest. Unlike memory difficulties, dysexecutive problems can have a 'personal' feel to them. This can be a source of conflict within groups, both for members and facilitators.

For those with organizational difficulties, an organizational period before and at the end of the group, during which the client is prepared for what will happen in the group and in what order, can be helpful. A session outline on a one-page handout may be beneficial, and this handout can be referred to in the session to provide a framework for the client. At times, the therapist may need to be more directive. The use of hand signals to indicate any inappropriate behaviour may be helpful, but would need to be sensitively agreed with the client beforehand. Citing the client's name may also assist those tangential clients that need refocusing.

Deficits in abstract reasoning and problem solving are likely to hamper the delivery of CBT groups unless aspects are modified. Language may need to be more concrete and pertaining to the individual. Existential concepts such as choice and responsibility will need to be made concrete, with relevant applications made to the client's life. It will help if the therapist or other group members can supply or suggest 'alternative' cognitions. More concrete and accessible techniques of CBT, such as 'behavioural activation' (scheduling in activities to encourage patients to approach activities that they are avoiding), may be beneficial (Mitcheson, Maslin, Meynon, Morrisson, Hill, & Wanigaratne, 2010).

Difficulties with inhibition and turn-taking (shown through interrupting others or not sharing time within the group) can feel rather alienating and cause annoyance to other groups members. Here it is necessary for facilitators to use very explicit reinforcement of turn-taking in the group and encourage feedback from other group members. Those who have difficulty with shifting topics can be helped if facilitators alert group members before shifting the topic and summarize at each end of the topic, i.e., 'We have finished talking about x, now let's discuss y'. For those groups for which planning is required (for example, planning for a job interview), the use of a planning guide where each step is clearly delineated may be beneficial.

Apathy or lack of motivation may be a key limiting factor. It is therefore vital at the beginning of group therapy, when engagement takes place, to spend time building a therapeutic alliance, particularly when the client has significant cognitive deficits and feels hopeless about the future.

Specific cognitive remediation groups

Although memory training groups and computerized cognitive training strategies that 'exercise memory' have shown improvement on tests, unfortunately there is little evidence that such improvements generalize to everyday life. Sadly, restoration is presently an unrealistic goal (Glisky, Schacter, & Tulving, 1986) and compensatory approaches are the treatment of choice (Robertson & Murre, 1999).

Groups can helpfully offer specific psycho-education regarding the mechanisms of cognitive damage, likely cognitive difficulties, and compensatory strategies that can be used (Scheurich et al., 2004). Such groups can be readily integrated into a substance misuse group programme.

Case examples

The client with ADHD, self-regulation difficulties and poor social skills

A 25-year-old client with pre-morbid ADHD and co-morbid cocaine and alcohol dependency interrupts the group facilitator and other group members continually throughout a group session. When the therapist stands up to signal the end of a session, he raises his voice and starts to talk about how others have not offered much to the group today. When the group facilitator asks him to summarize what he has learnt from the group, he says he cannot remember.

Strategies

- Individual time with the client to discuss group goals that may relate to maintaining focus and self-monitoring.
- Reduce distractions in environment—keep group room clutter-free and minimize external noise.
- Explicit focus at the beginning of the group on social skills that are required in groups, such as turn-taking, sharing and listening skills, and strong reinforcement when clients demonstrate this.
- Visual cues on flipchart to focus attention during the group session.
- Salient, directive statements when the client has interrupted in the session, commenting on the process 'you are interrupting me'. Encouragement of other group members to give regular feedback to the client.
- Break half-way through group.

The client with alcohol-related brain damage and memory difficulties

A 56-year-old client with alcohol-related brain damage showed difficulties in remembering information from the groups. He was not able to summarize the information that he learnt in the group and was not able to retain information to use in his recovery. He became apathetic and depressed, and felt that he was not gaining much out of the group programme. He began craving alcohol and requested to be discharged.

Strategies

- Client keeps notebook during the group and records key words.
- Facilitators highlight key words on a whiteboard.
- Enhancement of encoding via repetition, summarizing, and the use of visual prompts.
- A handout summary of the session to be read with client in one-to-one session.
- A post-group follow-up to reinforce information. The client is asked to recall what he has learnt and how this applies to his own recovery.
- The use of activity scheduling (with strong rewarding activities) for depressed mood. Client to have a 'review of the day' to summarize key messages from groups and to record pleasurable activities from the day.

Conclusions

Research has demonstrated that substance misuse can lead to varying types and degrees of neuropsychological dysfunction, which have immense psychological and social importance in the process of rehabilitation and recovery. Clinical experience suggests that cognitive deficits in attention, memory, and executive functioning compromise engagement in rehabilitation, treatment efficacy, and recovery. Although very motivated to change, clients with cognitive impairments are vulnerable to experiencing poorer functioning and may be more vulnerable to relapse. Integrating individuals with varying levels of cognitive ability into recovery groups can be achieved with minor modifications and adjustments. This can help improve the function of impaired clients without adversely affecting less-impaired clients.

References

Ardila, A., Rosselli, M., & Strumwasser, S. (1991). Neuropsychological deficits in chronic cocaine abusers. *International Journal of Neuroscience, 57*, 73–79.

Baddeley, A. D., & Wilson, B. A. (1994). When implicit learning fails: Amnesia and the problem of error elimination. *Neuropsychologia, 32*, 53–68.

Bechara, A., Dolan, S., Denburg, N., Hindes, A., Anderson, S. W., & Nathan, P. E. (2001). Decision making deficits linked to a dysfunctional ventromedical prefrontal cortex, revealed in alcohol and stimulant abusers. *Neuropsychologia, 39*, 376–380.

Brandt, J., Butters, N., Ryan, C., & Bayog, R. (1983). Cognitive loss and recovery in long term alcohol abusers. *Archives of General Psychiatry*, *40*, 435–442.

Burgess, N., & Alderman, P. (2004). Executive dysfunction. In L. H. Goldstein & J. E. McNeil (Eds.), *Clinical neuropsychology. A practical guide to assessment and management for clinicians*. Chichester: Wiley.

Charness, M. E. (1993). Brain lesions in alcoholics. *Alcoholism: Clinical and Experimental Research*, *17*, 2–11.

Clare, L., Wilson, B. A., Carter, G., Roth, I., & Hodges, J. R. (2002). Relearning face-name associations in early Alzheimer's disease. *Neuropsychology*, *16*, 538–547.

Fals-Stewart, W., Schafrer, J., Lucente, S., Rustine, T., & Brown, L. (1994). Neurobehavioral consequences of prolonged alcohol and substance abuse: A review of findings and treatment implications. *Clinical Psychology Review*, *14*, 755–778.

Gerhart, K. A., Mellick, D. C., & Weintraub, A. H. (2003). Violence-related traumatic brain injury: A population-based study. *Journal of Trauma*, *55*, 1045–1053.

Glisky, E. L., Schacter, D. L., & Tulving, E. (1986). Computer learning by memory-impaired patients: Acquisition and retention of complex knowledge. *Neuropsychologia*, *24*, 313–328.

Jernigan, D. H. (1991). Alcohol and head trauma: Strategies for prevention. *Journal of Head Trauma Rehabilitation*, *6*, 48–59.

Knight, R. G., & Longmore, B. E. (1994). *Clinical neuropsychology of alcoholism*. Hove: Lawrence Erlbaum.

London, E. D., Ernst, M., Grant, S., Bonson, K., & Weinstein, A. (2000). Orbito-frontal cortex and human drug abuse. Functional imaging. *Cerebral Cortex*, *10*, 334–342.

Manning, V., Wanigaratne, S., Hill, R., Reed, L. J., Strang, J., Gossop, M., Marshall, E. J., & Best, D. (2008). Changes in neuropsychological functioning during alcohol detoxification. *European Addiction Research*, *484*, 1–8.

Mitcheson, L., Maslin, J., Meynon, T., Morrisson, T., Hill, R., & Wanigaratne, S. (2010). *Applied cognitive and behavioural approaches to the treatment of addiction: A practical treatment guide*. Chichester: Wiley-Blackwell.

Parkin, A. J., Hunkin, N. M., & Squires, E. J. (1998). Unlearning John Major: The use of errorless learning in the reacquisition of proper names following herpes simplex encephalitis. *Cognitive Neuropsychology*, *15*, 361–375.

Parrott, A. C., & Lasky, J. (1998). Ecstasy (MDMA) effects upon mood and cognition. *Psychopharmacology*, *139*, 261–268.

Pope, H. G., & Yurgelun-Todd, D. (1996). The residual cognitive effects of heavy marijuana use. *JAMA*, *275*, 521–527.

Powell, J. (2004). The effects of medication on cognitive functioning. In L. H. Goldstein, & J. McNeil (Eds.), *Clinical neuropsychology. A practical guide to assessment and management for clinicians*. Chichester: Wiley.

Robertson, I., & Murre, J. (1999). Rehabilitation of brain damage: Brain plasticity and principles of guided recovery. *Psychological Bulletin*, *125*, 544–575.

Rosenthal, T. L., & Meyer, V. (1971). Behavioral treatment of clinical abulia. *Integrative Psychological and Behavioral Science*, *6*, 22–29.

Ryan, C., & Butters, N. (1986). Neuropsychology of alcoholism. In D. Wedding, A.

M. Horton Jr, & J. S. Webster (Eds.), *The neuropsychology handbook*. New York: Springer.

Scheurich, A., Müller, M. J., Szegedi, A., Anghelescu, I., Klawe, C., Lörch, B., Kappis, B., Bialonski, H.-G., Haas, S., & Hautzinger, M. (2004). Neuropsychological status of alcohol-dependent patients: Increased performance through goal-setting instructions. *Alcohol and Alcoholism*, *39*, 119–125.

Solowij, N. (1998) *Cannabis and cognitive functioning*. Cambridge: Cambridge University Press.

Tarter, R. E., Butters, M., & Beers, S. R. (2001). *Medical neuropsychology*. New York: Springer.

Teichner, G., Horner, M. D., Roitzsch, J. C., Herron, J., & Thevos, A. (2002). Substance abuse treatment outcomes for cognitively impaired and intact outpatients. *Addictive Behaviours*, *27*, 751–763.

Wilson, B., & Moffat, N. (1984). *Clinical management of memory problems*. London: Croom Helm.

Chapter 15

Co-morbidity in groups

Rachel Davies

Introduction

'The term 'dual diagnosis' covers a broad spectrum of mental health and substance misuse problems that an individual might experience concurrently' (Department of Health, 2002, p. 9). The term 'co-morbidity' is also used to describe dual diagnosis (Department of Health, 2007) and, as the European Monitoring Centre in Drug Dependence and Alcohol (EMCDDA, 2004) states, can encompass the presence of substance misuse with psychiatric or personality disorders. There are a range of mechanisms that describe the complex relationship between substance misuse and mental health issues. These include:

1   A primary psychiatric illness precipitating or leading to substance misuse.
2   Substance misuse worsening or altering the course of a psychiatric illness.
3   Intoxication and/or substance dependence leading to psychological symptoms.
4   Substance misuse and/or withdrawal leading to psychiatric symptoms or illnesses. (Department of Health, 2002, p. 9)

There is a high prevalence of dual diagnosis among clients attending mental health services and vice versa. Weaver et al. (2003) found that 44% of their sample of patients attending mental health services self-reported problematic drug use, and/or were assessed as having used alcohol at hazardous or harmful levels in the past year. They also found mental health problems among 75% of clients within the drug services and 85% of clients within alcohol services. EMCDDA (2005) found that 80% of individuals with a drug dependency diagnosis have co-morbid psychiatric disorders. It has been suggested that mental health needs may not be sufficiently treated within substance misuse services (Weaver et al., 2003) and vice versa. Furthermore, dual diagnosis is associated with a range of negative and complex factors, including higher rates of completed suicides, worsening psychiatric symptoms, housing instability, poorer levels of social functioning including negative impact on carers and family, less compliance with treatment, and increased contact with the criminal justice system (Department of Health, 2007).

There are several hypotheses that offer explanations for the close link between substance use and mental health problems. Arguably, the most important of these is the self-medication hypothesis formulated by Khantzian and Albanese (2008). Essentially, the self-medication hypothesis suggests that individuals use a drug of choice to relieve symptoms of an underlying disorder or condition, such as anxiety or depression. The obverse of this is that the use of drugs and alcohol actually cause such disorders, and while this chapter does not explore the 'recursive interface between psychopathology and drug use', interested readers can refer to a number of useful texts on co-morbidity (Stewart & Conrod, 2010; Versta, Brady, Galanter, & Conrod, 2011). The primary aim of this chapter is to offer some practical ideas of how to manage co-morbidity within a group, whatever its cause.

Clients with anxiety disorders

How to recognize common anxiety disorders

Anxiety disorders cover a wide range of problems, including panic disorder, social phobia, generalized anxiety disorder, and obsessive compulsive disorder. While post-traumatic stress disorder is also classified as an anxiety disorder, this will be discussed in a separate section.

Panic is a sudden episode of fear with physical symptoms plus a feeling of impending disaster. Panic attacks are discrete episodes of anxiety that cause physical symptoms of increased heart rate, chest pain, nausea, difficulty in breathing, sweating, dizziness, feeling faint, tingling of the fingers, hot and cold flushes, trembling, difficulty swallowing, and a strange feeling of unreality. Because of these strange and severe feelings, most people have a specific fear about what would happen if the attack continued, e.g., dying, choking, fainting, losing control. While many people with panic disorder will function perfectly well in groups, they may experience discomfort being in a closed space or room for any length of time, difficulties in talking in front of others (elevated heartbeat may be mistaken for a panic attack), and feel the need to sit near to or in sight of the exit.

Social phobia is a type of anxiety provoked by exposure to specific social or performance situations that typically leads to avoidance behaviour. Social phobia is a highly prevalent anxiety disorder, particularly among clients with alcohol dependence and by its very nature means that work done in any social or group setting is difficult. Possible behaviours include agitation, restlessness, difficulties sitting still, avoidance of eye contact, and difficulties sharing in front of others. Clients may also place themselves in an unobtrusive place, e.g., choosing to sit in the corner so that they feel safer and do not feel too exposed. They may also try to avoid groups altogether, or excuse themselves from it once started. It is important to recognize that this is not a motivational issue, but one intimately connected to the illness or disorder.

Generalized anxiety disorder is an anxiety disorder that is characterized by persistent and excessive anxiety and worry. Clients suffering from generalized anxiety disorder are likely to report distress because of constant worrying about everyday eventualities. In the group they may appear restless, agitated, have difficulty concentrating, and become tired easily.

Obsessive-compulsive disorder is characterized by obsessions (which cause marked anxiety or distress) and/or by compulsions. Unless particularly severe, these are not likely to interrupt group participation, although some clients may have difficulty attending punctually if they are caught up in rituals, or they may show some rigidity in the way things are done, particularly when participating in tasks. Rigidity is likely to be particularly evident in those individuals with obsessive personality disorder; this is discussed later in the chapter.

How to work with anxiety

As a group facilitator you will need to weigh up and judge whether having a very anxious person in the group is in the best interests of the individual themselves and of other group members. If group attendance is compulsory and an anxious client has a negative group experience, that person is even less likely to participate in subsequent groups. You also run the risk of losing their trust and damaging your therapeutic alliance, and that client may even leave treatment. Keep in mind that confronting fears, in the absence of alternative coping strategies to manage anxiety, may also increase 'cravings' for alcohol/substances and might result in lapse. You might wish therefore to consider a graded approach to group attendance and participation. A good first step on the hierarchy might be to encourage attendance at didactic/teaching groups, where less participation is expected, or groups with smaller numbers of participants. If at all possible, offer the groups in the same environment with a set structure so the client knows what to expect and is prepared for activities.

It may be beneficial to start the group by guiding the members through a relaxation exercise. It is helpful to give clear instructions in a matter-of-fact and logical manner, avoiding hasty presentations and lots of changes during the activity. It will help anxious group members if you as a facilitator can remain calm. It is important that group facilitators are aware of clients' anxieties and only encourage clients to speak and participate when they feel ready; refrain from 'pouncing' on them and directly asking for their participation. Remember that anxiety may show itself in agitated behaviour or fidgeting, and that it will be unhelpful to call attention to this during the group. Similarly, excessive talking that stems from anxiety may be best diverted by encouraging others to join in the conversation.

It can be helpful to meet afterwards to discuss their experience, evaluate new beliefs, and agree their next step that will build on their confidence.

Clients with traumatic past experiences

How to recognize possible signs of past trauma

Post-traumatic stress disorder or PTSD is the name given to a pattern of symptoms that happen after someone has experienced or witnessed a traumatic event. The trauma can vary from natural disasters such as floods and earthquakes to man-made events like traffic accidents, wars, violent attacks, rape, and sexual abuse.

An event is called 'traumatic' when it is 'outside the ordinary range of human experience' and involves actual or threatened death, injury or safety of the self or another person.

The main symptoms of PTSD are:

- Re-experiencing: feeling as though the trauma is happening again. This can take the form of nightmares and flashbacks where pictures or thoughts related to the trauma flash through your mind.
- Avoidance or numbing: trying to avoid situations/feelings/thoughts that are reminders of the trauma, or feelings of numbness and inability to feel or enjoy life.
- Hyper-arousal: where people feel restless, on edge, jumpy, unable to sleep or concentrate.

In a group setting such clients may manifest the following behaviours:

- Avoidance of thoughts, feelings, and conversations about anything that reminds them of the trauma. They may avoid talking about certain topics, places, people, or personal history that reminds them of the trauma; conversations might feel guarded or disjointed with significant information missing.
- Become distressed by what other people might see as 'nothing' but for the individual was a reminder of the trauma. Individuals are unlikely to be able to explain this within the group setting.
- Be hyper-vigilant. Individuals may arrive early at groups to make sure they can sit where they can see the exits and watch people arrive to make sure the group feels safe for them. They might seem jumpy and on edge.

- Seem lost in thought, distracted, not following the group process. This can happen when the client is re-experiencing an event from the past.

How to work with clients showing signs of trauma

Sometimes clients with traumatic past experiences find it difficult to attend groups and would therefore rather avoid them. This can be because it is simply too painful to think, feel, or talk about their traumatic experiences and they may have strong fears of being overwhelmed by emotion. While being careful not to dismiss their real sense of distress, it may help to explain to the individual that they are not alone in their experiences and that unfortunately many clients entering substance misuse treatment have experienced a great deal of trauma and will understand their struggles. You may wish to ask the client whether they want to discuss these experiences on an individual basis outside the group, and reassure them that they will not be expected to discuss them within the group. You may further wish to agree a phrase such as 'that is not something I want to talk about now', which indicates to the group facilitator that the issue relates in some way to the trauma and is not appropriate for the group discussion. Clients may also benefit from learning some 'here-and-now' coping strategies to respond to flashbacks during the group, such as grounding techniques.

Clients with depression

How to recognize signs of depression

Although depression can manifest itself in a number of ways, there are often a number of typical symptoms and these would include:

- Persistent low mood.
- Difficulties concentrating.
- Feeling restless, agitated, or irritable.
- Loss of appetite and weight, or gaining weight.
- Feeling hopeless about the future.
- Not wishing to be around other people.
- Loss of confidence.
- Physical aches and pains, e.g., back ache without physical cause.
- Loss of interest in sex.
- Feelings of worthlessness or excessive guilt.

In the group context, clients experiencing depression may:

- Become tearful or distressed.
- Only focus on their failings and what they have done wrong.

- Express a high level of negative thoughts and/or feelings.
- Seem unmotivated and reluctant to participate in any activities or conversations, even pleasurable activities.
- Appear as though everything is an effort.

How to work with signs of depression

Firstly, it is important to realize that it may take enormous effort for someone suffering depression to even attend a group, let alone participate in activities. They may further look like they do not want to be helped, when actually they are longing for someone to care and listen. Someone feeling depressed may need extra time to react to events and express their ideas. They are also likely to find it difficult to take in positive feedback and for this reason it is helpful to find clear ways to give genuine positive feedback for any effort made in the group. It can be helpful to incorporate some pleasurable activities or tasks in the group that have a guaranteed chance of success, since the satisfaction of achievement can boost mood and is also good modelling to generalize outside the group.

If a group member becomes tearful or distressed, it is helpful to acknowledge their distress. I find it helpful to ask the client whether they would like to talk a little about what is distressing them in the group or would prefer to wait until after the group. Although offering support may sometimes mean side-tracking from the specific topic of a structured group, I have learned not to ignore distressed behaviour since the group can perceive this as uncaring facilitation and can then take on the role of 'counsellor' focusing on the distressed client. I would be mindful of the balance between offering time to explore feelings and creating opportunities for group members to discover shared experiences, while directing away from self-preoccupied talk which may limit group interaction and alienate other group members.

You can also offer individual support after the group session. You should always take suicidal threats and ideas seriously and follow up on these after the group, checking in with the client, making safety plans, and ensuring that you report concerns to others involved in the client's care. Clients attending substance misuse services can be vulnerable and may feel desperate enough to attempt suicide.

Clients experiencing a manic episode

How to recognize signs of mania

A manic episode is defined as a distinct period in which there is an abnormally and persistently elevated, expansive, or irritable mood. You may notice that the person shows an inflated self-esteem or grandiosity, a decreased need for sleep, is more talkative than usual or show a pressure to keep talking. They may demonstrate flight of ideas or a subjective experience that thoughts are racing while being easily distracted. They may display an increase in goal-directed activity or psychomotor agitation and excessive involvement in pleasurable activities that have a high potential for painful consequences.

In the group they may:

- Not stop talking! (Even if you directly ask them to stop talking and ask them to give others a turn.)
- Think they have all the answers and know best.
- Keep changing topics and find it difficult to stay on subject even when encouraged to.
- Finish tasks very quickly but perhaps incompletely or incorrectly.
- Be unable to sit still and want to move about the room.
- Create a 'buzz' in the group and get the other group members excited.

How to work with signs of mania

Without prior experience, you might think that having a 'very happy' person in the group is wonderful. However, manic group behaviour has the potential to be destructive for both the group and individual. Someone who is experiencing mania or elated mood may easily become frustrated and irritable, and express this through an aggressive outburst. Their responses may seem out-of-proportion to the situation or stimuli in terms of intensity and duration. This can influence group processes and many clients can also later regret words said or actions taken during a manic episode. As facilitators, it will help enormously to remain calm, consistent, and matter-of-fact. This might mean providing clear boundaries around unacceptable behaviour like aggression or domineering in the group. However, manic behaviours may not be controllable and it may be necessary to ask the member to leave the session on this occasion. This not only helps the group to keep on track, but also offers some protection to the person who is experiencing mania.

If the client is talking about a lot of different things at once, then you can handle their distractibility and flight of ideas by constantly bringing the client's attention back to the topic of the group. This also opens up the discussion to other group members. If the group member is expressing grandiose or inaccurate ideas, I find it helpful to say something like 'I know that is what you believe, but that is not the same way that I see it.' By saying this, I avoid agreeing with what they are saying and reinforcing their beliefs while also avoiding direct confrontation that may lead to aggressive outbursts.

Since individuals with mania experience time as moving faster than objective time, it can help to offer short-focused groups where gratification and task satisfaction are guaranteed. Activities that demand a wide range of movement can also be used to channel energy.

Clients with schizophrenia or psychosis

How to recognize schizophrenia and psychosis

Schizophrenia is a serious mental illness that lasts for at least six months and includes at least one month of symptoms such as delusions, halluci-nations, disorganized speech, grossly disorganized or catatonic behaviour, or negative symptoms.

In an addictions setting, you are unlikely to have clients with acute symptoms in the group, but are more likely to see negative symptoms of schizophrenia. Negative symptoms include affective flattening (where the person's face appears immobile and unresponsive and there is reduced eye contact and body language), alogia (limited speech, where responses are brief and empty), and avolition (where they are unable to initiate and persist in goal-directed activities).

In the group they may show negative and/or positive symptoms.

Negative symptoms:
- Unmotivated to do anything.
- Find it hard to make decisions.
- Likely to stop an activity the moment this becomes slightly difficult, or if they have to work at it.
- Only respond with short answers with little emotion.

Positive/acute symptoms:
- Exhibit peculiar behaviour (responding to something you cannot hear or see).
- Express strange ideas and concepts.
- Be paranoid and misinterpret what others say or do.

How to work with schizophrenia and psychosis

Since individuals with schizophrenia typically find it difficult to select and order incoming stimuli, they may become overwhelmed or distracted by multiple stimuli. It is therefore important that you hold the group in a neat, well-structured area with as few stimuli as possible. Arranging the seating in a circle encourages socialization.

While such clients are likely to have difficulties making decisions, this is an empowering process when opportunities with clear limited choices are offered. Clients are likely to find it hard to engage in activities and will respond well when any effort is affirmed and rewarded.

As a general rule it helps to be calm and friendly. Try not to enter into the hallucinations or delusions, accept that they are real to the client, validate their distress, but tell the client that you do not see or hear the same thing. Find ways to bring clients back to reality by referring to something within the group like 'coming back to what 'John' said about . . .'. If they become very distressed, it may be best for them to leave the group. It may be worth considering avoiding note-taking when working with someone showing signs of paranoia or invite them to read your notes. If they misinterpret what someone has said, encourage them to check or clarify what the other person intended.

Clients with attention-deficit hyperactivity disorder (ADHD)

How to recognize ADHD

ADHD is characterized by prominent symptoms of inattention and/or hyperactivity-impulsivity. Symptoms can include failing to pay close attention to detail, difficulty sustaining attention, difficulties in listening and following instructions, difficulty in planning tasks and activities, fidgeting or being always 'on the go', and difficulties in waiting one's turn.

In the group they may:

- find sitting still for any length of time impossible
- be unable to concentrate and follow instructions
- not be able to focus on what is being said, even if they are interested in the group
- be easily distracted by anything
- interrupt others rather than wait for their turn to speak.

How to work with ADHD

Recent research has suggested that people with ADHD perceive time to pass more slowly than those without ADHD and this may help explain their restlessness on tasks. With this in mind, it will help to offer short focused groups. If possible you may want to grade the group in terms of length of time attending or engaging in the group; an initial step may be to attend for 15 minutes or that after 15 minutes they can stand up and walk around the room.

If possible, ensure that the group is made up of short tasks; it helps if activities demand movement to channel their energy. If you have discussed this with the individual before the group sessions, it may be appropriate to allocate the individual a task such as writing down ideas on the whiteboard so that they have something physical to do in the group. Please be mindful that many clients with ADHD will have had negative school experiences and may be reluctant to do activities that remind them of school. If you use worksheets, handouts, or give 'homework' in the group, you need to explain that, unlike school, there are no right or wrong answers and that they can choose to share their work if they want to, but they are not obliged to. Just as with clients with mania, encourage the client to bring their attention back to the group topic.

Clients with a personality disorder

How to recognize personality disorders

EMCDDA (2004) found that in clinical prevalence samples 50–90% of the drug users were reported to suffer from a personality disorder. Within this population, we most commonly meet with clients who have a borderline personality disorder and this is discussed in Chapter 17. We are also likely to work with clients with antisocial personality disorder, dependent personality disorder, avoidant personality disorder, and obsessive personality disorder. The next section provides a brief outline of the key characteristics and some suggestions for working with these within a group setting.

- Antisocial personality disorder is characterized by a pattern of disregard for and violation of the rights of others.
- Dependent personality disorder is characterized by an excessive need to be taken care of and submissive behaviour.
- Avoidant personality disorder is characterized by feelings of inadequacy, and hypersensitivity to negative evaluation resulting in interpersonal avoidance.
- Obsessive-compulsive personality disorder is characterized by a preoccupation with orderliness, perfectionism, and control.

People with personality disorders have deeply ingrained maladaptive behavioural patterns and tend to react in a stereotyped way to a variety of life stresses. Although they may appear to be coping, behind their façade they could be struggling to cope with stress, feeling lonely and isolated, have low self-esteem, and also be struggling to form meaningful relationships.

Key considerations when working with individuals with personality disorder within a generic group

- When working with this client group, ensure that you have an up-to-date risk assessment because you need to be aware of whether they pose a risk to themselves or others, and have an appropriate plan in place.

- This client group is likely to evoke a range of strong emotions within you and it is essential that you are mindful to remain consistent, show acceptance, concern, genuineness, and empathy.
- Remember that 'having a personality disorder' is not a choice but rather is a result of earlier experiences, is way of coping and of 'being'. Individuals cannot be different just because you ask them to be.
- This client group is likely to divide teams because they evoke different emotions in different people. It is in the best interests of the client that you regularly discuss their treatment as a team and share your differing views of the client.
- Regular supervision is essential when working with this client group.
- Ensure that you set clear guidelines for the group, with realistic objectives and goals.
- Establish boundaries for acceptable and unacceptable behaviour within the group and be explicit about the consequences of these behaviours. You may have to ask a group member to leave the group if they become aggressive or abusive.
- Reinforce that just being in the group can be a useful experience in terms of being with other people and adhering to boundaries.
- It can be helpful to map out the personality disorder profile with the individual's reasons for using drugs and alcohol (this can be followed up in individual sessions rather than form part of the group focus).

'Specific' versus 'generic' groups within addictions services

There is an interesting debate to be had about specific versus generic groups within addiction. By 'specific' groups, I mean that group membership relates to the mental health disorder and that the group are also dependent substance misusers. By 'generic' groups, I mean groups for substance misusers. Integrated treatment is considered the model of excellence in the treatment of dual diagnosis (Department of Health, 2002). This is when psychiatric and substance-misuse interventions are provided in a coordinated manner by the same staff member (or clinical team) working in a single setting. There is, however, a debate as to whether separate groups should be offered to address the different needs of this client group. There are, of course, advantages and disadvantages to offering specific groups for specific diagnoses or symptoms. On the positive side, clients may feel less isolated, less 'different' within the group, and more comfortable discussing their difficulties when they know all the other group members have similar experiences. They may engage more fully with the treatment if they believe all their needs are being met, not just addiction needs. This might also allow staff to be trained to manage specific situations that are likely to occur with a particular client group, e.g., very socially anxious clients, rather than applying general training to meet all possibilities. It may also allow the group to be structured to best meet the needs of the particular client group, such as a shorter group that includes active tasks and opportunities to move around for clients with ADHD.

However, specific groups might make these clients 'special', cause segregation within the client group as a whole, and also runs contrary to the Mental Health and Social Exclusion Report (Social Exclusion Unit, 2004) that aims to reduce stigma and discrimination among dual diagnosis clients. There is also the potential to get caught up in attempts to 'fix' or 'cure' the mental health issue and lose sight of the addiction, even though there may be a direct cause-and-effect relationship between these issues. Furthermore, if clients with dual diagnosis are only asked to attend groups specifically for them, this may create an artificial environment that does not reflect the communities they will return to or will face daily. Due to the variety of different diagnoses among substance misuse clients, it is also likely that there may not always be sufficient numbers of clients to run a therapeutic group. Last, but definitely not least, are the resource and financial implications of offering specific groups to a small minority of clients.

If your service is fortunate enough to have the resources to enable you to offer specific groups, then I would focus my attention on offering: (1) groups that meet the majority of clients' needs; (2) specific groups for clients who are unable to tolerate generic group situations, such as those with social anxiety; and (3) specific groups for clients whose presentation is too disruptive for generic groups, such as ADHD and mania.

Conclusion

This chapter does not tell you how to run groups for specific mental health disorders since this would require several books in their own right, but rather I hope that it has provided an overview for readers working with generic groups to consider in their group practice. I also hope that through reading this chapter, it will encourage facilitators to view behaviours associated with co-morbidity not as 'intentional', disruptive behaviour to be 'punished', but more as useful information about where the client is and their complex needs. Facilitators can hold this information in mind, safely hold the client and group, and feed back pertinent information into ongoing treatment systems. Client presentation during the group will add useful information to individual work and specific needs that arise, particularly when you notice changes in behaviour or mood. For example, it is essential to feed back to the team working with a group member if they start exhibiting signs of paranoia or hallucinations because this may indicate a deterioration of their mental state and may require their medication to be reassessed. Furthermore, some information disclosed within the group may not be appropriate for the group and should therefore be discussed on an individual basis.

I further hope that I have been able to communicate that clients with co-morbidity are likely to be grappling with complex and long-standing difficulties, both in their internal and external worlds. Frequently this struggle becomes magnified within a group context. Ambivalence about changing substance misuse is expected among clients without mental health difficulties; ambivalence can also be anticipated from clients with dual diagnosis, clients for whom the prospect of 'giving-up' long-standing, well-used coping strategies may induce deep fear and uncertainty about their ability to cope. As the group facilitator, it is essential to convey the belief that they have the ability to make changes and learn to cope, while being aware and accepting of their uncertainties.

References

Department of Health (2002). *Mental health policy implementation guide. Dual diagnosis good practice guide.* London: Department of Health Publications.

Department of Health (England) and the devolved administrations (2007). *Drug misuse and dependence: UK guidelines on clinical management.* London: Department of Health (England), the Scottish Government, Welsh Assembly Government and Northern Ireland Executive.

European Monitoring Centre in Drug Dependence and Alcohol (2004). Selected issue 3: Co-morbidity. In *Annual Report 2004: The state of the drugs problem in the European Union and Norway* (pp. 94–102). Luxembourg: European Monitoring Centre for Drugs and Drug Addiction. Office for Official Publications of the European Communities.

European Monitoring Centre in Drug Dependence and Alcohol (2005). Co-morbidity—drug use and mental disorders. *Drugs in Focus*, 14. Lisbon: European Monitoring Centre for Drugs and Drug Addiction.

Khantzian, E. J., & Albanese, M. J. (2008). *Understanding addiction as self medication: Finding hope behind the pain.* New York: Rowman & Littlefield.

Social Exclusion Unit (2004). *Mental health and social exclusion report summary.* London: Office of the Deputy Prime Minister.

Stewart, S. H., & Conrod, P. (2010). *Anxiety and substance use disorders: The vicious cycle of comorbidity.* New York: Springer.

Versta, J. C., Brady, K., Galanter, M., & Conrod, P. (2011). *Drug abuse and addiction in mental illness: Causes, consequences and treatment.* London: Humana Press.

Weaver, T., Madden, P., Charles, V., Stimson, G., Renton, A., Tyrer, P., Barnes, T., Bench, C., Middleton, H., Wright, N., Paterson, S., Shanahan, W., Seivewright, N., & Ford, C. (2003). Comorbidity of substance misuse and mental illness in community mental health and substance misuse services. *The British Journal of Psychiatry*, *183*, 304–313.

Chapter 16

Working with drug users in the criminal justice setting

Tim Meynen and Nancy Akrasi

After recent changes in the UK criminal justice system, a greater number of offenders now access addiction treatment services. Although there are still conflicting views as to what constitutes effective treatment for this clinical population, there is emerging evidence from both the addiction and criminal justice literature that structured group work can be effective in reducing drug use and criminal activity, especially when based on Cognitive Behavioural Therapy principles. This chapter draws together ideas from the UK literature and our experience in the field to help those designing and running groups for offenders based in partnership addiction treatment services. Four main issues are considered: (1) partnership working; (2) support systems for group facilitators; (3) group content; and (4) effective ways to deliver groups.

Background

Substance users have more frequent contact with the criminal justice system than the general population (McSweeney & Hough, 2005). There is also clear evidence that substance use is linked to criminal behaviour (e.g., Liriano & Ramsay, 2003). Typically, this link occurs when offences are committed through possession, when criminal activity is used to obtain money for substances, or when offences relating to the substance-using lifestyle occur, e.g., anti-social behaviour caused by intoxication, drink driving, and violent behaviour. In recognition of this and the potential to 'treat' offenders perceived to have substance misuse problems, there have been some significant changes made to both the policy and structure of the British criminal justice system since the early 1990s. Changes such as the creation of the Drug Intervention Programme in 2003, testing on arrest or charge in 2005, and restrictions on bail in 2003 have dramatically increased the numbers of offenders with drug and alcohol problems given the opportunity to engage with treatment services.

While there have been some conflicting results from meta-analyses as to whether treatment of substance use and offending behaviour is effective (e.g., Holloway, Bennett, & Farrington, 2005), some major UK studies have produced encouraging results (Gossop, 2005; McIntosh, Bloor, & Robertson, 2007). Other meta-analytic reviews have found evidence to suggest that structured, cognitive behavioural groups delivered by highly trained staff in well-organized treatment programmes can be effective in addressing criminal behaviour in general and in reducing rates of re-offending (McGuire, 2002; Wilson, Allen Bouffard, & Mackenzie, 2005; Morgan & Flora, 2002). 'Reasoning and Rehabilitation' (Ross & Fabiano, 1985) and 'Think First' (McGuire, 2000) are good examples of structured cognitive behavioural programmes; they assume a link between cognitions and offending, and aim to promote new thinking styles that facilitate pro-social behaviour. They largely focus on exploring and developing positive personal and social values, increasing social problem-solving skills, promoting reflective thinking, critical reasoning, and challenging attitudes and beliefs that support criminal behaviour. These programmes emphasize how new learning is promoted by repeated exposure to material and encouraging homework exercises, as well as using interactive teaching methods like role-play and rehearsal.

Programmes to specifically address substance misuse have also been developed in the Probation Service, one of which, Addressing Substance-Related Offending (ASRO; McMurran & Priestley, 1999, 2004), was developed for group work. It is a cognitive behavioural group designed to address motivation to change current substance use and offending, to closely examine this reciprocal relationship, and to increase knowledge and confidence in using skills to manage drug/alcohol use.

The recovery movement in the substance-use field (e.g., White, 2005) and the desistance narrative in the criminal justice literature (e.g., McNeil, 2006) have highlighted how similar processes play a crucial role in supporting long-term behaviour change. Firstly, both literatures view long-term change as a process that can take place over many years. Group programmes can introduce offenders to ideas and skills to change. However, these are time-limited and what happens after the group is of equal significance in determining whether the new knowledge and skills are used by the offender to help them develop more pro-social roles and opportunities away from substance and/or offending. Secondly, the literature stresses that change can be stimulated and sustained by shifts in personal identity and values (Kearney & O'Sullivan, 2003), and the development of pro-social activities and relationships that foster a feeling of social inclusion (Farrall, 2002). Thirdly, the literature highlights the cognitive aspects of long-term behavioural change, arguing that while events are important in helping a person change, the individual's perception of these events is more important.

Partnership working

The following section raises some issues that are important to consider when offering groups to offenders within partnership addiction treatment services.

Firstly, it is important to be aware that the success of group work will be determined by the quality of the relationship between the treatment provider and criminal justice system. This relationship should be built on systems that promote a collaborative understanding and working alliance, maximizing the potential for effective communication between the services. Unfortunately, these basic concepts can easily be forgotten, since the goals of the treatment provider are very different from their criminal justice partners: whereas the treatment provider is focused on rehabilitation and recovery, the criminal justice system is guided by protecting the general public, primarily through punishment. This difference in core philosophies sometimes creates difficulties for criminal justice staff, treatment providers, and offenders that are hard to reconcile. The following considerations help to safeguard against this.

- Group facilitators should be fully aware of the legal issues associated with group attendance and the implications of non-attendance or non-participation. Roles also need to be clearly delineated so that the treatment provider is responsible for the safe management of the group, but not for addressing the implications for non-attendance and legal issues.
- Regular communication between the group facilitator, criminal justice staff, and offender is essential. This can be supported by clear joint working protocols for sharing clinical information and regular inter-agency meetings to clarify inter-agency goals and problem-solve any difficulties. This will foster collaborative working and appreciation of one another's roles. Group facilitators will need to feed back to criminal justice staff information about attendance and adherence to court orders; it is also helpful to provide clear treatment care plans, progress updates, and summaries of clinical progress for court reports.
- Many offenders will have no previous experience or solely negative experiences of treatment, and will benefit from receiving a clear explanation of what they might gain from participating in the therapeutic group programme. This might include clear instruction at the pre-group assessment phase about treatment goals, exploring what the offender thinks they might learn from participating, and clarification as to what would be expected of the offender and how participation relates to their court order.

Secondly, while there will be contractual and practical pressures on treatment providers to engage all offenders within the group programme as part of their court orders, not all offenders will be suitable or capable of group participation. Obvious examples include those with mental health problems, such as social phobia or post traumatic stress disorder, who may find attending groups with others an aversive experience. It would also be necessary to judge how appropriate it would be for a lone female to attend a male-dominated group. A pre-group assessment is therefore a good opportunity to understand what issues may be pertinent for each individual presenting for treatment, to determine their suitability for the programme and also prepare them for group work. This interview might focus on the offender's perception of group work, what they would like to gain from participating, exploration of previous group experiences and exploration of any possible barriers they can foresee in using the group. It is also a chance for the facilitator to assess how the offender relates to others, to inquire what they might positively contribute and how they might use the experience of their peers to further their own development, and to recognize any obvious anti-social behavioural traits that may hinder group engagement. The interview can be used to clarify practical points about attendance, confidentiality, group rules, and so forth, to correct any obvious misunderstandings about the nature of the group, help problem-solve any difficult issues, as well as collect baseline outcome measures.

Thirdly, when designing groups and selecting clients for group work it is helpful to keep in mind the typical characteristics of this population.

- **Motivation**: Individuals who are coerced into treatment have lower motivation than those who voluntarily enter treatment (Brecht, Anglin, & Wang, 1993). Group treatment is more effective when it incorporates a motivational element, particularly for younger offenders (Sinha, Easton, & Kemp, 2003).
- **Dual diagnosis**: Offenders have a high rate of dual diagnosis and associated psychosocial, educational, and interpersonal difficulties (e.g., Banerjee, Clancy, & Crome, 2002). Antisocial personality traits are commonly found among this population (Leukefeld & Tims, 1993). Women are more vulnerable to psychiatric difficulties (Zlotnick, Clarke, Friedmann, Roberts, Sacks, & Melnick, 2008). Assessment will help judge how co-morbid conditions may affect an individual's ability to engage and benefit from group work, and how the group may be sensitively adapted.
- **Age-related factors**: Younger offenders tend to show lower intelligence levels in combination with a higher incidence of learning difficulties, difficult temperament, more antisocial cognitions, delinquent peer-group, and residence in impoverished neighbourhoods (Sullivan, Veysey, Hamilton, & Grillo, 2007). Older offenders show greater awareness of substance-use problems. These factors can contribute to less favourable treatment outcomes for younger offenders (Sinha et al., 2003).

- **Gender-differences**: Traditional substance use programmes have been designed for men (Kassebaum, 1999); however, there has been an increase in the numbers of female offenders undergoing treatment (27% of those entering treatment in 2008/2009; National Drug Treatment Monitoring System). Emerging research reports the effectiveness of gender-specific treatment (Zlotnick et al., 2008). Interestingly, studies have highlighted gender differences that may influence how group work for offenders is implemented. Lardén, Melin, Holst, and Långström (2006), for example, found that adolescent girls held fewer antisocial cognitive distortions and more moral judgements than boys their age.
- **Factors related to socioeconomic background**: Drug-related crime is often committed in areas of poverty and unemployment (Peck & Plant, 1986). High concentrations of black and minority ethnic groups (BME) in England reside within these areas and data for 2003 from the National Treatment Agency show an increasing prevalence of drug use within the BME population. There is also a suggestion that BME groups are unfairly over-represented within the criminal justice system (Goodman & Ruggiero, 2008). Predisposing factors that increase the risk of problem drug use, particularly in younger populations, include homelessness, a history of offending, having a disrupted education, and previously being in local authority care (Lloyd, 1998). Poor problem-solving skills, particularly coupled with low educational attainment, is a predictive factor of repeated offending among the offender population (LeBlanc, 1994). These findings highlight the importance of providing a group programme that is realistically pitched at the needs of the group members seen in the service locality.

Support systems for group facilitators

Group work with offenders can be a demanding task and facilitators are likely to encounter a number of interpersonal behaviours, such as extreme anti-social behaviours, that pose challenges for running therapeutic groups. For example, offenders may be verbally abusive to facilitators or 'test out' new relationships towards those in authority. However, there are ways of dealing with this, and over the course of our careers we have identified a number of considerations that help support staff in their group facilitation.

Firstly, it is important that groups are run by at least two facilitators, since this allows for the monitoring of both process and content while the group is underway. Secondly, it is essential that the system protects time for pre-group planning and post-group debriefing, particularly since facilitators are often required to perform competing duties such as providing manda-tory drug testing and recording attendance for the criminal justice service. A third area for input is through regular, ongoing supervision and training (individual and peer). As well as enhancing staff confidence and skills, this also helps to minimize staff turnover and to promote consistency in the therapeutic programme. Staff training will be most effective when it encompasses the delivery of the group content and group skills, builds on Motivational Interviewing (MI) skills (Miller & Rollnick, 1986), and allows discussion of real-life scenarios. It is useful to discuss scenarios that raise issues, such as how to identify and manage glorification of criminal activity, disclosure of 'insider information', and disclosure of past and future offences. Other aspects that training might usefully cover are how to support women in a male-dominated group, manage members who are constantly challenging the group rules, suspected dealing among clients during break times, intoxication, or lateness. MI skills are important for encouraging staff to avoid falling into a confrontational and overtly chal- lenging style that many offenders have learned to ignore or resist. MI skills also help foster therapeutic alliances and counteract perceptions of treat- ment as an activity to resist.

Group content

The focus on cognitive behavioural principles to treat offenders has been based on two factors. Firstly, there is an assumption that offenders lack pro-social values, attitudes, and social problem-solving skills needed for pro-social adjustment. Secondly, reductions in criminality and substance use are often accompanied by changes in personal values and development of pro-social identities. Here we suggest some ideas for group sessions that use cognitive-behavioural principles to break the reciprocal cycle of drug- taking and criminality.

Enhance self-control and self-management

Here we find it helpful to present the idea that we tend to operate on 'automatic pilot' and often react to our environments and events without much thought. The group are asked whether they believe this to be true for substance use and/or offending, and how operating on 'automatic pilot' has led them into trouble or difficulties. The group can be given the analogy of stopping a car at red traffic lights to demonstrate that it is often a good idea to 'Stop and think before acting on initial impulses and gut feelings'. The group can be given ways to help them achieve this: for example, before taking drugs, getting into the habit of asking 'Do I really need this today? Is using going to create further problems for me?'

Delay short-term gratification to receive long-term gain

Many caught in the cycle of offending and substance use are living from hand to mouth. Money/resources that are 'earned' are immediately spent on substances at the expense of other basic needs like rent, food, and heating. The group can examine the pros and cons of living like this. Ideally, the members would then generate new ways of controlling this impulse (e.g., paying for all bills before using drugs) or develop new rules or standards to live their life (e.g., 'My needs come first, before the drugs').

Increase social problem-solving skills

Many offenders show cognitive deficits in pro-social problem-solving skills. The 'Reasoning and Rehabilitation' treatment programme, for example, dedicates many of its sessions to guiding offenders through ways of recognizing problems, generating a menu of solutions, assessing the impact of each solution, and then following an appropriate response (Ross & Fabiano, 1985). As most problems will be solved by dealing effectively with other people, it can also be helpful to discuss questions such as 'What are the pitfalls of dealing with others to get problems solved?' and 'What helps?'

Increase empathy

Pro-social problem solving also requires recognition and consideration of others. Facilitators can use the group to stimulate a discussion as to what the offenders have done to others because of their substance use or offending. In these discussions it will be important to acknowledge personal responsibility for actions, explore the reasons for the associated shame and guilt, and acknowledge any emotional impact on others. For example, 'So when you stole from your family, how did that make you feel? How has it affected your relationships?' During these discussions offenders may also talk about self-imposed limits to their offending behaviour: for example, that it is okay to steal from small corner shops but not from their family. It is really useful to explore why they hold these standards in order to re-inforce pro-social behaviour and also use peers to challenge anti-social standards, such as it's okay to commit fraud, rob from others in the street, use weapons, assault others while intoxicated, and so forth.

Promote reflective thinking

In order to problem-solve effectively, we all need a degree of cognitive flexibility in how we think in order to differentiate between subjective opinion and facts. Too often, our immediate actions and decisions are based on our initial emotional reactions to events or are distorted by self-serving interests. It can therefore be useful to discuss this with the group and explore occasions when their initial reactions were wrong and based on poor judgement, and occasions when others have made bad judgements about them based on biased opinion. The facilitators can also explore ways to help members separate thoughts from facts. One strategy is offering a way of self-questioning, asking 'What's really going on here? Am I jumping to conclusions? Do I need more information to solve the problem?' Typically, with cognitive behavioural therapy work, facilitators will also take time to highlight common thinking errors and explore with members particular errors they may have, such as emotional reasoning, mind reading, personalization, and all or nothing thinking (Mitcheson, Maslin, Meynen, Morrison, Hill, & Wanigaratne, 2010).

Promote positive social and personal values

Theory and research suggest that behaviour change is initiated and sustained by how people view themselves and their social self (Fishbein & Ajzen, 1975; Kearney & O'Sullivan, 2003; McNeil, 2006). This assumes that behaviour is often predicted by an individual's social values and their attitude towards the behaviour and its consequences. Below are some ideas of how to introduce and explore these concepts within the group.

- Examine the pros and cons of 'continuing' versus 'discontinuing' a lifestyle attached to offending and/or substance use.
- Ask the group how well the above theory and research fits with their own experiences and how much of their current or past behaviour is driven by their personal and social values.
- Explore discrepancies between offenders' 'core values' versus 'current lifestyle' (associated with substance use and/or criminality).
- Explore ideas of the 'self now' ('How do you see yourself now?') versus 'future self' ('Where do you see yourself in five or ten years time?').
- Use a values card sort exercise to identify core personal values (Miller, C'de Baca, Matthews, & Wilbourne, 2001).
- Initiate conversations about how to engage in more fulfilling, positive community activities that will provide a sense of purpose and support meaningful change. It is important to acknowledge some of the difficulties with initiating change (for example, ceasing drug dealing also involves loss of income and social role) and spend time problem-solving how to initiate and sustain positive changes.
- Explore offenders' views of their personal strengths in order to re-inforce feelings of self-efficacy and instil hope and ideas as to how to achieve a better future.
- Explore the group's perception of the possibility of change through asking questions such as: 'Is change possible? Do you have the personal resources, skills, or commitment to make those changes? Do you have past examples of where you have made successful changes? What

personal attributes allowed you to make those changes? Have you seen changes in other drug users or offenders who you least expected to see change?'

- Encourage attendance at recreational, vocational, and educational groups. While therapeutic groups stimulate and initiate the recovery journey, other groups provide positive pro-social experiences to develop personal reasons to change.

Effective ways to deliver groups

The importance of group rules

Group members are essentially in treatment because they have already chosen to break some of society's rules. Establishing clear group rules is essential to any therapeutic group and this plays a particularly critical role in establishing a positive therapeutic atmosphere for this client group. Since group members may feel forced into treatment and perceive any system of rules as punitive rather than containing and helpful, it is helpful to reflect on how group rules are made and enforced, while retaining a therapeutic alliance. This may mean developing the rules with the group as well as discussing the respective roles of facilitators and group members in enforcing these. We have found if care and attention has been used in developing collective ownership of the rules, in most situations the group members themselves will challenge peer rule-breaking. In a community-based treatment setting the most common infringement of rules is likely to be arriving late and attending while under the influence of substances. It is important that any infringement of group rules is immediately acknowledged and addressed, because consistent failure to do so will weaken the facilitators' position and create dysfunctional norms within the group. While the group facilitators should make it clear that they are obliged to record group attendance, they also need to clarify that they are not responsible for enforcement issues around attendance. Facilitators can sometimes feel overly responsible for offenders who do not engage with their treatment order, and it is helpful to recognize that the offender has a right not to engage with treatment and that it is not the facilitators' role to protect them from potential negative consequences.

Clear understanding of confidentiality

From the outset, group facilitators must make it clearly known that they have a responsibility to share clinical information from the group with their wider team and to share treatment progress with the criminal justice staff managing the offender. Since clinical information may become a public record when incorporated into documents (e.g., court reports), the level of detail must be arranged locally and clearly communicated with the group. Once the group members are clear about confidentiality, they can then make their own decisions about what information to disclose. Facilitators need to be clear about when offences (past and present) will be automatically disclosed to the police or criminal justice service as a matter of risk to others. It can be helpful to provide an information sheet explaining these points and carefully explain different scenarios during the group covering examples such as 'What if someone were to tell the group that they were still shoplifting? Would that information be passed on to the criminal justice service? And if yes, what would this mean?'

The importance of motivation

Low motivation is a serious barrier to achieving positive outcomes in group work among offenders coerced into treatment. Such individuals are likely to present with low motivation to change, participate less in treatment, and hold more negative views of professionals.

As a starting point, external incentives applied by court orders can be viewed as a useful way to introduce many previously naive problematic substance misusers into treatment. The next key issue is how to generate internal incentives to change. Using a MI style during the pre-group assessment interview offers an opportunity to enhance internal incentives; it will also enhance treatment engagement, reduce resistance to treatment, promote responsibility for change, and begin to build a strong, empathic therapeutic relationship (Carroll et al., 2006). Visual maps may also be valuable during this assessment to produce useful, and essentially motivational, conversations about the potential for change.

Some group sessions will require offenders to contemplate significant lifestyle changes. These will not be easy decisions to make and need careful consideration. The decisional balance is a useful MI technique that can be employed in groups to explore the pros and cons of: offending and/or substance misuse, breaking ties with social networks to remain abstinent, losing potential sources of income, loss of status by dropping criminal activity, or seeking employment with criminal records and few professional qualifications.

Motivation to change is also influenced by one's confidence in the ability to make changes. This is particularly the case when an offender believes that change is unlikely or impossible because of factors now outside their control, such as past failure to gain educational or professional qualifications, an inability to secure a legitimate job because of a list of criminal convictions, or a succession of failed attempts to control substance use. In these circumstances it can be very useful to use the 'ruler' MI technique to measure levels of importance to change these behaviours and confidence in their ability to make changes. The group can be asked questions such as:

- 'How committed do you feel about wanting to stop offending? Please rate where you would place yourself on a scale of 1 to 10, where 1 is 'Not at all' and 10 is 'Very much'.'
- 'How confident do you feel about being able to break ties with, or say 'no' to, all your substance-using friends? Please rate where you would place yourself on a scale of 1 to 10, where 1 is 'Not at all confident' and 10 is 'Very confident'.'

These scales could also be used to elicit further 'change talk' by asking the group members to give their reasons for their rating and not a lower score, or what would have to happen in their lives to increase the rating to a higher score.

Another useful MI technique to consider with offenders who are less ready to change is to ask them a hypothetical question. Such questions, like the ones below, will encourage change talk.

- 'What would it take for you to decide to stop offending?'
- 'For one moment, just imagine that you are no longer caught up in the routine of substance use and offending. How might things be different?'
- 'If you did decide to turn your back on offending, what would you have to do to make this happen?'

Visual maps could also be used in the group programme to address ambivalence about making changes to lifestyle and stimulate small group exercises to explore specific topics.

The selection of group methods

In contrast to other clinical populations, offenders who use substances may present with lower academic attainment (Butzin, Saum, & Scarpitti, 2002), have lower thresholds of concentration (Hiller, Knight, Leukefeld, & Simpson, 2002), have less experience of peer-led classroom-like discussions, have more anti-authority tendencies (Onifade, Smith Nyandoro, Davidson, & Campbell, 2010), and have fewer references for pro-social skills. The success of group work with offenders may therefore be influenced by *how* the information is presented and the choice of exercises used to stimulate learning.

While it can be helpful to use the whiteboard and incorporate written exercises into the group, be mindful that this may elicit negative experiences of 'being taught' at school, and that some clients may have reading and writing difficulties. It is good practice to ask group members at the pre-group assessment about their schooling experiences and gauge reading and writing abilities, to explain how groups are conducted, and to identify any problems with their involvement. This information can then be used to tailor the group delivery to the individual's needs.

Since group work can be cognitively and emotionally demanding, it helps to be realistic about how much can be learnt in the allocated time. Group information is more likely to be retained and reflected on when the content and key messages are kept as simple as possible. In general, avoid using textbook jargon, limit learning to three key take-home messages per session, and use examples and points of reference that members will relate to rather than invent new concepts. Handouts can be used to stimulate conversations, highlight important points, and act as resources for group members to refer to after the group.

Meaningful homework assignments will promote learning and increase an offender's responsibility for their own recovery. For those attending community settings, these assignments can be made more realistic by making them apply to real-life scenarios, such as going to the gym or cinema. Assignments are more likely to be successful when they are simple and easy to understand, and when the assignment and its relevance have been talked through during the group, i.e., doing something rewarding and pleasurable without using substances. It is important that time is allocated in later groups to review individuals' progress with their assignments and acknowledge their successes and positive learning.

To avoid unnecessary confrontation between facilitators and group members, it is important that facilitators learn how to resist automatic impulses to challenge and confront group members on their initial vocalization of personally unhelpful and/or antisocial behaviours. Offenders are constantly being told what to do and how to behave and are likely to switch off or resist when feeling challenged. It is often better, therefore, to ask the peer group for their reactions or comments on another member's statement and opinion.

The importance of evaluation

Finally, it is always a good idea to evaluate the effectiveness of a group treatment programme to ensure its ongoing quality. This may be achieved by evaluating the usefulness of individual group sessions to the group members or monitoring changes in target areas after the overall programme. Evaluation may measure motivation, confidence in ability to change specific values and attitudes, or behavioural outcomes such as engagement, retention, and involvement in pro-social vocational, recreational, or educational activities. DeLucia-Waack and Bridbord (2004) provide a useful review of potential outcome measures within a criminal justice setting.

Chapter summary

With the increase in the number of offenders now accessing support for substance use, it is likely that group programmes will continue to be a primary treatment method. Facilitators will therefore be under pressure to create and deliver effective group programmes with a clinical population who present with diverse needs and many challenges. This chapter highlights key themes and core elements of what might help equip the group members with knowledge and skills to challenge both substance use and continued offending behaviour. Although there are many challenges in treating this under-served clinical population, the rewards can be significant when working in a well-designed group programme.

References

Banerjee, S., Clancy, C., & Crome, I. (Eds.) (2002). *Co-existing problems of mental disorder and substance misuse (dual diagnosis): An information manual.* London: Royal College of Psychiatrists' Research Unit. Report to the Department of Health.

Brecht, M. L., Anglin, D., & Wang, J. (1993). Treatment effectiveness for legally coerced versus voluntary methadone maintenance clients. *American Journal of Drug and Alcohol Abuse, 19,* 89–106.

Butzin, C., Saum, C., & Scarpitti, F. (2002). Factors associated with completion of a drug treatment court diversion program. *Substance Use and Misuse, 37,* 1615–1633.

Carroll, K., Ball, S., Nich, C., Martino, S., Frankforter, T., Farentinos, C., Kunkel, E., Mikulich-Gilbertson, S., Morgenstern, J., Obert, J., Polcin, D., Snead, N., & Woody, G. (2006). Motivational interviewing to improve treatment engagement and outcome in individuals seeking treatment for substance abuse: a multisite effectiveness study. *Drug and Alcohol Dependence, 81,* 301–312.

DeLucia-Waack, J. L., & Bridbord, K. H. (2004). Measures of group processes, dynamics and climate, leadership behaviors, and therapeutic factors: A review. In J. L. Delucia-Waack, D. Gerrity, C. Kalodner, & M. Riva (Eds.), *Handbook of group counselling and psychotherapy* (pp. 338–350). Thousand Oaks, CA: Sage Publications.

Farrall, S. (2002). *Rethinking what works with offenders.* Cullompton: Willan.

Fishbein, M., & Ajzen, I. (1975). *Belief, attitude, intention, and behavior: An introduction to theory and research.* Reading, MA: Addison-Wesley.

Goodman, A., & Ruggiero, V. (2008). Crime, punishment, and ethnic minorities in England and Wales. *Race/Ethnicity: Multidisciplinary Global Perspectives, 2,* 53–68.

Gossop, M. (2005). *Drug misuse treatment and reductions in crime: Findings from the National Treatment Outcome Research Study (NTORS).* London: National Treatment Agency for Substance Misuse.

Hiller, M., Knight, K., Leukefeld, C., & Simpson, D. (2002). Motivation as a predictor of therapeutic engagement in mandated residential substance abuse treatment. *Criminal Justice and Behavior, 29,* 56–75.

Holloway, K., Bennett, T., & Farrington, D. (2005). *The effectiveness of criminal justice and treatment programmes in reducing drug-related crime: A systematic review*. Home Office online report 26/05. London: Home Office.

Kassebaum, P. A. (1999). *Substance abuse treatment for women offenders*. Rockville, MD: Center for Substance Abuse Treatment.

Kearney, M. H., & O'Sullivan, J. (2003). Identify shifts as turning points in health behaviour change. *Western Journal of Nursing Research, 25*, 134–152.

Lardén, M., Melin, L., Holst, U., & Långström, N. (2006). Moral judgement, cognitive distortions and empathy in incarcerated delinquent and community control adolescents. *Psychology, Crime & Law, 12*, 453–462.

LeBlanc, M. (1994). Family, school, delinquency, and criminality: The predictive power of an elaborated social control theory for males. *Criminal Behaviour and Mental Health, 4*, 101–117.

Leukefeld, C. G., & Tims, F. R. (1993). Drug abuse treatment in prison. *Journal of Substance Abuse Treatment, 10*, 77–84.

Liriano, S., & Ramsay, M. (2003). Prisoners' drug use before prison and links with crime. In M. Ramsay (Ed.), *Prisoners' drug use and treatment: Seven research studies* (pp. 7–22). Home Office research study 267. London: Home Office.

Lloyd, C. (1998). Risk factors for problem drug use: Identifying vulnerable groups. *Drugs: Education, Prevention and Policy, 5*, 217–231.

McGuire, J. (2000). *Theory manual for Think First*. Prepared for the Joint Prison Probation Accreditation Panel.

McGuire, J. (2002). Integrating findings from research reviews. In J. McGuire (Ed.), *Offender rehabilitation and treatment: Effective programmes and policies to reduce re-offending* (pp. 3–38). Chichester: John Wiley & Sons.

McIntosh, J., Bloor, M., & Robertson, M. (2007). The effect of drug treatment upon the commission of acquisitive crime. *Journal of Substance Use, 12*, 375–384.

McMurran, M., & Priestley, P. (1999). *Addressing substance-related offending (ASRO) and programme for reducing individual substance misuse (PRISM). Section 1: Theory, evidence and evaluation.* Unpublished document, Home Office Pathfinder Unit.

McMurran, M., & Priestley, P. (2004). Addressing substance-related offending (ASRO): A structured cognitive-behavioural programme for drug users in probation and prison services. In B. Reading & M. Weegmann (Eds.), *Group psychotherapy and addiction* (pp. 194–210). London: Whurr.

McNeil, F. (2006). A desistance paradigm for offender management. *Criminology & Criminal Justice, 6*, 39–62.

McSweeney, T., & Hough, M. (2005). Drugs and alcohol. In N. Tilley (Ed.), *Handbook of crime prevention and community safety* (pp. 563–594). Cullompton: Willan.

Miller, W. R., & Rollnick, S. (1986). *Motivational interviewing. Preparing people for change.* New York: Guildford Press.

Miller, W. R., C'de Baca, J., Matthews, D. B., & Wilbourne, P. L. (2001). University of New Mexico. Retrieved from http://www.motivationalinterview.org/library/valuescardsort.pdf

Mitcheson, L., Maslin, J., Meynen, T., Morrison, T., Hill, R., & Wanigaratne, S. (2010). *Applied cognitive and behavioural approaches to the treatment of addiction: A practical treatment guide.* Oxford: Wiley-Blackwell.

Morgan, R. D., & Flora, D. (2002). Group psychotherapy with incarcerated offenders: A research synthesis. *Group Dynamics: Theory, Research, and Practice, 6*, 203–218.

Onifade, E., Smith Nyandoro, A., Davidson, W., & Campbell, C. (2010). Truancy and patterns of criminogenic risk in a young offender population. *Youth Violence and Juvenile Justice, 8*, 3–18.

Peck, D. F., & Plant, M. A. (1986). Unemployment and illegal drug use: Concordant evidence from a perspective study and national trends. *British Medical Journal, 293*, 929–932.

Ross, R. R., & Fabiano, E. A. (1985). *Time to think: A cognitive model of delinquency prevention and offender rehabilitation.* Johnson City, TN: Institute of Social Sciences and Arts.

Sinha, R., Easton, C., & Kemp, K. (2003). Substance abuse treatment characteristics of probation-referred young adults in a community-based outpatient program. *The American Journal of Drug and Alcohol Abuse, 29*, 585–597.

Sullivan, C., Veysey, B., Hamilton, Z., & Grillo, M. (2007). Reducing out-of-community placement and recidivism: Diversion of delinquent youth with mental health and substance use problems from the justice system. *International Journal of Offender Therapy and Comparative Criminology, 51*, 555–577.

White, W. (2005). Recovery: Its history and renaissance as an organizing construct. *Alcoholism Treatment Quarterly, 23*, 3–15.

Wilson, D. B., Allen Bouffard, L., & Mackenzie, D. L. (2005). A quantitative review of structured, group-oriented, cognitive-behavioral programs for offenders. *Criminal Justice and Behavior, 32*, 172–204.

Zlotnick, C., Clarke, J., Friedmann, P., Roberts, M., Sacks, S., & Melnick, G. (2008). Gender differences in comorbid disorders among offenders in prison substance abuse treatment programs. *Behavioral Sciences & the Law, 26*, 403–412.

Chapter 17

Acceptance and change

Working with complex cases

Elly Farmer and Deepti Shah-Armon

Introduction

In this chapter we describe two groups for clients who are engaged in our substance-misuse service: (1) a group for female survivors of childhood sexual abuse (CSA) and (2) a dialectical behaviour therapy (DBT) group for those with borderline personality disorder (BPD) or related difficulties.

Overview of childhood sexual abuse and substance misuse

A significant proportion of individuals seeking support with drug or alcohol misuse report sexual abuse in their childhood years and continue to live with the impact of this in their adulthood. For example, one review found that women with substance misuse problems compared with those without such problems were twice as likely to report having suffered CSA (Simpson & Miller, 2002). Indeed, CSA is more strongly associated with substance dependence than with any other psychiatric disorder (Kendler, Bulik, Silberg, Hettema, Myers, & Prescott, 2000). The experience of CSA and subsequent invalidation can profoundly shape the beliefs that survivors develop about themselves (e.g., 'I am flawed, defective, damaged'), their emotions (e.g., 'My feelings are not important'), and other people (e.g., 'People close to you betray you'). Such abuse also impacts on developmental tasks such as attachment, forming peer relationships, and emotion regulation, and forces children to develop survival strategies that are likely to be maladaptive once the abuse has ceased. Finkelhor and Kendall-Tackett (2008) have noted how adult survivors typically experience difficulties in multiple areas of their lives, including intense and easily triggered negative emotions, dissociation, intrusions, numbing, self-harm, eating disorders, aggression, obsessionality, chronic pain, sexual changes, and disrupted relationships.

Case study 1: A group for survivors of childhood sexual abuse

Clinically, we have found that it is best to deal with CSA independently of other forms of childhood trauma such as emotional neglect and/or physical abuse. There are three main reasons for this. Firstly, survivors of other forms of abuse often perceive themselves as less impacted than those who have experienced CSA, and this can create an unhelpful, erroneous 'hierarchy of abuse' in a group (Kennerley, 2008). Secondly, those who have suffered CSA tend to report particularly significant difficulties relating to shame, stigma, self-blame, and sexual relations (Feiring & Taska, 2005; Feiring, Taska, & Lewis, 2002; Lemieux & Byers, 2008). These issues can be made a legitimate, central focus of attention when the group only includes CSA survivors. Thirdly, group members find it easier to risk disclosing thoughts, feelings, and behaviours when surrounded by others dealing with similar experiences.

The group limits itself to female clients because fewer men disclose CSA, and also because female survivors frequently request female-only groups as their abusive experiences often lead them to distrust men. That stated, we are aware that including men could provide a revelatory experience for female survivors, as well as facilitating a powerful therapeutic journey for the men; thus, this decision is always under review. We also ask that members have sufficient control over their substance use so they can tolerate discussions and thinking about difficult childhood experiences without resorting to drug or alcohol use. They may be stable on a prescription, abstinent, or able to usually limit their substance use to certain times of the day or week. When lapses do occur, they are addressed through problem-solving, contracting, and relapse management strategies. Frequent use that significantly impedes a client's group participation may, however, mean that they will defer group attendance to later in their treatment.

The group is designed as a closed group for a maximum of nine members. It runs for 24 weeks and is held on a weekly basis, lasting for an hour and three-quarters, with a brief break halfway through. The overall orientation behind the group is cognitive behavioural, but also draws on systemic, psychodynamic, and narrative perspectives.

At the beginning of the group programme, we discuss different models of how CSA impacts on people. The group is constructed as a safe place for group members to: (1) learn and test out new skills; (2) develop adaptive understandings of themselves; and (3) facilitate new experiences in the present. Examples of how these are achieved are outlined below. Group members are given a copy of *Recovering from childhood abuse: therapy workbook* (Kennerley, Whitehead, Butler, & Norris, 1998) at the start of the programme, from which they complete reading and exercises between group sessions. Each week's session starts with a relevant issue.

Teaching new skills

These skills are drawn from mindfulness and DBT therapies and aim to help clients adaptively manage high levels of negative emotion. Clients are encouraged to plan self-nurturing and self-soothing activities. Although these tasks are simple, clients often find them intensely challenging because they act against entrenched self-beliefs. Since group members find it hard to even generate ideas of ways to soothe or nurture themselves, we hand out a list of activities to stimulate the group's thinking. Clients typically begin with a simple endeavour such as a pleasant walk, listening to music, or cooking a meal. In cognitive-behavioural fashion, group members are encouraged to plan these tasks in a stepped manner, gradually increasing the degree or length of time spent on self-soothing. Facilitators emphasize how doing things differently can in the end mean thinking and feeling differently.

There are often lengthy discussions on each member's plans for these tasks; we pay particular attention to identifying and challenging any sabotaging self-critical aspects that have been introduced. For example, the nurturing powers of a bath with pleasant bath oil, music, and candles might be nullified by adding abrasive cleaning agents or painful scrubbing. We find that survivors rarely disclose the full extent of self-punishing behaviours and that our naming of these common behaviours helps members share and thereby reduce their shame, stigma, and isolation.

We discuss another set of key skills that we describe as 'dipping in and out of flashbacks'. Clients frequently experience unpredictable and intrusive flashbacks from past abuse that can trigger involuntary and more voluntary forms of dissociation, such as amnesia and substance misuse. This leaves the content of the flashbacks unprocessed, emotionally raw, and therefore likely to intrude again (Brewin & Holmes, 2003). While trauma-focused individual therapy may be necessary to fully process such memories (National Collaborating Centre for Mental Health, 2005), we safely encourage clients to exert control over flashbacks by their choosing to allow material from flashbacks to fully enter into their consciousness for a pre-planned amount of time. Grounding strategies to help with this include actively focusing on aspects of the present environment using each of the five senses, or entering an imaginary safe place (Kennerley, 1996). Practice in and out of group sessions is necessary before such skills are accessible as a tool during the flashback moment. Audio recordings of clients describing their safe place (typically in response to therapist questions focusing on the sensory detail of the place) or asking themselves grounding questions can be useful aids. The result of survivors actively allowing themselves to 'stay with' their flashbacks for a certain length of time, knowing that they can then voluntarily take themselves out of them, helps not only to begin the task of processing the memories, but also imparts a sense of control—

thereby reducing feelings of powerlessness and fears of losing one's mind. These aims are also achieved through choosing to remember through writing and sharing in the group.

Developing new understandings

A central task is for group members to come to accurate, affirmative, and adaptive views of themselves. We use discussion to help members to recognize their negative beliefs and how these are understandable and shared, and this is followed up through completion of situation/thought/feeling diaries. The discussion continues by talking about when negative self-beliefs began, and their fears about letting go of them. Clients often come to perceive negative beliefs as an understandable consequence of abuse and invalidation, and realize that these are not statements of truth, but that, rather, they might be holding onto them out of fear of facing the true nature of the abuse. Once group members name such fears, the fears tend to reduce and can be overcome. For example, they may come to realize that they are holding on to self-blame to avoid the anger and sadness of knowing that the abuse was undeserved. Clients often hold judgements about themselves while expressing compassion towards others, i.e., 'inconsistent reasoning'. By repeatedly drawing attention to these discrepancies, facilitators and other members help clients judge themselves more kindly.

Psychoeducation about abusive dynamics and consequences further paves the way for more affirmative self-beliefs. For example, when members hear that sexual arousal during abuse is a common, physiological reaction quite separate from free choice, they find it easier to share any such experiences with one another and come to challenge them as evidence that they were to blame or are 'dirty' (Munro, 2004). Sharing information about traumatic reactions helps to challenge beliefs members hold about their psychological difficulties; for instance, that nightmares and flashbacks are signs of their madness or punishment. Instead, these reactions come to be seen as evidence that each person's mind is attempting to process the past in order to heal itself. Symptoms are seen as part of a compassionate mind, rather than a disordered or vindictive one.

Facilitating new experiences

Consistent with cognitive behavioural theory, our clinical experience suggests that it is the new relational and emotional experiences that are the most powerful means by which people recover from past abuse. Members are often ambivalent about sharing personal stories, fearing breaches of confidentiality, negative judgements, and their own emotional reactions. At the same time they sense the relief sharing could bring. This is addressed through: (1) open discussions about this dilemma (pros and cons of 'sharing' versus 'remaining silent'); (2) psycho-education about emotional reactions (for instance, that emotions are necessary and will not overwhelm clients if expressed rather than blocked); and (3) teaching strategies to promote safety. While we encourage sharing, we make it clear that we respect each member's right to decide how much she discloses.

When members feel able to share their experiences of abuse, they may choose to do so through art, poetry, a written story of their memories and their feelings, a 'letter' to someone significant in their lives, or a simpler verbal account. Sharing might happen in one substantial piece, or through fragments shared across many sessions. To facilitate this requires therapists to balance discussion of the weekly topic with conversations that follow clients' (sometimes subtle) indications that they are ready to share some of their story. This balance appears to be containing by clients. The process of sharing helps to change intrusive, affect-laden fragments into more manageable parts of a life-narrative, thereby reducing nightmares, flash-backs, and voices. Clients also experience being cared for, non-blamed, and understood in the context of revealing memories normally linked with views of themselves as bad or shameful. This provides a new relational experience that can transform their view of themselves and others. Both self-disclosure and listening to others engenders a sense of connection, reduces feelings of isolation and defectiveness, and stirs compassion towards others that we encourage members to also extend to themselves.

Clients often do not find it easy to take on board affirmative messages. For instance, a group member who discovers through the reactions of others that she can be cared for also discovers, by implication, that her parents could have cared for her but did not. This 'acceptance' of past realities can bring with it intense, yet appropriate, feelings of loss, grief, and anger. Although group members are each discovering different truths leading to different emotions (some feeling anger, others vulnerability, still others sadness), all are on a journey in which they experience and integrate feelings that were previously feared and avoided.

Maintaining safety

Members need to feel safe in the group in order to take the significant risks involved in attempting new thinking, skills, and experiences. This involves trusting other members not to share anything spoken about in the group outside, and it also means keeping group relationships focused on the recovery process, as healing (not harming) relationships. These aspects are facilitated through consensually agreed group rules. These include: (1) confidentiality; (2) contacting group facilitators for support for oneself and, if concerned, for other group members; and (3) not drinking or using drugs together. While some members have commented that this last rule feels rigid and disrespectful of their autonomy, we have found that not retaining this rule leads to facilitators being positioned as the 'neglectful parent', group members feeling vulnerable to peer pressure, and relationships losing their supportive centre.

Many group members will have harmed themselves and attempted suicide in the past and we remain mindful of current risk, particularly during moments spent focusing on past memories, trying out new skills, and avoiding behaviours previously used to cope. The risk of self-harm and suicide is reduced by each member, with help from the group, constructing a crisis plan consisting of concrete actions they would take in different possible moments of risk. Facilitators also monitor feelings in the group, guide members to offer positive advice and encouragement to others feeling this way, offer one-off individual support sessions or telephone calls if necessary, and co-construct 'safety contracts' in which the client promises not to take specified risks before the next meeting. Lastly, the safety inherent within the supportive group relationships is prioritized at all times. Facilitators encourage clients to hear each other in any disagreements, and come back to points of commonality and a baseline of respect.

Overview of dialectical behaviour therapy

A high proportion of individuals attending substance misuse services meet the diagnostic criteria for a personality disorder. A recent UK study showed that 37% of clients in drug and 53% of clients in alcohol treatment services met the criteria for personality disorder and that the ICD-10 Cluster B Borderline Personality Disorder (BPD) was particularly prevalent (Bowden-Jones, Iqbal, Tyrer, Seivewright, Copper, Judd, & Weaver, 2004). DBT is a particular therapeutic approach designed by Linehan (1993a, 1993b) for clients who meet criteria for BPD. Although designed to help individuals with BPD learn to manage overwhelming negative emotions and build a life worth living, it is useful for a much broader range of clients struggling with intense emotional reactions and impulsive behaviours. For clients with drug misuse and BPD, it has good treatment retention rates and proven effectiveness in reducing drug use and improving global and social functioning (Linehan, Schmidt, Dimeff, Craft, Kanter, & Comtois, 1999).

Several premises lie behind DBT techniques and processes. Firstly DBT suggests that individuals with borderline difficulties have often experienced invalidating environments in which their emotional needs are denied, disrespected, and inconsistently responded to (Bezirganian, Cohen, & Brook, 1993; Zanarini et al., 1997), leading individuals to experience intense emotional reactions and develop maladaptive interpersonal and emotion regulation skills. Secondly, that individuals are doing the best they can at all times. Thirdly, that progress is dependent on both the therapeutic relationship and attention to key dialectics, a dialectic being the truth or wisdom that emerges from the synthesis of two opposing viewpoints. DBT views clients as struggling with central dialectics such as tensions between 'acceptance' and 'change', between 'gaining skills' and 'losing needs', and between 'validating their current beliefs and skills' and 'developing new ones to achieve change'. Therapy helps free clients from these unhelpful either/or stances in order to come to a more useful synthesis.

A further major focus of DBT is its behavioural aspect, sharing many similarities with cognitive behavioural therapy (CBT) with its focus on problem-solving, behavioural experiments, Socratic questioning, and logical reasoning (this might, for example, be used to draw clients' attention to the untenable nature of their self-criticism in light of their compassion towards others in similar predicaments).

Elements that are particularly characteristic of DBT include the way in which therapists mix warmth, matter-of-fact irreverence, and strategic self-disclosure to motivate clients, as well as the emphasis on clients accepting themselves in the moment ('radical acceptance'). There is also a focus on diminishing therapy-interfering behaviours, such as self-harm, late attendance, interrupting others, and the use of substances before group. This might be done through the use of 'arbitrary reinforcers', in other words, responding to positive change with consciously chosen rewarding behaviours (for example, a therapist might offer a longer telephone conversation if a client agrees to stop drinking that day), or 'contracting', namely writing out formal contracts with clients in which they commit to not self-harming within a specified time period that they feel confident about.

Case example 2: Running a DBT group in a substance misuse setting

This group is run weekly as a closed group with a minimum of three members and a maximum of nine. The group is open to service users at all stages of their treatment, even if they are ambivalent about their substance use or regularly using, since these clients are often those who are struggling the most with emotional dysregulation and therefore most in need of DBT. However, we find it is unhelpful for the group when clients regularly attend visibly under the influence of substances and address this as described in the previous case example, as well as considering additional one-to-one sessions and telephone support.

The group lasts 90 minutes; the first hour focuses on skills training and the last half an hour on specific issues related to the past week. Members can stay for two cycles of the group, each cycle containing four modules: (1) distress tolerance skills; (2) emotional regulation skills; (3) interpersonal relationship skills and (4) mindfulness skills. New members can join at the start of each module.

Distress tolerance skills

This module communicates ideas and skills that help clients to accept unavoidable aspects of life and to tolerate and survive crises. The guiding philosophy is that pain is an unavoidable part of life, and that inability to accept pain leads to needless suffering. Typically our clients have avoided distress by using substances and we often find that clients initially struggle to take on board the 'polar opposite' approach of acceptance. We facilitate repeated in-depth discussions in order to fully convey the radical, different, and potentially transformative power of acceptance. It is helpful to use metaphors and examples to illustrate the wisdom of acceptance. For example, we might compare the usefulness of a client 'accepting' versus 'refusing to accept' that they have been unfairly banned from accessing hospital facilities. 'Non-acceptance' leads to rebellion, difficult emotions for the individual, and possibly impulsive behaviours. On the other hand, 'acceptance' leads to constructive action such as seeking healthcare elsewhere and making a formal complaint. The idea of acceptance is also conveyed through mindfulness exercises that involve each group member simply focusing on the present moment—'accepting' it for what it is without reference to past or future.

As can be seen in the above examples, we aim to introduce acceptance in a way that is empowering and calming, ensuring that acceptance is not misunderstood as approval. DBT does not advocate forgiveness, passivity, or endorsement of past injustices, but rather a true appreciation and awareness of life in order to change it. As clients become familiar with this idea, they often begin to feel that their emotions and fate feel less dependent on the people and systems around them. So, for example, a client might change from extensively discussing how unhelpful her friends were in encouraging her to drink, to deciding how she could spend less time with them, based on an acceptance that they are unlikely to change these unhelpful proclivities. Similarly, a client betrayed and hurt by a family member might allow herself to simply be aware of these feelings, rather than using strategies involving 'blocking' or impulsive 'catharsis'.

Emotion regulation skills

Individuals with BPD and substance misuse often struggle to understand emotional experiences without acting on them in impulsive ways and/or avoiding them. The aim of this module is to develop clients': (1) understanding of emotions and the functions they serve; (2) awareness of their own emotional reactions; and (3) conscious control over how they react to them. We focus this module particularly on self-harm, because this is one of the most frequent and yet most risky means by which group members respond to negative emotional states. As clients gain control over their substance use, it is not unusual to see an increase in these self-destructive behaviours and we remain vigilant for any signs of this, for example by carefully reading diary worksheets, exploring how changes in mood may have been acted on, and regularly asking about self-harm in a compassionate yet direct fashion. We also encourage clients to be honest about their struggles; this is best achieved by group members observing the benefits of this approach through facilitators and other members being non-judgemental, emphasizing that each individual is doing the best she can, and focusing on solutions they feel able to attempt. Facilitators may offer additional telephone or therapeutic support when necessary.

An additional emphasis within this module is on reducing vulnerability to negative emotions by taking care of oneself even when life is going well—for example, by scheduling rewarding activities, as well as routine health checks. We do, however, discuss how visits to the dentist or doctor can cause flashbacks of trauma for some clients, and think together how these may be avoided.

Interpersonal relationship skills

Overall the aim of this module is to promote an understanding of ways in which relationships can be more satisfying and less frequently a cause of suffering. The skills taught on this module focus on achieving three central goals in relationships: (1) obtaining the changes one wants; (2) maintaining positive relationships; and (3) upholding self-respect. Often one or more of these three aims is lost when individuals engage in avoidance or impulsive behaviours. Meeting all three aims involves being able to keep each of them in mind while using the skills of the other three modules and social skills that cluster around the theme of assertiveness.

Many clients tolerate abuse in relationships and do not believe they deserve to have self-respect and their needs met. Clients' negative schemas about themselves and others can block their testing out of new inter-personal skills and in order for this module to be effective, we find that we need to challenge such schemas. We highlight the small steps by which people sacrifice their needs and self-respect in order to maintain relationships, so that cumulatively they arrive at a point where they have little left. If this happens clients may feel completely controlled by the relationship—one client described this situation as 'him having the remote control for my head' and group members used this metaphor to continually remind each other of why this type of relationship is worth avoiding. Group discussions also explore the seeming paradox that prioritizing your own needs at times can help to forge better, mutually respectful relationships. This can be challenging to apply, because at times it may mean risking relationships, especially those in which the other person is insufficiently thoughtful or respectful. The central learning point is that meeting all three of the relationship goals is a juggling act, and different circumstances call for one or other of the goals to be prioritized.

Extensive role-plays based on clients' experiences are invaluable in turning these principles into lived experience. These appear to be most helpful when they centre on topics that have some relevance to clients' lives but without being too emotive, so that clients are engaged yet not so emotionally involved as to be unable to attempt new ways of interacting in their role or think about underlying principles. Examples include a client asking for money owed from a friend, or a client talking to her father about his criticism of her child. Group members describe role-playing as most useful when they observe the facilitators doing it first. We introduce role-playing spontaneously to avoid anticipatory anxiety, and this is also reduced by the subsequent discussions of learning points focusing on the skills exhibited rather than on any perceived shortcomings.

Mindfulness skills

Mindfulness is very much a core part of DBT and is woven throughout the other modules. Mindfulness skills are taught at the beginning of each module, and at least one mindfulness exercise is practised every session. Through discussion, clients become aware of the mindfulness skills they already have, for example clients who use drugs are very much 'in the moment' when seeking and using their drug, and are taught to generalize these skills to other aspects of their lives as a way of living in the present without being overwhelmed by their emotions (Christensen, Riddoch, & Huber, 2009).

Conclusions

Clients with personality disorders, childhood sexual abuse, and substance-misuse problems are often seen as having problems that are too complex or too severe to treat. This chapter has illustrated some of the group approaches that have helped many of these clients achieve substantial positive change and wellbeing. Anonymous feedback suggests that the majority of those who attend both groups report feeling generally calmer and more able to regulate their emotions (for example: 'I feel more able to recognize how I'm feeling and can now put skills into practice, I feel more placid and haven't self-harmed'). While DBT group members tend to also highlight positive changes to their relationships (particularly greater mutual respect), those in the group for survivors of CSA emphasize having more affirming understandings of themselves both in the past and present, and freedom from shame (for example: 'I no longer feel ashamed about the sexual abuse. So I am now feeling the need to inspire, support, and encourage other survivors. It affects me in the sense that I put it to good use to help others'). It seems likely that these positive changes combined with the impact of the social networks that develop between group members contribute to substantial reductions in substance misuse.

In this chapter we have focused on two groups that have been useful in reducing substance misuse and comorbid difficulties in complex clients attending a drugs and alcohol service. However, the techniques, skills, and approaches outlined are applicable to all work in substance misuse, whether group or individual, whether with addictions of complex or more straight-forward aetiologies. We have found that clients frequently make important steps towards change when they can make sense of the paths that led to their substance misuse. This can be accomplished by learning and practising new interpersonal skills, finding new ways of handling intense emotions, and experiencing a therapist who both fully accepts them for who they are and fully believes in their ability to make the changes they desire. The most generalizable principles are those of validation combined with reinforcement of behaviours that move clients forward, in other words, acceptance and change.

Thank you enormously to Michele Head for all her clinical wisdom; it played a crucial role in developing the approaches described in this chapter.

References

Bezirganian, S., Cohen, P., & Brook, S. (1993). The impact of mother–child interaction on the development of borderline personality disorder. *American Journal of Psychiatry, 150*, 1836–1842.

Bowden-Jones, O., Iqbal, M. Z., Tyrer, P., Seivewright, N., Copper, S., Judd, A., & Weaver, T. (2004). Prevalence of personality disorder in alcohol and drug services and associated comorbidity. *Addiction, 99*, 1306–1314.

Brewin, C., & Holmes, E. (2003). Psychological theories of posttraumatic stress disorder. *Clinical Psychology Review, 23*, 339–376.

Christensen, K., Riddoch, G. N., & Huber, J. E. (2009). *Dialectical behaviour therapy skills, 101 mindfulness exercises and other fun activities for children and adolescents: A learning supplement*. Bloomington: AuthorHouse.

Feiring, C., & Taska, L. S. (2005). The persistence of shame following sexual abuse: A longitudinal look at risk and recovery. *Child Maltreatment, 10*, 337–349.

Feiring, C., Taska, L. S., & Lewis, M. (2002). Trying to understand why horrible things happen: Attribution, shame and symptom development following sexual abuse. *Child Maltreatment, 7*, 26–41.

Finkelhor, D., & Kendall-Tackett, K. (2008). Developmental impact. In D. Finkelhor (Ed.), *Childhood victimization: Violence, crime and abuse in the lives of young people* (pp. 65–91). New York: Oxford University Press.

Kendler, K. S., Bulik, C. M., Silberg, J., Hettema, J. M., Myers, J., & Prescott, C. A. (2000). Childhood sexual abuse and adult psychiatric and substance use disorders in women: An epidemiological and co-twin control analysis. *Archives of General Psychiatry, 57*, 953–959.

Kennerley, H. (1996). Cognitive therapy of dissociative symptoms associated with trauma. *British Journal of Clinical Psychology, 35*, 325–340.

Kennerley, H. (2008). Personal communication.

Kennerley, H., Whitehead, L., Butler, G., & Norris, R. (1998). *Recovering from childhood abuse: Therapy workbook.* Oxford: Oxford University Press.

Lemieux, S. R., & Byers, E. S. (2008). The sexual well-being of women who have experienced child sexual abuse. *Psychology of Women Quarterly, 32*, 126–144.

Linehan, M. M. (1993a). *Cognitive behavioural treatment for borderline personality disorder.* New York: Guilford Press.

Linehan, M. M. (1993b). *Skills training manual for treating borderline personality disorder.* New York: Guilford Press.

Linehan, M. M., Schmidt, H., Dimeff, L. A., Craft, C., Kanter, J., & Comtois, K. A. (1999). Dialectical behavior therapy for patients with borderline personality disorder and drug dependence. *The American Journal on Addictions, 8*, 279–292.

Munro, K. (2004). *Sexual feelings during sexual abuse.* Retrieved on September 8, 2009, from http://www.kalimunro.com/sexual_feelings_abuse.html

National Collaborating Centre for Mental Health (2005). *Posttraumatic stress disorder (PTSD): The management of PTSD in adults and children.* NICE clinical guideline 26. London: National Institute for Health and Clinical Excellence.

Simpson, T. L., & Miller, W. R. (2002). Concomitance between childhood sexual and physical abuse and substance use problems: A review. *Clinical Psychology Review, 22*, 27–77.

Zanarini, M. C., Williams, A. A., Lewis, R. E., Reich, R. B., Vera, S. C., Marino, M. F., Levin, A., Yong, L., & Frankenburg, F. R. (1997). Reported pathological childhood experiences associated with the development of Borderline Personality Disorder. *American Journal of Psychiatry, 154*, 1101–1106.

Chapter 18

Reflections on running a women's group on an inpatient alcohol detoxification ward

Ernestine Nhapi and Josephine Shaw

> Thus it may be the repeated experience of being understood in depth that builds up the sense of self, based upon the capacity to evoke feeling and thought in the other.
>
> (Mollon, 1993)

Introduction

This chapter explores the role of women's groups for clients with alcohol dependence. Much of this account is based on evaluations, self-reports, and observations made in an inpatient alcohol detoxification ward, where women attended a weekly women's group during a 2–4-week inpatient admission. Each group was attended by an average of four to six women aged between 16 and 75 years and from a diverse range of social backgrounds and ethnicities. The chapter explores three main themes: (1) the rationale for women-only groups; (2) the role of the female facilitator; and (3) common themes and issues.

The rationale for running women-only groups

The National Institute on Drug Abuse (1998) has identified a number of findings from its ongoing research into gender-specific addiction treatments and concludes that the 'one size fits all' approach in the assessment and treatment of addiction is not as effective as that which addresses gender differences. Our own clinical experience in a number of different substance-misuse treatment centres also indicates that groups that are specifically gender-structured are more beneficial than those that are not. This appears to be related to the differences between the genders in the biological and co-morbid factors that predispose to addiction. For instance, emotional factors such as anxiety, depression, suicidal ideation, and susceptibility to many adverse effects of alcohol on the body, such as liver and brain damage, are known to be more prevalent in women (National Institute on Alcohol Abuse and Alcoholism, 1992).

The majority of people who become dependent on drugs and alcohol have experienced a number of critical issues, such as childhood abuse and other traumas. The inability to adequately address these issues in any treatment environment increases the risk of relapse. While mixed-sex treatment and groups do provide a safe and supportive means of looking at relapse prevention techniques, they often fail to address the unique characteristics of each gender, which aid the discovery of the self lost in time through the misuse of drugs and alcohol (Denzin, 1984). Women in such treatment facilities are more likely than their male counterparts to have low self-esteem because of guilt and self-blame, have a personality disorder and/or other mental health problem (Miller, Downs, & Testa, 1993).

Jack Kline, the Executive Director of Four Circles Recovery Center in the USA, defines women's groups as a place where women can provide and experience 'a compassionate, non-judgmental environment . . . to share their stories, fears, struggles, and life lessons with other women who have walked in their shoes', thereby resulting in 'a unique setting for women to begin exploring who they are, physically, mentally, emotionally and spiritually' (www.fourcirclesrecovery.com/gender_specfic.html).

There are a number of other reasons for offering a women-only group. During the course of alcohol detoxification, women can feel physically and emotionally vulnerable, and those who have experienced loss or past trauma are likely to report feeling extremely fragile and sensitive. Without the assistance of alcohol or other substances to numb painful memories, it is perhaps not surprising that memories of abuse, kept at bay over weeks, months, or years, may begin to resurface. We have also witnessed or become aware of occasions within the ward when male clients verbally abuse or directly or indirectly undermine their female peers (although of course, the reverse can happen). Men can, for example, appear domineering through ensuring their choice of television programmes in the communal lounge or appear intimidating through their use of inappropriate and/or obscene language and even at times be verbally abusive. It can be highly detrimental to a woman's recovery if she feels unable to live alongside, let alone to challenge, her male peers in the community. Furthermore, we have seen how sometimes difficult and often quite disturbing issues are either ignored or inadequately explored by women in a mixed-group setting. One possible explanation for this is the different styles in which men and women communicate within groups. Sometimes it has become apparent to us that women can feel uneasy when men dominate discussions in an aggressive way and that this then dissuades them from raising distressing personal concerns within the group. This can, we believe, lead to disillusionment, resentment, and sometimes a degree of fear among the female members of the group. At the same time, it is important to acknowledge that some women in the group may relate in a more positive way to their male peers, who may provide much-needed role models of how men can be kind, helpful, and fatherly. This can be reinforced by positive interactions with male members of staff.

A space for women to relate to each other in a female-only setting can therefore act as a forum where difficult feelings of fear, anger, and other powerful emotions may be safely explored. Additionally, a women's group can be another forum for facing up to life's problems and developing strategies for recovery, and for rediscovering strengths lost through years of addiction. Notwithstanding age, race, or sexual orientation, the shared problem of alcohol addiction links women together for the purpose of much-needed understanding and mutual benefit.

The role of the female facilitator

Our women's group was always facilitated by two female staff members, both of whom regularly worked on the ward and therefore knew the group members relatively well. We found that through experience it was easier to synthesize what was being shared in the group and, while not self-disclosing too much, make contributions relating to our own experiences and knowledge. We felt this helped group members to recognize that the facilitators were part of the group and minimized, but did not of course eradicate, the imbalance of power that exists between professional staff and clients. In terms of theoretical stance, we took what can be best described as an integrative approach, drawing on supportive person-centred approaches and cognitive behavioural therapy.

Previously, groups were held once a fortnight, and on occasion only when staffing resources permitted. However, the rotas were amended so that every Wednesday there were adequate female staff to facilitate these groups. We soon learnt that the groups were more effective when held regularly and consistently at least once a week for an hour. If the group was allowed to go on longer than the hour, there was a tendency for individuals to run out of things to say and allow themselves to be easily distracted by external stimuli. The group was also in danger of becoming emotionally draining for both the women and facilitators. It was important to have the group in a setting where women felt comfortable and relaxed, and away from distractions. On the unit, the group was held in the female lounge, which was away from the communal areas of the ward, including staff offices. Some of the boundaries that apply to the mixed-gender groups, such as discouraging drinks and nibbles, were dispensed with so as to encourage an atmosphere conducive to openness.

Perhaps it is fair to say that, before any group, anticipatory anxiety on the part of facilitators was not unusual. However, in our experience this appeared less prevalent in female staff when preparing for the women-only group. Sometimes in the general community life of the ward, negative transference can lead to inappropriate and difficult attitudes or behaviours. On balance, this occurred less frequently with staff facilitating the women's group.

The group began with the facilitator asking members to go through the basic ground rules. These included issues of confidentiality and respect followed by a brief outline of the purpose of the group, explaining how it differed from other mixed- gender groups held on the unit. The facilitator then reviewed the issues previously worked through. Further items for discussion were then raised along with the introduction of new members. It was also important to name the possible emotions that group members might experience during the group, which in turn encouraged greater participation and exploration of feelings.

In order for the women to feel relaxed in the group setting the session might commence with an opening preamble, for example the weather or an item of news. This could lead into a discussion of an important relevant issue. Alternatively the facilitator might introduce a particular subject or theme ensuring that this was not focused on any particular client. The matter of exclusive relationships would only be raised if several members of the community were involved. Participants were encouraged right from the outset to engage as fully as possible and to be forthcoming about what was important to them. This in itself can be quite significant for the individual group members. Although this may seem like a small step, we believe that this taking of responsibility highlights ways in which some control could begin to be reclaimed or developed by members of the group.

In order that women felt safe to engage and explore personal issues, ground rules such as confidentiality and respect for one another were emphasised. Whilst women were encouraged to share, this was always guided by what they felt most comfortable with. The facilitators ensured that no direct or indirect pressure was placed on participants to speak about their own personal experiences or emotions unless they wanted to.

Confidentiality was particularly relevant when issues connected to abuse were shared, as many women feared being judged or having their disclosures related back to others on the ward. On those occasions that women asked for issues to remain within the group, we the facilitators would reiterate the confidentiality group rule explaining that relevant information was shared within the team.

Due to the deeply personal issues often explored during this group we learnt the importance of remaining mindful of our own reactions and keeping an empathic and non-judgemental stance. We also joined in discussions and helped to interpret what was being said and this hopefully helped the group members to feel understood and listened to, a rare experience in some of our clients' lives. Through experience and supervision, the facilitators became aware of any negative or counter-transference issues. This was necessary as difficult emotions may be invoked subsequently impacting upon the group's functioning. It involved working through one's own reactions to certain behaviours. Some members of the group have the potential for causing disruption through breaking ground rules. Facilitators thus need to understand how to work with the anger and contempt sometimes displayed by clients. It was important to recognise that such behaviour and attitudes were sometimes a much needed defence against feelings of low self-esteem.

In the initial stages of establishing a women's group, we recommend that at least one of the facilitators should be experienced in running groups of this nature. We also recommend that those wishing to facilitate women's groups would benefit from and best serve the group by developing their own knowledge. This includes awareness of the multi-factorial nature of addiction in women. Issues effecting women such as domestic violence, sexual abuse and custody of children are also important aspects for consideration, as well as some understanding of the criminal justice system.

Common themes and processes

It is interesting that women who are often quiet in the mixed-gender group setting become more vocal in an all female group. It may well be that the dynamics of women's groups tend to foster a caring, family-like atmosphere, where strengths are recognised and weaknesses tolerated. Some of the women, regardless of what stage they are at in their treatment, appear quite instinctively to adopt a maternal role. They demonstrate a certain empathy and are emotionally available to their distressed peers. Others are happier remaining quiet onlookers, a behaviour perhaps rooted in their past where children were seen and not heard. The more vocal women may endeavour to encourage more diffident members of the group or to shield them by speaking for them.

The safe and supportive environment of the women's group can lead to disclosure and discussion which women choose not to, or find difficult to express in mixed-gender groups. For many women there may be feelings of guilt related to how alcohol misuse has affected their families, particularly their children. This issue is quite frequently explored in the group. Hopefully, it is through this sharing of past experiences that, for at least some women, feelings of shame may begin to lessen or become more tolerable. Personal growth involves the management of overwhelming and difficult thoughts, and this in turn is an important step towards the achievement of happiness and wellbeing.

Notably many of our clients have experienced personal trauma during their early life, for instance, abuse, poor parenting, emotional and physical neglect and abandonment. Physical, emotional and sexual abuse at the hands of authority figures have resulted in some clients living the long years of childhood without any appropriate role model. It is also not unusual for there to be a number of clients of both sexes with forensic histories. Some will have committed grievous or actual bodily harm often in association with alcohol. This not only gives some indication of the sort of issues that can emerge during a women's group, but also highlights how women might perceive staff in light of their previous experience of authority figures.

It is through staff taking every step to develop positive therapeutic relationships with clients that unhelpful beliefs and attitudes can be altered to ones that are more trusting and appropriate to the here-and-now. We believe that the women's group may provide the environment for such development, not least because women display a willingness to be guided in the way in which their group is conducted. Such groups can open up the possibility for developing healthier relationships with others and thereby new peer networks, particularly when groups adopt a person-centred approach. Caring for and really trying to make sense of each other's needs is therefore a major component of the group process. It is as if this pervasive need to be the 'good enough mother' (Winnicott, 1960) both within the ward as well as in life beyond, is in part a clue to the cohesive nature of the women's group. In spite of disrupted pasts, many of our female clients are good listeners and excellent builders of rapport. Such qualities render them 'helpful' participants and this in turn enhances the group's coherence. As we have already described, facilitators frequently witness the women express a great level of empathy and understanding. This encourages us to believe that the therapeutic environment of the group is conducive to the discovery of inner strengths as well as a rekindling of hope for the future. We have seen and heard from many women how they have experienced a great deal of personal change and reclaimed lost identities through participating in this type of group.

Conclusion

Both authors have around ten years experience working within an inpatient alcohol detoxification ward. Running a women's group has led us to the conclusion that this exclusive focus on women's needs in a group context does indeed have a place in a treatment facility catering for both genders. We believe that gender-specific groups are not only of value to the individuals themselves, but also enhance the ward atmosphere and hopefully contribute towards effective treatment outcomes.

Our involvement with women's groups has been a rewarding and enlightening experience. Many women with whom we have worked have demonstrated a deeply caring instinct to support and motivate each other in their struggle with alcohol addiction. We as their group facilitators appreciate all that we have learned from them.

References

Denzin, N. K. (1984). *The alcoholic self.* New York: Sage.

Miller, B. A., Downs, W. R., & Testa, M. (1993). Interrelationships between victimization experiences and women's alcohol use. *Journal of Studies on Alcohol (Suppl.), 11*, 109–117.

Mollon, P. (1993). *The fragile self: The structure of narcissistic disturbance.* London: Whurr.

National Institute on Alcohol Abuse and Alcoholism (1992). *Moderate drinking.* Alcohol alert no. 16 PH 315. Bethesda, MD: US Department of Health and Human Services, Public Health Service, National Institutes of Health, NIAAA.

National Institute on Drug Abuse (1998). Men and women in drug abuse treatment relapse at different rates and for different reasons. *NIDA Notes: Research Findings, 13*, 4.

Winnicott, D. W. (1990). *The maturational processes and the facilitating environment.* London: Karnac.

Chapter 19

Psychodynamics in groups or psychodynamic groups?

Martin Weegmann

Introduction

This chapter explores a subtle but important grey area, namely psycho-dynamics in groups versus dedicated psychodynamic groups. It is argued that all groups (indeed, all group situations), while non-analytic in aim, contain complicated psychodynamics and group-dynamic elements. Wisely and wittily, Freud (cited in Ferenczi, 1909) was reported to have said, 'we may treat a neurotic any way we like, he always treats himself . . . with transferences' (glossary). In other words, the unconscious is always there, in the background of all clinical encounters, influencing how the client sees the world and others. Correspondingly, a good measure of psychodynamic awareness and thinking by group therapists, and the supervisors who support them, is an important aid to greater clinical sensitivity and understanding.

Part One provides examples of group situations and non-analytic groups conducted, supervised, or witnessed by the author: (1) inpatient ward rounds; (2) after-care discussion groups during inpatient detoxification; (3) preparing clients for AA groups in Twelve-Step Facilitation Therapy; and (4) cognitive behavioural, relapse prevention groups. Part Two briefly summarizes the nature of formal psychodynamic groups, which, it is argued, can play an important role in medium-term and long-term recovery, at least for some clients. All clinical material is of a composite, anonymized nature.

Part One

Ward rounds

Ward rounds during detoxification are central arenas in which staff and clients address needs and review treatment progress. Although the primary task is precise and objective, psychodynamic understanding can still help staff be more responsive to what can be a stressful experience for the client, in which they are the subject of close scrutiny. Some possible fears that can affect clients in a ward round are:

1   fear of group situations and of being 'outnumbered'
2   fear of professional authority and power, both real and imagined
3   anxiety about 'giving over' control and separation from the drug of choice and
4   'abstinence phobia' and fears concerning loss of the drug (Hall, 1984).

Although professionals act as helpful agents and offer reassurance, how we see ourselves is not necessarily the same as how clients see us; in the throw-away words of a client entering the ward round, albeit with pre-emptive humour, 'Ah, the Spanish inquisition again. . .!' Another client was convinced that 'the medics' had already made decisions about him and his views carried no weight, assumptions that increased his (defensive) anger in dealings with them. A bereavement metaphor of recovery in addiction (discussed in Part Two) is a useful reminder that all change involves actual and anticipated experiences of loss, particularly in this case, separation from drug(s) of choice and the threat to a previous lifestyle, hitherto central to a person's identity. However voluntary detoxification may be (and 'voluntary' is paradoxical in states and settings where patients are often very ill and dependent), substance misusers are psychologically threatened by relinquishment of the drug. Consequently, in attachment terms (glossary), they unconsciously experience us as taking something away from them, as we threaten the addictive bond. Further, they are often unconvinced and/or under-confident that the alternatives offered to drugs are compelling, attractive, or workable. 'Our abstinence', so to speak, will not necessarily seem preferable to 'their' drugs.

Groups during detoxification

Groups during inpatient drug and alcohol detoxification typically include educational groups, coping skills, relapse prevention, introductory AA/NA, community meetings, recreational groups, and so forth. The format of such groups is simple and structured; beyond the specific task, they also implicitly aim to help clients recover thinking ability and to tolerate group situations. The reasons for structure and an inevitable degree of repetition are that such clients are uncomfortable, distracted, preoccupied, and often, but hopefully only temporarily, cognitively compromised. Groups are remarkable opportunities for support, encouragement, and mutual learning; they further act as preparation to face the ordinary and extraordinary challenges of moving into the next stage of recovery. There is a question, however, in that even though emphasis is rightly placed on safety and a framework of clear, respectful boundaries, many clients do not, at least at first, experience groups as being in the least bit safe, comfortable, or secure. While 'holding a mirror' (glossary) may in ideal situations prompt interpersonal learning, it is equally regarded with fear and repudiation. What will happen in this unpredictable situation? Will I be exposed? What if I don't like my peers? What if I am (a)shamed?

In the following examples, two particularly difficult group dynamics are described, with reflections on how they were understood and responded to.

Example 1

There was a great deal of expressed resistance as the group was called, with one person peering into the group room, and saying, in jest, 'So who's put the chairs so close . . . we going to be holding hands, then?' As the group assembled, one person, Jason, remained outside. On being asked to join the group, he bluntly stated, 'I'm not talking in there and I'll leave if I want to'. As the group unfolded, there were further references to hugging and hand-holding. Jason walked out, much to the amusement of his fellows, but one adding, 'We've got to stop making fun of the guy; we know he has issues. . .'.

The dynamics before the start of this group will be familiar to those who work in detoxification settings. There is often a climate of ritual reluctance or protest, although, notwithstanding, this is frequently resolved and disappears once groups get underway. 'Crossing the threshold', so to speak, and settling people in a formal group situation is the first challenge. The group carves formal discursive space, interruptive of the informal spaces from which the clients have been called (including woken from). Reluctance can be seen, among other things, as both a wish for control, not to 'give in' to the staff, and as an amplified group process among peers, communicating something like, 'Let's not be seen as being enthusiastic'. My style is to accept reluctance when it occurs with good humour while also communicating clear expectations; the group, after all, was mandatory. I begin all groups with a brief, though not mechanical, explanation of the group task and invite first-name introductions, never assuming that everyone knows each other. We must also not forget that we are often new figures or strangers in their eyes.

Although the group described was designed to discuss aftercare options, the group climate was mocking, both of the primary task of the group and of Jason; the challenges played on homophobic anxieties, and, knowing that Jason 'had issues', other members took advantage of his sensitivity. Although making light of their actions purchased relief, it was followed by expressions of regret and guilt. Seeing, or 'unconsciously electing' (glossary) a particular group member as the 'weak', 'problem', or 'needy' one enables others to disown vulnerabilities. Furthermore, the two (male) facilitators were also challenged. How would we respond to mockery? Could we protect the task of the group and reach out to Jason, who had, after all, done what he had warned by walking out?

In the after-group discussion, we, the facilitators, were concerned that Jason had been excluded (or excluded himself) and been set up to encounter the very thing he most feared. On the other hand we were partly relieved that, with persistence, the group discussion became productive and was able to acknowledge shared anxiety, not confined to Jason, regarding fears of being in group situations that invited (and would continue to invite in the future, e.g., in rehabilitation) emotional intimacy. We wondered about the role of macho defences in substance misusers and what happens when clients can no longer 'fight' or no longer wish to see themselves as powerful or invulnerable figures. Might we represent the kind of 'soft' male figures that they felt threatened by? Importantly, there are always 'out of the room', co-occurring dynamics that are part of the context of ward living. When informal hierarchies emerge, even periodically gang-like structures, rival leadership, or destructive pairing, this can increase postures of resistance, such as being 'either with us or against us' (Bion, 1961). In such circumstances, it is doubly difficult for clients to lose face, revealing problematic aspects of their lives.

Example 2

> The theme of the group in question was 'Where Next?', exploring discussion of future directions and plans. As the group unfolded, one member, Tony, questioned the value of 'talking'. He voiced dislike of groups and announced his determination to 'sort it out myself, I won't be back here again, that's for sure'. He said that he did not like 'shrinks' (he knew I was 'a psychologist or psychiatrist') and that he can 'suss who's a soft touch and who isn't in staff'. Jokingly he said that he 'steers well clear of X' (the author), as he does not think he has 'problems'. Although others countered his view and defended the role of the group, Tony became talkative to the point of domination. It was only when I responded, 'I think I'm authority in your eyes, and therefore not someone to be trusted. And you're also finding it hard to listen to what your fellows are saying about themselves and about you as well', that Tony began to listen. On leaving, he commented that the group had, in fact, been 'Alright', and, glancing at me, added, 'Nice one, I hope you don't take it personally mate, you seem an OK bloke'.

Reflections

Tony undermined the basic task of the group and communicated distrust of authority figures. Perhaps he was threatened by the controlled, quiet situation of the group and felt the need to re-assert his power by discharging talk and opinions. Unfortunately, Tony's idea of talking was tantamount to domination, so that for a while the group effectively became a container used for the purposes of his 'psychic evacuation' (glossary). It is important to remember that the ridding of 'toxic feelings' (glossary) is a frequent dynamic that accompanies the physical detoxification (Winship, 1999). The other members were devalued and responded with frustration, resentment, or resigned by switching-off. There was a strong element of bravado in his comments, but what was notable was that, after my intervention, Tony was more settled, or at least compliant, and thus the group was able to return to purpose. Was it that his feelings of mistrust had been acknowledged, alleviating his need to (ex)press his position? In his parting comment, Tony appeared to be trying to equalize our relationship, to make it 'matey'; he evidently viewed relations with staff as involving power struggles and his reference to 'soft touches' demonstrated a potential for splitting.

There is always a group behind the individual (just as behind each professional is an multi-disciplinary team group and service), with important issues of how people 'present face' to the peers with whom they are temporarily living. Groups, whether formal or informal, are crowded places and working out one's place within them is stressful. Not showing 'weakness' may be a well-practised skill, so as to minimize the chances of being taken advantage of. Defensive requirements of this kind must be understood with empathy, such as a client's need to maintain a semblance of dignity in an anxiety-provoking situation. The sociological notion of 'footing' is useful, concerning as it does the social presentation, position, and alignments of individuals to each other (Goffman, 1981). Whereas professionals already occupy positions and exercise particular speaking rights within their routines, as it were, clients in this setting are 'ill people' and so start from a different footing and may test the environment to find out where they stand. The existence of such formal and informal Ward hierarchies is ignored at one's peril. Detoxification is more than physical recovery, and if all goes well, formerly 'ill' clients are assisted to gain a more secure footing and to gain more equal 'speech rights'. For many, it will have been a long time since they were last sober/clean and able to clearly and consistently communicate their needs; groups are an important means by which clients can be helped to regulate themselves differently and build coherence.

Twelve-Step Facilitation Therapy

Twelve-Step Facilitation Therapy (TSFT) is a professionally-led therapy that assists clients to understand and to actively engage with Fellowship groups, such as AA/NA (Nowinski & Baker, 2003). Usually the client in question commits to regular AA/NA attendance, talking through their impressions with the professional, but TSFT is also an opportunity for anxious and avoidant clients to explore their preconceptions, myths, and sources of resistance.

Example 3

Andy was seeing a counsellor in a Twelve-Step programme, and, while interested in 'Twelve-Step ideas', was highly wary of commitment to AA meetings. Before the discussion that follows, Andy spoke about contradictory views of himself as both a 'superior' and 'inferior' person, which the counsellor had related to the distortions of an alcohol-misuse lifestyle over the years. The counsellor's inner reactions ('counter-transference'; glossary) to Andy were of annoyance to his haughty attitude: 'it is as if Andy wants to be seen as staff rather than patient', the counsellor reported.

Counsellor: 'Tell me, what's your image of an AA meeting?'

Andy: 'Well, I guess people sit around in a circle and talk. It's obvious isn't it! I wouldn't want to be put on the spot, not by a load of strangers. I'm not going to be as bad as those guys in there, that's for sure. . .'.

After further discussion, the counsellor inquired, 'So, now we have talked more about it, do you reckon you might go to the AA meeting this Monday?' Andy looked anxious, saying, 'I might not be ready, I'd kinda feel they'll see right through me, right to the rotten core'.

Reflections

Ambivalent clients can feel the pressure of their own declared interest, as if they are afraid of talking *themselves* into something, a process easily disowned and projected on the counsellor, who is then experienced as the one who 'really wants it'. This creates an unconscious compliance trap (glossary), so that if a client like Andy does not cooperate, they may believe that the counsellor will be dissatisfied with them. Conversely, if they do cooperate, they might imagine that the counsellor is 'pleased', adding a further layer of expectations to the therapeutic relationship.

Andy gave clues as to the nature of his ambivalence when he referred to different self-concepts as (1) different and 'better' to other service users and (2) as a despicable 'fraud' who had exploited people to further his aims. Within the terms of TSFT, there are useful guidelines that could assist Andy, some used by the counsellor. Among these are:

1   acknowledging normal fears about entering any new, group situation
2   offering correctives, such as explaining the AA ethos of 'no cross talk', confrontation, or pressure to talk on members, newcomer or otherwise

3   encouraging a person to practise the AA principle 'look for the simi-
    larities, not the differences' and
4   empathically acknowledging that people with addiction frequently
    experience guilt and shame, and so on.

A psychodynamic formulation of Andy's presentation might read
something like this. Andy deploys characteristic defences of superiority to
deal with the anxiety of inferiority, provoked by the prospect of a situation
that might associate him ('group' him, as it were) with others (e.g., fellow
service users, the as-yet-unknown others of an AA meeting). This is because
he fears being judged, but also because of his *own* actively judgemental
stance, to self and others. His comment about being seen through, 'to the
rotten core', testifies to the strength of a critical super-ego (glossary) and
the likelihood of feeling exposed to the same judgemental process he applies
to others (one could label this a 'return of persecution' (glossary). So, on
the one hand, Andy sees himself as a 'bad individual', beyond remedy, but
on the other, regards himself as 'better' than others. In the transference to
the counsellor, Andy may fear that he will be 'seen through' and regarded
as unworthy, to be penalized if he decides not to attend the meeting. In
grandiose mode (glossary), Andy may wish to be seen as like a member of
staff and would resist activities that might compare him to other service
users. All in all, the AA group in Andy's mind represents a persecutory and
denigrated object (glossary), something that might expose him to (paradoxically helpful) uncomfortable truths and something to look down on,
for defensive purposes. By placing AA meetings in this light, Andy does not
have to face anything that might threaten his psychic equilibrium
(glossary).

Once again, listening with a psychodynamic ear can help clients like
Andy to identify their unconscious fears and premonitions, with the hope
that some of them might be eased, if not resolved.

Relapse-prevention groups

Typically, relapse prevention groups are semi-structured, cognitive-
behavioural groups, that are time-limited or allow for renewable
membership. Some of the areas addressed in such groups are:

- models of relapse process
- lapse/relapse distinctions
- high-risk emotions and high-risk situations
- coping responses and efficacy
- 'set ups' and cognitive distortions or justifications
- management of cravings and
- lifestyle imbalance.

While the original model does not place significance on the mode of delivery, relapse prevention is commonly delivered on both an individual and group basis and as Wanigaratne and Keaney (2002) and Reading (2004) point out, group dynamics are always present in relapse-prevention groups and exert an influence 'to a greater or lesser degree' on the process. They make the further point that if such dynamics are ignored, this could reduce the potency of such groups.

Example 4

An anxious individual, Peter, joined a well-established, largely abstinent relapse-prevention group with a stable, core membership. Peter, also abstinent, was immediately convinced that the others were 'far ahead' of him and worried about being a 'burden'. Two group responses were evident. On the one hand, some members implied (e.g., through glances and small talk before he arrived) that Peter was 'not ready' for the group and might upset their stability; and on the other hand, other members enacted (verbally and non-verbally) a protective, 'let us look after you' response. Peter did not commit to the group and in subsequent discussion with his key worker confessed to feeling that (1) they 'did not like him' and (2) that he was anxious about 'making them worry' about him. Although the key worker encouraged Peter to continue with the group, Peter replied that he does best in 'one-to one'.

Reflections

Newcomer dynamics are interesting: how does the new member join a pre-existing group and how do the existing group members respond to the newcomer? Such transitions are full of fantasy, including expectations and untested projections, which go both ways. With a degree of anxious 'distortion', Peter would have picked up a version of the group's response and so, in response to *their* responses, may have protected himself from possible psychological injury by returning to the safety of the one-to-one relationship. With the benefit of hindsight, had Peter been better prepared for likely psychological discomfort and by anticipating his likely fantasies and avoidance, the key worker might have succeeded in assisting him to manage the newcomer situation.

Example 5

In the same group, somewhat later, we (the group conductors) were aware of the emergence of what we playfully named, in after-group discussion, a 'star-in-her own mind' client who wanted to present as having succeeded, beyond all doubt, in recovery. Whatever the topic of the group, Mary always had 'the answer' and did not hesitate in advising others of her insights. Predictably, Mary became ever more unpopular among them, as well as engendering uncomfortable counter-transference responses in ourselves in her seeming bid to be better than us at running the group. The group's hostility proved hard to contain, such as Bill's openly stated wish (before she arrived) that 'she should be brought tumbling down with an almighty crash'. Mary eventually left, adding that she had 'exhausted the group' (an interesting expression, given her presentation). Subsequently, Bill reflected on his confessed 'nasty and aggressive side' and how these constituted 'high-risk' reactions. Bill admitted that he was afraid of 'coming crashing down'.

Reflections

Mary's formidable characterological defences would have been a test for any group and any group therapist. Yalom's (1970) analysis of the difficulties presented by the 'self-righteous' patient is useful, in which the self-justification of always 'being right' and 'in the right' is the predominant need. Such patients are soon disliked, getting under the skin of anyone who tries to be the equal or to offer them another point of view. This 'dislike' was strongly evidenced in Bill's hostile reaction, which in testimony to his insight, he could relate to his fears, although it took Mary's departure for this to happen.

For those running such groups, simple things help, such as ensuring that co-therapists have a protected and maintained time both before a group begins and after, so that there can be ongoing reflection concerning 'what is going on for our clients, for us and between us?' The presence of strong counter-reactions (glossary) or transference is a clue to the power of groups, whose spontaneity catches us unawares. The group therapists' reaction to Mary is a case in point, as she pushed them into believing that they might be redundant; she may have also brought out their competitive side and challenged their desire to take the helping position. It is difficult to sustain empathy for clients who are themselves unempathic, even though this trait might itself be an important way that they maintain the upper hand; of course, the self-defeating aspect of the self-righteous defence is that clients find themselves surrounded by *more* criticism, with the professional often unwittingly drawn into trying to bring the client down 'a peg or two'. One has to accept that one cannot hold all clients in therapy and groups, especially when their posture is resolutely counter-dependent (glossary), although one hopefully succeeds in helping their fellows to look at their own responses. Just as complacency or arrogance (Mary's stance?) is, in relapse prevention language, a high-risk position to adopt, so too, anger and intolerant hostility to others is a high-risk reaction (Bill's stance?).

Part Two

Psychodynamic group therapy

Formal psychodynamic group therapy is a relatively open, interpretive form of therapy in which group members are invited to talk freely about their addiction and associated problems of living. They are also encouraged by the work of the group to make links between the past and present, and links between what happens outside the group with feelings aroused within the therapy group. In this regard it is a rather particular form of reflective space. Psychodynamic groups may be 'homogeneous', in which all the members have a primary disorder in common (as in substance-use disorders), or 'heterogeneous', in which members present a diversity of primary problems (e.g., substance-use disorder, anxiety disorders, depression, personality disorder, etc.). Whereas the former, when available, is likely to take place in a specialist setting, such as a community addiction service or residential rehabilitation, the latter may take place in, say, a psychotherapy department. Psychodynamic groups are relatively long term in nature (e.g., including up to several years); they may be 'slow open', with a gradually evolving membership (and requiring notice, both to join and to leave) or 'fixed term' (e.g., six months, sometimes with a fixed membership). Group frequency is likely to be weekly, even more often in rehabilitation settings, and should not, in the view of the author, preclude membership of concurrent groups (e.g., AA).

Criteria for membership to psychodynamic groups might include:

- an appropriate period of abstinence or stability (this varies according to setting)
- a commitment to maintaining abstinence or stability
- a willingness to work on the self, self-in-relation to others, and addictive patterns, so that underlying feelings and fantasies can be thought about rather than acted on and
- an ability to commit to time, attendance, and group norms.

A third type of group, common in practice, is the psychodynamically-informed 'support group', in which the group therapist draws on analytic thinking without adopting an actively interpretive role in the group itself. In this and all other variants, supervision is crucial.

There are a number of time-honoured and increasingly researched psychodynamic group models available, drawing variously on attachment-oriented therapy (hereafter AOT; Flores, 2004, 2006), interpersonal traditions (Leighton, 2004), modified dynamic group therapy (hereafter MDGT;

Khantzian, Halliday, & McAuliffe, 1990), and applied group analysis (Sandahl, Busch, Skarbrandt, & Wennberg, 2004; Weegmann, 2004, 2006). For a more detailed illustration of how such groups can work, the reader is referred to Weegmann and English (2010). These models share an emphasis on safety and clear boundaries, adapting to differing needs at different stages of recovery, rather than an ethos of indiscriminate disclosure or emotional expression, per se. In the same way that there are dynamic elements within non-analytic groups, so too, non-analytic mechanisms of change (e.g., cognitive re-structuring, social modelling) occur within analytic groups. One useful analogy for thinking about the purpose of psychodynamic groups in recovery is that of building moral and psychic 'muscle', so that the depletion and demoralization associated with addiction can be addressed and remedied (Baumeister, Vohs, & Tice, 2007; Elliot, 2003). This leads to a strengthening of self and, hopefully, an increased flexibility in the use of defences.

The following diagram illustrates how psychodynamic groups might figure in the lives of individuals struggling to overcome addictions.

Drugs as objects of habit, desire, comfort, nostalgia

Group as affiliation, sober dialogue, change

The centre of the diagram represents the 'push/pull', 'change/threat' dynamic at the heart of addictive disorders. This conveys how group members are often torn between aims (e.g., the wish to be sober versus the desire to use substances socially) and/or between different parts of the personality seeking different aims (e.g., parts of the personality seeking relief and developmental short-cuts versus parts seeking growth and maturation). The psychodynamic model, akin to motivational interviewing, places emphasis on core 'ambivalences' of change, but, unlike motivational interviewing, postulates the active role of non-conscious psychic forces and patterns that influence the individual in various ways (Weegmann, 2005). For this reason, con-sciously articulated 'reasons to change' are not always to be understood at face value.

The top of the diagram points to the presence of drugs as powerful objects of desire, comfort, and nostalgia: feelings and associations that symbolically hover over each group session. In the words of one group member, 'it's like they never leave me be, they're still there, inside, some-where, even though I haven't used for a very long time'. Sometimes, whole groups can enact a talking 'high' through the recollection of past using, drug effects, and the use of 'memorabilia' (glossary) (Weegmann & English, 2010). Nostalgia can be explicit, as in reports of strong desires to use or euphoric recall, but on other occasions, the psychic or group 'pull' towards drugs is more subtle, 'underground' if you will, with memories encoded in feelings or through indirect, split-off idealizations of drug use. In terms of self-medication (Khantzian, 1997), particular drugs are compelling for the very reason that they seemingly meet (or once met) important psychological needs, addressing 'gaps' in the structure of the self. 'Psychological relapse' often, if not invariably, precedes actual relapse, although need not lead to an actual relapse if such preparation for using and build up can be identified and arrested in time. Not surprisingly, the idea of an 'immediate effect', a short-cut means of changing how a person feels, competes with the ethos of the group, which represents different values: re-building the self, painful working-through of problems, and the move towards greater psychic integration.

Recovering individuals negotiate a process akin to bereavement, in that giving up drugs represents a loss. The shadow of addiction is a long one, and rather than negotiate bereavement, the drug user may be tempted to short-circuit loss by lapse, or to maintain the lost substance through some form of vicarious identification. A client in a psychodynamic group commented that, although clean for a long time, she found herself forever reading crime books and sensational crime reports in the newspapers, because, she came to realize, it reminded her of past, drug-linked criminality, with all the associated excitement and violence. Giving up drugs is like losing a part of oneself, but, unlike loss occasioned by death or unbridgeable separation, the user can always return and be re-united with drugs. Funerals need not happen; re-using substances is one, serious step on from vicarious identification with a lost world. Reading makes the point that under conditions of stress, the attachment behavioural system is activated; correspondingly, such systems 'geared to the maintenance of proximity to the drug will also become activated when the addictional bond is threatened' (2002, p. 28). Locating and discussing this missing, pining, and nostalgic pattern is one component of psychodynamic groups, which encourage concerted discussion focused on what it is like to give something up and to move into new, uncharted territories. In this regard, groups mirror a forward/backward, backward/forward pattern, with the working-through of many crises, actual or threatened relapses, and the consolidation or otherwise of the new, 'recovering' identities.

The struggle to move forward is signalled at the bottom of the diagram, with psychodynamic groups promoting 'sober dialogue', based on improving contact and toleration of different parts of the self and others (Weegmann, 2006). In a different context, Canham (2002) draws a useful contrast between 'group states of mind', in which individuals can tolerate, explore, and value differences and alternative viewpoints, and 'gang states of mind', in which thinking and creativity is undermined, with the individual/ group locked into a primitive identity or outlook.

Addicted individuals present complex needs and distorted motivational systems, in which the drug stages a psychic 'take over' of the personality: other interests, commitments, and relationships become secondary, or may even be extinguished. Complex defensive structures built over the years serve to reduce dissonance and justify continuation. In psychodynamic terms, the individual is caught in a web, trapped by their own attempts at self-treatment and omnipotence (Weegmann, 2002; Director, 2005). Psychodynamic groups may, in time, provide a much-needed alternative (re-)source of affiliation and attachment, the (becoming) 'safe base' in which healthy exploration of life can resume. 'Recovery' is seldom a singular trajectory and it is hard to convey the continuing back-and-forth processes that figure in the lives of those in recovery, echoed at the level of the group as a whole. Within groups there are usually constant struggles and retreats, even, in some situations, the formation of 'anti-dialogue' (glossary) that challenges the very principle of sober dialogue.

It is in the harnessing of the therapeutic potential of groups, with all their destructive and constructive possibilities, that the real labour of psychodynamic groups lies. There is a balance to be struck. MDGT, for example, as a resolutely non-confrontational approach, emphasizes the cultivation of cohesion. In group terms, achieving cohesion is the equivalent of the 'positive therapeutic alliance' of individual therapy. In this model the group conductor aims to direct the group's efforts to four therapeutic areas: (1) affect tolerance; (2) building of self-esteem; (3) working on and improving interpersonal relationships; and (4) the development of better capacities of self-care and self-comfort. By way of contrast, though not contradiction, AOT predicts that dysynchrony, conflict, and successful resolution are integral to healthy relationships, Flores noting that 'Because group therapy is inherently more frustrating than individual therapy, its increased potential for dysynchrony provides more opportunities for individuals to learn that conflict and resolution can deepen the affective bonds of a relationship' (2006, p. 22). When difficult affective states, adverse interpersonal styles, and conflicts are identified and worked on, this is an aid to emotional learning and to improved self-regulation in the future. The therapist, approaching groups with confidence, acceptance, and even a degree of respectful humour (irony, for example, can help), helps to make the process of learning enjoyable to all.

Conclusion

Washton and Zweben capture the complexity and value of group work clearly: 'Setting up and running substance abuse groups is a highly challenging but rewarding task requiring skilful handing of various issues that emerge during different stages of the group process. The therapeutic power of groups is often quite remarkable' (2006, p. 257). This chapter has maintained that psychodynamic and group-dynamic understanding is of considerable benefit to workers running groups and to their supervisors. Indeed, substance-misuse professionals in general can benefit greatly from this perspective as they seek to understand the internal worlds and suffering of their clients. Part Two summarizes the contribution of formal, long-term, dynamic psychotherapy groups, particularly how such groups wisely help clients to overcome avoidance and counter-dependence, and thus to foster emotional and relational growth.

Glossary of psychodynamic terms

Anti-dialogue A refusal to learn and non-openness to others in a group situation, leading to the reinforcement of prejudices and established patterns.

Attachment theory This is concerned with the human need to seek, maintain, and provide affectional bonds with close others, through which requirements to be responded to, cared for, and supported are met (Bowlby, 1988). Addictions distort such needs, replacing attachment to others by attachment to substances.

Counter-dependence A defence by which individuals act or believe as if they do not require human interdependence. Substance misuse erodes normal capacities for attachment and affiliation.

Counter-reactions/counter-transference In the therapeutic relationship, strong, often automatic reactions are aroused in the therapist to clients and their modes of presentation. Such reactions can become a block and hindrance to the work or, when understood and contained by the worker, are a highly useful source of information about the client.

Critical super ego The presence of a judgemental 'inner voice' that subjects the client to criticism or devaluation.

Denigrated/persecutory object A defence through which a person holds another person (or service or opportunity) in contempt by devaluing them. Seen in a denigrated light, the person might believe that they have 'got rid' of the other (see 'psychic evacuation'), but may also worry that the other (person, service, etc.) will wish to enact revenge or rejection. Thus a denigrated experience might become a persecutory one.

Grandiosity A defence in which a person believes that they possess superior attributes and are thus in some way better, or better-off, than others.

This can take extreme forms, as in grandiose delusions, or may operate less dramatically, as in an underlying conviction of moral superiority. This is a brittle defence that can easily collapse, flooding the person with opposite feelings of worthlessness and self-denigration.

Holding a mirror In group therapy, one way that learning takes place is through successive experiences of 'mirroring', i.e., seeing an aspect of oneself in another, and another seeing something of themselves in us. The image of 'holding a mirror' encapsulates this process of self-reflection.

Memorabilia A way of designating evocative memories, associations, and positive expectancies about previous drug use. Individuals in recovery can easily 'hold onto' a stock of such memories, both consciously and unconsciously.

Psychic equilibrium The notion that the mind seeks homeostasis and that unexpected or disruptive experiences are perceived as threats to this balance. The challenges of treatment alter the equilibrium, often with increased (initial) resistance to change.

Psychic evacuation The wish to 'get rid' of difficult feelings and experiences from the self. A person may try to 'discharge' such feelings through, say, a rageful outburst or a chronic stance of blame. See also under 'toxic feelings'.

Return of the persecuted A process whereby particularly difficult feelings and shameful self-beliefs, that have previously been denied, re-appear in conscious life, making the person feel inwardly persecuted, bad, or haunted. This is a variation on Freud's (1915) notion of the 'return of the repressed'.

Sober dialogue People with substance-misuse difficulties need to get used (or re-used) to being both free of chemicals and to engaging in sober, responsible conversations. This creates conditions for new dialogue and a re-building of the self.

Toxic feelings The notion that individuals can associate negative emotions (e.g., hurt, anger, let down, etc.) with inner 'toxins', because they are unbearable; a response to such feelings is the effort to rid them from the mind.

Transference The process whereby emotions are redirected or displaced from one person or situation to another. This is often unconscious and automatic, such as a client who experiences a ward as the children's institution in which they grew up or who sees the professional as a threatening authority figure.

Unconscious compliance trap The process by which a client can feel pressured in the therapy to submit to their therapist or comply with a 'demand' they find problematic. How this is handled depends a great deal on the therapist's skill and empathic insight.

Unconcious election A process observed in groups whereby another person is scapegoated, volunteered, or regarded as problematic in some way. This can take negative forms, such as setting someone up as the 'weak' person in the group, or can take other, often ambivalent forms, such as coming to rely on someone as 'the only one who speaks out and protests on our behalf'.

References

Baumeister, R., Vohs, K., & Tice, D. (2007). The strength model of self-control. *Current Directions in Psychological Science*, *16*, 351–355.

Bion, W. R. (1961). *Experiences in groups*. London: Tavistock.

Bowlby, J. (1988). *A secure base: Clinical applications of attachment theory*. London: Routledge.

Canham, H. (2002). Group and gang states of mind. *Journal of Child Psychotherapy*, *28*, 113–127.

Director, L. (2005). Encounters with omnipotence in the psychoanalysis of substance users. *Psychoanalytic Dialogues*, *15*, 567–586.

Elliot, B. (2003). *Containing the uncontainable: Alcohol misuse and the personal choice community programme*. Chichester: Wiley.

Ferenczi, S. (original work published in 1909). Introjection and transference. In *Contributions to psychoanalysis* (1916) (Ernest Jones, Trans. pp. 30–80). Boston: Richard G. Badger.

Flores, P. (2004). Addiction as an attachment disorder: Implications for group therapy. In B. Reading & M. Weegmann (Eds.), *Group psychotherapy and addiction* (Chapter I, pp. 1–18). Chichester: Wiley.

Flores, P. (2006). Conflict and repair in addiction treatment: An attachment disorder perspective. *Journal of Groups in Addiction & Recovery*, *1*, 5–26.

Freud, S. (1915). Repression. In James Strachey (Ed.), *The standard edition of the complete psychological works of Sigmund Freud* (Volume 14, pp. 141–158). London: The Hogarth Press and the Institute of Psychoanalysis.

Goffman, E. (1981). *Forms of talk*. Philadelphia: University of Pennsylvania Press.

Hall, S. (1984). The abstinence phobias: Links between substance misuse and anxiety. *Substance Use and Misuse*, *19*, 613–631.

Khantzian, E. J. (1997). The self-medication hypothesis of substance use disorders: A reconsideration and recent applications. *Harvard Review of Psychiatry*, *4*, 231–244.

Khantzian, E., Halliday, K., & McAuliffe, W. (1990). *Addiction and the vulnerable self: Modified dynamic group therapy for substance misusers*. New York: Guilford Press.

Leighton, T. (2004). Interpersonal group therapy in intensive treatment. In B.

Reading & M. Weegmann (Eds.), *Group psychotherapy and addiction* (Chapter 6). Chichester: Wiley.

Nowinski, J., & Baker, S. (2003). *Twelve Step Facilitation handbook.* Minnesota: Hazeldon.

Reading, B. (2002). The application of Bowlby's attachment theory to the psychotherapy of addiction. In M. Weegman & R. Cohen (Eds.), *Psychodynamics of addiction* (Chapter 2). Chichester: Wiley.

Reading, B. (2004). A relapse prevention group for problem drinkers. In B. Reading & M. Weegmann (Eds.), *Group psychotherapy and addiction* (Chapter 7). Chichester: Wiley.

Sandahl, C., Busch, M., Skarbrandt, E., & Wennberg, P. (2004). Matching group therapy to patients' needs. In B. Reading & M. Weegmann (Eds.), *Group psychotherapy and addiction* (Chapter 4). Chichester: Wiley.

Wanigaratne, S., & Keaney, F. (2002). Psychodynamic aspects of relapse prevention. In M. Weegman & R. Cohen (Eds.), *Psychodynamics of addiction* (Chapter 8). Chichester: Wiley.

Washton, A., & Zweben, J. (2006). *Treating alcohol and drug problems in psychotherapy practice.* New York: Guildford Press.

Weegmann, M. (2002). Motivational interviewing: A psychodynamic appreciation. *Psychodynamic Practice, 8,* 179–195.

Weegmann, M. (2004). Alcoholics Anonymous and fellowship: A group-analytic appreciation. *Group Analysis, 37,* 243–258.

Weegmann, M. (2005). 'If each could be housed in separate identities. . .': Therapy as conversation between different parts of the self. *Psychoanalytic Psychotherapy, 19,* 279–293.

Weegmann, M. (2006). Tenuous to tenacious: Psycho-dynamic group therapy with substance misusers. *Journal of Groups in Addiction and Recovery, 1,* 51–67.

Weegmann, M., & English, C. (2010). Beyond the shadow of drugs: Group therapy for substance misusers. *Group Analysis, 43,* 3–21.

Winship, G. (1999). Addiction, death and the liver in mind: The Prometheus syndrome. *Psychoanalytic Psychotherapy, 13,* 41–49.

Yalom, I. (1970). *The theory and practice of group therapy.* New York: Basic Books.

Concluding thoughts

We have thoroughly enjoyed reading about our colleagues' experiences of running groups in addictions and hope that you have also found these chapters useful and interesting. It was always our aim to put together a fairly 'hands-on' type of book that could be used to inform everyday group work practice, as well as to highlight some of the key principles informing such work. We therefore thank all of our contributors for taking up this challenge with alacrity and good grace.

Finally, while a conventional conclusion might aim to summarize what went before, we instead wish to leave you with 19 questions that correspond to at least one chapter in the book and invite you to join us in reflecting upon these.

1 Why run groups for drug and alcohol users?
2 Why is motivation important when thinking about group work in addictions?
3 What are the latest ideas about relapse prevention? Which do you think are most important for your clients to know?
4 Health promotion can not only save lives, but can improve people's quality of life. How can you best impart such information to clients?
5 Recovery is a multi-faceted concept—what does it mean to you and how do you share this with clients?
6 Do you think that drug and alcohol users can benefit from mindfulness? If so, why?
7 What are your beliefs about Twelve-Step groups?
8 What group would you like to run in your service and how can you go about making this happen?
9 Have you ever avoided facilitating a group? Do you find that the level of anxiety you experience before a group matches the level you experience during the group?
10 How would you evaluate your groups and who would you share this with? Is there really such a thing as a 'bad group'?

11 What sort of behaviours do you find difficult when facilitating groups? When might self-disclosure benefit the group?

12 If you or your team are experiencing work-related stress, what can you do to reduce this?

13 What are your cultural beliefs and how do you think these may influence your perception of addiction and group work?

14 What might make you suspect a group member has a cognitive deficit associated with alcohol and drug use? What can you do with this information?

15 What mental health or personality issues do your clients commonly experience? How might you support clients with these when working in groups?

16 Are there any special considerations to take into account when working with offenders in an addictions group setting? Can people benefit from a compulsory group?

17 What factors help to create safety within the group?

18 Why have a women's group? Why have a men's group?

19 How might a psychodynamic understanding of group processes enhance your facilitation skills? How might understanding your own feelings benefit your facilitation skills?

And, as the Editors, we have taken the liberty of adding one more question:

If you could run a group on anything at all in the world, what would it be?

We wish you all the best on your journey in group work.

Index